A JOHN GRAVES READER

a John Graves Reader

UNIVERSITY OF TEXAS PRESS   AUSTIN

First edition, 1996

Requests for permission to reproduce material
from this work should be sent to
Permissions, University of Texas Press,
Box 7819, Austin, TX 78713-7819.

∞The paper used in this publication meets the
minimum requirements of American National Standard
for Information Sciences—Permanence of Paper for
Printed Library Materials, ANSI Z39.48-1984.

LIBRARY OF CONGRESS
CATALOGING-IN-PUBLICATION DATA

Graves, John, 1920–
A John Graves reader / John Graves.
        p.   cm.   —(Southwestern writers collection series)
ISBN 0-292-72795-X (cloth : alk. paper). ISBN 0-292-72796-8
(paper : alk. paper)
1. Southwestern States—Literary collections.   2. Texas—Literary
collections.   I. Title.   II. Series.
PS3557.R2867A6   1996
813'.54—dc20   96-123

This book is dedicated with affection
to BILL WITTLIFF,
for whom friendship is a lot more
than a matter of words

SOUTHWESTERN WRITERS COLLECTION SERIES

*The Southwestern Writers Collection Series originates from
the Southwestern Writers Collection, an archive and literary center
established at Southwest Texas State University to celebrate
the region's writers and literary heritage.*

CONTENTS

PREFACE

*S*UCH A BOOK AS THIS, made up of samplings from a rather sparse life's work, assembled with its author's cooperation, and published before he is even decently dead, can possibly be seen as exhibiting a degree of self-importance on said author's part. There is of course a measure of that unfortunate attitude in all writing intended for publication, which is a form of telling potential readers, I've got something to say and it's worth your listening to. But if any of it has spilled over into the anthology's contents, it has done so in spite of my best efforts. While I have my fair share of personal shortcomings, taking myself very seriously has never been one of them. I have taken most of the writing seriously, but that is another subject.

Someone in this region, I think McMurtry, once wrote with an apparent touch of pique that John Graves had never published his failures. I suppose that is partly true, for I have always been picky about my work. However, certain failures are being published here, though their deficiencies may be a little less striking than they were before I decided I had a right to tinker with older writing and improve it if I could.

In this connection I would like to invoke a patron spirit. I have mentioned him in my work before, somewhere, but I need him worse this time. He was a comfortably fixed Victorian named Frederick Locker-Lampson, a friend of Tennyson's who when young, in 1857, published a well-received book of verse called *London Lyrics*. Then he spent much of the rest of his life in revising this book and publishing its latest version. During the same stretch of time, for Locker-Lampson was rather popular, it was being pirated in the United States and elsewhere, so that in the end dozens of editions of *London Lyrics* existed, all different from one another in some respect, a book-collector's dream.

On an even more eminent level, the Spanish poet Juan Ramón Jiménez, whose work I admire, was famous or notorious for doing much the same thing—working over old poems of his whenever they were to be republished somewhere.

Although I do not otherwise equate myself with those sterling wordsmiths, the confidence engendered by their examples has freed me to add material and chop out passages and change content and form and language whenever I felt like doing so with individual pieces. Such a procedure is not very scholarly, but then neither am I. The stuff is mine, and as a self-critical and not highly productive writer I have not resisted the temptation to rewrite work from the past, in order to give it a somewhat better chance of accomplishing whatever I wanted it to accomplish when I wrote it in the first place.

I seem to have wound up as a "regional" writer, whatever that may be. It was not what I had in mind at the outset, but I find that this doesn't bother me much these days. After a good bit of floundering and wandering when younger, I found my principal vein of material in Texas and the Southwest where I had started out, and my concerns for the most part have not been momentously contemporary ones. So be it. I wrote what presented itself to be written, and the question of whence it derived does not loom very large to me at this point. The other question—the main one—of whether it turned out well or badly is for readers present and future to decide.

Persons familiar with my previous books will know that I don't always distinguish sharply between fiction and non-fiction, but often mingle them in a single piece of writing. In keeping with this perhaps reprehensible habit, examples of the two forms are not kept separate here, or labeled as one or the other.

Some surprises await a writer who starts to putter with his own past work. While examining my small assortment of old short stories for possible use in the book, for instance, I was startled to observe how often certain themes are repeated in them, and in some of the non-fiction as well. A main theme of this sort is friendship between a young man and an older one—and it shows up with variations in "The Green Fly," "The Aztec Dog," "A Valley," *A Speckled Horse*, and elsewhere. I suppose such friendships have been thematic in my own life, for I have been close to a number of older, often much wiser persons over the years and have been broadened by association with them. But I hadn't realized that those relationships had penetrated my work so deeply.

There are some overlaps of subject matter as well, which I have not troubled to eliminate and won't try to catalog. One sole example I will cite is the account of a sailboat cruise from Mallorca to Ibiza, dealt with first in the profile of my Spanish friend Pepe Mut, and again in shorter, fictionalized form in an excerpt from the unpublished novel *A Speckled Horse*.

One or another of the items in the book may be tied to a particular time during the era through which I have lived, and I assume that a reasonable reader can make allowance for this by noting the year of composition or publication. Dire datedness is a special pitfall for polemical writing, and largely for that reason none of my occasional sallies in that direction—practically all of them having had to do with threats to the natural world—are reprinted here. You help win a battle and your rhetoric, having justified itself, goes obsolete, or you pick the losing side and without the glow of victory the work is abruptly obsolete too. Few of us are Miltons or Swifts, whose preachments are still revered not for their conviction of righteousness or the causes they espoused, but for their pure and potent excellence as expression.

Other kinds of writing left out of the anthology include apprenticeship stories; slick fiction and commissioned articles written only for needed cash; correspondence; attempts at literary judgment in the form of speeches, book introductions, reviews, and reading notes; and uncharacteristic efforts like a screenplay, still unfilmed, based on my story "The Last Running." An assortment of such material, if anyone is ever interested in it, is preserved in the archives of the Southwestern Writers Collection at Southwest Texas State University in San Marcos.

I need here to express gratitude to certain people who helped me along the way, a number of whom are now dead. As a writer I have been mainly a lone wolf and the list is not very long, though it dates back a number of decades, like much of the anthology's contents. A strong debt to my college teacher George Williams is acknowledged in the section called "Some Friends." Others in earlier years who were able and willing to give good advice about my writing included Abe Rothberg, a bright friend from my time at Columbia University just after World War II, and Martha Foley, who more or less presided over a fertile clump of disorder she called a writing class at that same institution. My fine agent John Schaffner, when he believed in a piece of writing, would peddle it right down the list of high-paying magazines and finally to quarterlies that couldn't afford a fee of more than twenty dollars, if that. He cared, as did Harold Strauss and Ashbel Green at Knopf and some editors at various magazines, including *Texas Monthly*.

In terms of the anthology itself, I sincerely thank two persons—my dear friend Bill Wittliff to whom the book is dedicated for excellent reasons, and Shannon Davies, a most perceptive and sympathetic editor.

JOHN GRAVES
Hard Scrabble, Somervell County, Texas

Front matter pages and preface composed in Bembo types with Richelieu Cursive initial.

Looking Back

SELF-PORTRAIT, WITH BIRDS

A s a student and observer of birds I remain a fairly rank amateur despite longstanding interest in them, and I suppose it's for this reason that I have trouble separating bird memories from memories of people I've known. Some of these individuals were just around when birds were around also, while others furnished me with bits and scraps of ornithological knowledge, or tried to. A few of them knew a great deal, so that if I'd always been receptive to their instruction I might know much more now than I do. But personal interests have their seasons, and in these latter days I find that I'm grateful for just about any awareness that a rather casual pattern of life has let me acquire, without complaining too much about its quality and scope.

In the simpler times I knew when growing up in Fort Worth, even we town youngsters had some almost unpeopled pieces of countryside, in the Trinity West Fork bottomlands and elsewhere, that were ours in exchange for a bit of legwork and a degree of sangfroid toward the question of trespass. Later on there were Depression country jobs in summer for a dollar or so a day and keep—wheat harvest, fence-building, and so on—and I can't remember a time when wild live things weren't a part of consciousness and when knowing something about them didn't matter.

Not that this led me into much contemplation of birds as a pleasure in itself, except during an occasional standard moment of marveling at redness, blueness, the sweetness of a song, or the slow-wheeling gyrations of vultures. As kids will, I derived most of my attitudes from adults whom I liked, and in terms of birds the main adults involved were a couple of uncles in South Texas, whose enduring devotion to feathered creatures was of a restricted and traditional sort. Bird hunters rather than bird watchers, they had an intricate stock of lore acquired in an era of such casual plenty that market hunting had been common. They weren't bloodthirsty, those uncles, and in truth they were closer to natural things than many nature-lovers I've known. They believed in selective clean killing, in conservation, and in the game laws, and were somewhat amused by people not familiar with the appearance and general habits of the countryside's more noticeable common birds, from field larks and mockers to swallows and hawks and herons. But their real passion flowed toward dove and quail and waterfowl, game species that could be sought by rightful sporting methods, shot flying, and afterward served up on dinner tables.·

Good shotguns and good dogs were central in their lives, as were the patterns of terrain and weather. Loving the names of familiar hunting grounds—the Mustang Motte, Cheapside, Alexander's Bull Pasture, the Post Oak Tank—they would roll them off their tongues like poetry. At least it sounded like poetry to me, and the hunting that I did with them, though only occasional, was the finest I've ever known because their absolute faith in the ritual's rightness gave it so much meaning. Over half a century later, it is still easy for me to call up the half-scared exhilaration of trotting along a hillside with them toward a place where frozen spotted pointers aimed their heads at a patch of scrub live oak, wondering all the while if I would ever manage to drop two quail on a covey rise as the uncles did routinely.

Both of them were avid about their hunting—birds nearly always it was, never deer and such—but the health of the older one was failing a bit by the time I started going out much with them, and he was often willing to mosey and pause and explain things. It was he who once picked up and brought over to me a plump small-headed bird, streaked in brown and tan, that one of us had brought down by mistake during a flurry of shooting in a sunflower field full of doves. I asked what it was.

"Plover," he said. "I wanted you to see one. In my daddy's time they used to come through in thousands, millions maybe. Shooting, they said you could fill up a wagon, and a lot of damned hogs did." He gave a short whickering whistle that I'd heard myself without knowing what bird it came from. "You can hear them best on cloudy nights in spring and fall when they're flying over low," my uncle said. "It always makes me think about how things used to be."

The other uncle, a lawyer and sometime judge, was too single-minded about the chase to spend any time on instruction afield unless you used a gun carelessly or approached birds wrong, at which juncture his instructions could be pungent. What you learned from him you learned by example, and it always had to do with the hunting itself. To learn it you needed young legs and good wind, since he seldom stopped to rest and would often break into a lope when dogs came down on point. He kept at it hard even after his left arm was sheared off by a truck that sideswiped his car, handling a light twenty-eight-gauge double almost as well as he'd handled a twelve before. In his late forties his heart gave out quite suddenly at the end of a long day spent follow-ing his dogs after quail. If he had the time to reflect on it, I imagine that he must have seen that kind of death as right.

My father, on the other hand, had begun to ease away from hunt-ing before I got well started, and I suspect he'd have quit entirely long before he did if he hadn't wanted me to know some things that he had known. Two or three times each fall and winter we would drive three hundred miles for those outings with the uncles in the rolling, long-settled, very Southern region along the lower Guadalupe, where he had been born and reared and they still lived. All of his best stories were about growing up there in the 1890s and the early years of this cen-tury—about town characters and feuds and black people and quirkish buggy horses and such things. Death being the thing that lets you see a father clearly, I know now that a deep homesickness for that small and satisfying world stayed with him all his life, even though he'd had to get out young to escape my grandfather's old-style despotic love. But those are other matters.

By the time I had finished with college and a war, Papa had stopped hunting altogether and had turned into a bird watcher, albeit a somewhat unconventional one. My mother had always maintained a little feeder in winter, but now they had a big affair kept filled all year long, which hung from a hackberry limb outside their breakfast-room window. The neighborhood was an old one with trees and much shrubbery, and their seed mixtures and suet logs brought in some rather special birds like grosbeaks and house finches and nuthatches, in addition to proletarian throngs of English sparrows and a full assortment of other usual species. Without often using binoculars or leaving their yard for the purpose, they piled up a quite decent life-list of sightings during the next few years, a period when I came home only occasionally from wherever I was living at the time.

One winter and spring they even had a magpie, either a drastically misplaced vagrant or someone's escaped pet. Hopping and swaggering in gaudy black and white about the lawn, he uttered harsh or querulous sounds and terrorized smaller birds at the feeder, which interested him chiefly for that reason since he craved meatier sustenance than was provided there. Staunchly anthropomorphic, Papa named him Gus and doted on him, ignoring his bullying ways and his tendency to rob nests, and putting out grisly scraps of steak and raw liver and fried egg on the immaculate St. Augustine grass for his delectation. But in June Gus vanished for good, having either decamped toward his native high-Western climes or, as Papa grimly surmised, been assassinated by some youngster tiptoeing down the alley with a BB gun.

However, he kept a BB gun of his own and used it with enthusiasm on neighborhood cats that stalked his feeder, cackling in glee when a pellet bounced off one's hide and it leaped skyward and squalled and fled. Probably he'd have used worse weaponry on them if it hadn't been for my mother. The BBs were deadlier against sparrows invading his martin house atop the garage or the wren boxes nailed up here and there, and he hated bluejays as well, rather illogically since their evil ways were not much different from those of their corvine kinsman Gus. One of the few times I ever saw him truly enraged, shaking in fact, was when he sighted a jaybird that was methodically pecking out the brains of a baby dove snatched from its parents' nest. Papa shouted and hurled a garden trowel, the only missile at hand, and the criminal flew off screeching in either anger or derision. But the dovelet by then was so horridly damaged that it had to be coup-de-graced.

subsisted almost entirely on undomesticated meat ranging in flavor from possum to sandhill crane.

We hunted meat there too from time to time, most often by sneaking one of the ponds. This required slithering along on elbows and hipbones through mud and damp grass for a couple of hundred yards, then scrambling erect and firing as ducks rattled frantically skyward from the water, sometimes dark thick hordes of them. It was an anciently prodigal place, part of the belt of level, mild, humid richness where the continent played out against warm Gulf waters and hundreds on hundreds of thousands of geese and ducks and cranes and raptors and smaller birds brought their autumn migrations to a stop and spent the winter months.

Standard hunting, however, interested Jack much less than the bird projects he nearly always had going—catching and doctoring cranes that were afflicted one year with a strange limbernecked disease (he never managed to cure one), studying the pompous, lovely courtship rituals of prairie chickens atop low salt domes, noting the progress of eggs and chicks in nests that he'd found here and there. Being with him on the prairie, whether afoot or horseback or in a car, was often like trailing a madly surging force that dragged you along behind, though his exultation in seeking and seeing could infect you too and make it worth the trouble.

There is not room for all of Staub here, or maybe anywhere else. I remember him as he was then mainly in clear picture-bits of time. . . . With, for instance, blood running down his chin from biting crippled ducks in the head to finish them off, a technique he had learned from the prairie Negroes and liked because it was efficient and uncouth. He was bellowing directions as to a downed pintail's whereabouts at a mild and scholarly friend who had thought that going hunting with us might be fun, and looking at Jack's chin the friend bent over and was quite sick. . . .

Or somehow maintaining himself upright in the swaying, fragile, thorny branches of a mesquite tree and peering raptly at the young in a caracara nest, while I held our horses and the enraged parent birds wheeled screaming about his red head. . . .

Or waist-deep in stagnant brown water and mud at midnight,

waving a flashlight and shouting recriminations at Jim Burnett, who was shouting recriminations back at him while the rest of us white boys stood there, waist-deep too, listening to owls and frogs and wondering about alligators. There was whiskey along and old Jim had had more than his share, but I don't know which of them had led us to that miry impasse, while in the distance the bell voices of the hounds we were supposedly following grew faint.

"Blame *me!*" Jim yelled. "Run ever'body in the dad gum bayou and then blame *me!* We gwine see how many more coon hunts I takes you on!"

"What we'll see is if I God damn want to go!" cried the Horrible One.

But they did go out together after coon and bobcat for the rest of Jim's long life, both shouting a good bit of the way. Across the gaps of age and color and everything else they were astoundingly alike in some ways, and in those ways the old quarter-Cherokee black man comprehended Jack better than his other friends could, love him though we did.

During those Rice years I knew a few more normal bird people, among them George Williams, a quiet maverick who may have been the best English teacher I ever had. In early mornings and at other odd moments he haunted the undeveloped back section of the college's sprawling property, a lushness of trees and grass and interlaced thickets of Macartney rose, where small birds teemed and in spring their songs obliterated the growl of city traffic not far away. Much later I found out that Williams was a respected bird expert—being, for example, one of those called on to clinch identification of an Eskimo curlew, a nearly extinct species, that turned up in the Fifties on a beach of Galveston Island. Because I liked him and liked being out, I went with him to his rose tangles on occasion, but girls and the coming war and other matters were much on my mind just then, and I seem to have managed without much effort to avoid absorbing any real dose of the ornithological wisdom he would gladly have shared.

I do remember that there were lots of quail. You couldn't shoot there and it would have been impossible hunting in any case among the thickets, but the bobwhites' whirring rise still made my heart jump.

That area is now covered mainly by an enormous pink-brick stadium and its paved parking lots.

The truth is that the only thing I can be certain I came to know about birds back then, beyond the smattering left over from earlier years, was that people I cared for could be intensely interested in them in ways not related to killing. I suppose this was a seed.

[3]

Some military men, most of them imperial British I fear, have made use of tours of duty in remote and woebegone places to study and record the natural texture of their surroundings and thereby to swell humanity's store of knowledge. The islands of the Pacific Ocean during World War II were remote for certain and plenty of them were woebegone too, at least after the shooting had moved along elsewhere, but I don't recall that any of my associates in that era and place sought thus to enrich their minds and their time, unless you want to count as nature study the hand-grenading of an occasional reef to see what would float to the top. We did have among us a sprinkling of Gooney Bird authorities, people who had been stuck for a little too long on some minute islet with little to look at but water, coral sand, coconut palms, Quonset huts, and albatrosses, graceful birds in flight but comically awkward when taking off or landing. These experts' repertory usually included a canter down the length of a barroom while flapping their arms and squawking, and a final collapse into a kicking, jerking heap. It was a sort of drama whose appeal could wither quite fast.

No doubt the Horrible Doctor would have barged through to the gist of things even there. But he was a long long way from the Pacific islands, in medical school at Duke. I visited him there late in the war and found him studying obsessively, among other things, the genetics of fine blue-ticked coon hounds under the tutelage of an old bacteriology professor, who lived in a house in the woods with dogs and children and black people all around.

Neither was my time in graduate school in the East after the war much of a stimulus toward bird study. For the most part I thought little more about such things until the late 1940s in Austin, where I found myself functioning as a junior English instructor at the state university, with five freshman sections containing thirty students each—or at any rate that is my jaundiced and perhaps somewhat (but not much) swollen recollection. Like my fellow unfortunates I was afflicted with ungraded theme papers that formed thick, flat lumps of guilty reminder in the pockets of scholarly tweed jackets (doggedly traditional, we smoked pipes too) and piled up on the mantel at home. Our students seemed chiefly to be either affluent or athletic, and were in general contemptuous of teachers. Nor did our abject love of books, the chief reason we underpaid contemptibles were there, find much fulfillment except in relation to composition texts and an occasional simple novel such as *Babbitt* that even a freshman tackle could grasp.

If one adds to this a marriage not in the best of shape, a powerful but stalled compulsion to write undying prose, and a yen to shake the dust of old Texas from my shoes and roam the world, I suppose it isn't strange that with my background I fled for solace when I could to the pleasures of forest and stream. Austin at that time was not a bad place to be if you were partial to guns and rods. For me its main corridor of such activity was the river that flowed down from the reservoirs above the city. In those days before it was dammed and beautified and its banks converted to parks or prime real estate, this stretch of the Colorado was cluttered with old tires and iceboxes and car bodies and things, but it was also cool and copious and clear, and little frequented by people except around bridges and other points of easy access. Though most of my friends at the university had more scholarly tastes, if I wanted outdoor company I could usually find it among an assortment of fellow river rats on the Colorado itself, one of them a small dentist with a twisted spine and tremendous dexterity in the use of a fly rod.

Below the city during fall and winter good numbers of bluebill and teal and mallard and other ducks swam in tight rafts on smooth runs or fed in weedy shallows, and I would drift at them hiding in the bilge of a green canvas boat, a sort of coracle assembled lopsidedly from a mail-order kit. Or I might stalk squirrels in the riverside trees, or trudge along boggy islets seeking jacksnipe that rocketed from beneath my feet with a shrill unnerving cry and zigzagged clear of my shotshells' patterns at least three times out of four. In truth, all of that activity resulted in a fairly thin harvest of protein, but I remember it as having furnished a wealth of sanity and peace.

Corruption of a sort was setting in, however. I had started taking a field glass and a bird guide along on voyages in the catawampus coracle, and found myself doing other things that would have puzzled or annoyed my South Texas uncles, had they seen me. Things like letting a fly line lie on the water in idle curves at evening, while I listened to barred owls tuning up their sardonic laughter in the woods, or watched nighthawks and bats taking over command of the bottomland's moist cool green-smelling air, with its insects, from the swallows that had worked it all day.

I also came to know and like a quite skilled bird man, one of the senior figures in the university's English department. A North Carolinian and a specialist in the work of Spenser, he had austere ways that caused his graduate students to hold him in awe and a certain amount of fear, but I had no academic axes to grind and we got along well from the start. He was a widower, and rather oddly I met him through his fifteen-year-old son, whom some colleague had talked me into taking on one of my river expeditions.

This boy Tommy was a thoroughly improbable offshoot from such a father, full of a raging energy much like that of the Horrible Doctor. It was channeled toward uncivilized things like game and fish and rural Mexicans and cattle and combat with people who got in his way. We did a lot of shooting and fishing together, and years afterward, following college and a three-year head-butting contest with the United States Marine Corps, he managed with scant capital and a full supply of resolve to get started at ranching on leased land in the wild Mexican highlands near Torreón. There he hung on fighting obstacles, most of them climatic or political though he stirred up some personal ones too, for a decade and a half before dying far too early.

The last time I was with Tommy we met at Port Isabel on the border, for a visit and some speckled-trout fishing after years of not seeing each other. He was browned and hard and cursed the salt air blue in both English and slurred norteño Spanish, switching back and forth between them without being conscious of it. At one point he told

2316 8468

me, "The way things are shaping up, in ten years there won't be more than two Americans still ranching in Mexico. But those two will be rich sons of bitches, and I'm going to be one of them."

I suspect he would have been, too, if his body had been up to the drive and the will that had rammed it along through life.

One strays from the point, which is supposed to be birds. (Damn right one does, at one's present age and looking back at people and things that have mattered. . . .) In those earlier years at Austin, the professor sometimes came afield with me and Tommy if we weren't using the lopsided boat, which held two people precariously and three not at all. While we bent ourselves to the ritual pursuit of meat, he would stroll off with his binoculars, and in time I often found myself going with him and letting Tommy hunt or fish by himself. On the cedar-furred heights west of Austin he gave me my first conscious glimpses of golden-cheeked warblers and vermilion flycatchers and other small splendid creatures, and without ever bubbling or exclaiming he had a gift for making them matter. Or maybe I was just ready to have them matter. His special aptitude was for songs and notes—being able to tell from a grating cheep or a snatch of warbled melody what hidden bit of fluff was sounding off, and often why. In the academic status-game of publication, he made a good many points during one period with learned papers discussing references to birds and birdsong in the works of the English poets.

It was the professor, I think, who first pointed out to me a gangling, otherworldly figure on the campus one day and identified it as Edgar Kincaid, who even then, still in his twenties, was on his way to becoming known as the obsessed, eccentric prince of Texas birders. Though I met Edgar at some point during that time, I hardly knew him until a decade later when I was a friend of his aunt and uncle the Frank Dobies, with whom he lived. But I heard the humorous legends that had begun to grow up around him and got to see one in the process of formation.

It involved a screech owl nest in an upper-story cranny of one of the university buildings. Edgar had apparently noticed the owls as they built it, and thereafter at least once a day and often two or three times, he would ooze from a third-floor hallway window onto a narrow stone ledge, and would inch spread-eagled along it for thirty feet or so to the nest for the purpose of observation. Since he kept this up for a period of weeks before the owls coaxed their young out to broader realms, word of it got around, and often while Edgar was absorbedly studying owls a clump of student and faculty aficionados, myself sometimes among them, would gather below to study Edgar. Both sides, I guess, achieved edification. What the screech owls got out of it is uncertain, unless it was some expanded human sympathy toward their posterity, for a part of whatever Edgar learned about them there and elsewhere must afterward have gone into his million-word abridgement and up-dating of the late Harry C. Oberholser's monumental life work, called *The Bird Life of Texas.*

That was all long ago, and lovable, strange, now departed Edgar Kincaid with his owls is queerly linked in my mind to another bird memory from the same era. It has to do with a roadrunner, as obsessed as Edgar and looking not unlike him, who developed a violent hatred of his own mirrored image in one single pane of one single window. This small rectangle of glass was on the second floor of a building a few yards across a courtyard from a room where I was trying three times a week, at eight o'clock in the morning, to convince a class of freshmen that the language of Shakespeare and Keats was still worth trying to use right.

Not inching spread-eagled but racing full tilt, Br'er Chaparral would come tearing around the building's corner on a windowsill ledge like Edgar's, and at the fateful spot would veer into an assault on his detested reflection, hoping to catch it by surprise. Pecking and spurring at the glass until he knocked himself backward, he would tumble into a hedge below and then down onto grass. Dazed and clearly unhappy, he would take time to rearrange his feathers before trudging back around the corner and instituting another charge. Because I was as in-terested in him as were my usually languid Pi Phi and Kappa Sig pledges and budding gridiron heroes, his performance did a pretty good job of neutralizing instruction for a week or two. Then he quit showing up, either having suffered so much concussive brain damage that he couldn't find the building any more, or having been cowed at last by the foe who was always waiting in that window and hot for strife.

[4]

Austin dropped behind with the good and bad I'd found there and some other things as well, including matrimony and the brief illusion that I was geared for an academic life in leather-patched Shetland tweeds. Farther along I would do more college teaching with less illusion and more pleasure, but what came in the meantime was an unreasonably protracted, pigheaded, impecunious, lone-wolf writing apprenticeship lasting for several years and conducted, in the main, more or less on the move and far from my native region.

During those years New York, England, Spain, Mexico, and various other locales felt my tread, not that any of them took notice of it or that I expected them to. All I wanted was to shuck off a few old guilts and inadequacies, and to see and learn and live a bit while engaged in a belated effort to make my work come right. In this war with enemies living inside myself I often felt like a loser with feathers awry, though a little of my writing was being accepted and published from time to time. By rights it should have been a miserable period, and I think it would have been if putting words on paper had been my whole point in life.

It wasn't, though, and still is not, and in truth the period was far from miserable. Those years were loaded with a sense of liberation from old limits, and loaded also with ten thousand things worth doing, from books and museums and places radiant with ancient meaning, to being on trains bound for towns or countries I hadn't seen before, to friends who knew things I didn't and whose minds were alive, to wine and music and bullfights and bright fair ladies.

What they weren't loaded with was the study of birds and other natural phenomena, though after Austin I did maintain a low-grade chronic case of this disease and its symptoms erupted from time to time. Two summers in a row while living in New York I went down to North Carolina to spend some time with my friend the austere Spenserian professor, at a cabin he owned in the high, cool, green country near Asheville. Wordsworth's ideal of "plain living and high thinking" governed in that place—cot beds, cold washtub baths, turnip greens with cornbread, fine book talk, and much communion with the birds that were everywhere in the moist mountains. An old notebook in my desk tells me that in those environs I not only came to know with some confidence, for the moment anyhow, thirty-odd local species ranging from Maryland yellowthroats to indigo buntings, but was also trying with less success to memorize and set down the songs that were known so well to my host. One drizzling misty afternoon we drove fifty miles or so to Mount Mitchell, one of the few sites south of Canada where the winter wren nests and can be heard tootling its complex, high-pitched music, and did hear the song without sighting the songster, and drove back to the cabin at evening well pleased. . . .

Another year there were three months in Devonshire not far from Plymouth, where a chum from graduate school, abroad that year on a foundation grant, was summering with his family in a thatched stone cottage. Because they had small children and no excess of space, I took a room at a pub with beams salvaged from the Armada's wreckage, whose owner kept fighting bulldogs and a Riley sportster and would pour free whiskey down you after hours. I suppose it was as rosily trite and anachronistic a summer as Americans on the mother island could have dreamed up for themselves, but nonetheless fine for all that.

Most of the day Sam would work at his papers and I at mine, and afterward we would amble through hedge-bordered lanes, up rocky streams, and along cliffs overlooking the sea, trying between long, wrangling, usually literary conversations to identify plants and birds and such. In some part this effort was literary too, because if you have grown up within the glow of British writing, thickly adorned as much of it is with themes and images from nature, when you get the chance you need to explore for yourself the reality of things like rooks and yellowhammers and hedgehogs and scarlet pimpernels. The local vicar, a civilized Scot with whom we sometimes tritely had scones and huge strawberries and clotted cream at tea, was no naturalist-ecclesiastic like old Gilbert White of Selborne, but he had a feel for that vein of inquiry and lent us some helpful field guides. As I recall that interlude, we learned much less about birds than about wildflowers, which don't hop around and hide in foliage and fly away. But we did log up a fair number of avian specimens (who, after all, can miss a skylark or a raven or the word of fear a cuckoo speaks?) and derived a certain leering and unscholarly American satisfaction from recognizing a slightly oversized chickadee known in Britain as the great tit.

Spain, however, was where I spent most of my time on that side of the water, and Spaniards in general, like other Mediterranean peoples—and like, for that matter, most Americans—tend to view nature, if at all, in terms of what it can do for or against them. Somewhere in that tawny and pleasant land there must have been some native bird-lovers, but I met none of them and was only occasionally in rural places. From time to time I did go fishing in the Pyrenees or on the short, swift, cold rivers running down to the Bay of Biscay from out of the Cantabrian range, where foreigners were seldom seen and a local angling doctor or priest or cobbler was usually happy to show me good pools and runs. The birds I saw and heard along those rivers were often of sorts that Sam and I had half-learned that summer in Devon (including, I swear, a great tit), and their familiarity was an agreeable part of being there. But my mind like those of my Spanish companions was chiefly fixed on trout—themselves an obsessive study to which numerous human lives, or at any rate large segments of them, have been devoted without regret. And for perhaps most trout people, birds matter mainly in terms of the feathers they furnish for tying flies.

Thinking back on Spain in ornithological terms, in fact, I see scant further learning or awareness on my part, but mainly just episodes and people with some connection to birds, such as those that follow here. . . .

A softspoken decent man in beret and smock encountered one day as I walked down a swale in the rolling untimbered foothills of the Guadarrama . . . He was lying at ease on the slope, a short distance away from a collection of small birds that were warbling and cheeping in wicker cages or from twigs to which they were leg-tethered. On the grass he had spread fine-meshed nets to be sprung when enough wild ones had gathered to these decoys. He got very little recompense for his catch, he said, but it was what he did, his living and his father's before him. Species didn't matter much—thrushes, finches, larks, whatever came—because the wineshops in Madrid that bought them from him would pluck them anonymous and gut them and fry them crisp in oil. I had seen them in such places in platters on the bar, and the accepted etiquette seemed to be to bite the head off first and crunch it with relish before devouring the remainder, bones and all.

Dark, quick, forktailed swallows that would flit in hundreds above a bull ring in late afternoon, diving and twisting and seizing the flies that formed a pall over the violent arena's blood and manure and us sweating enthusiasts in the stands . . .

An English painter, a friend who occasionally went for country rides with me on a motorcycle I had . . . He particularly liked one road that wound through General Franco's favorite and heavily stocked shooting preserve outside Madrid. There at some point he would nudge me to stop, and after looking about for gamekeepers would pot a fat redlegged partridge beneath a bush with a small catapult he carried, stashing the kill afterward in a pocket of his baggy tweeds. He used ball-bearings as pellets and seldom missed, having picked up the knack in youth from a gypsy poacher in Surrey. In the slum studio where he lived with an intelligent and mettlesome Spanish wife, he kept a kestrel on a perch beside his easel, and with Britannic understatement would give me to understand that its talent for hunting was huge. More often than not, though, when we carried it hooded to a park or other open space near the city and launched it at some unlucky sparrow or thrush or whatnot, too many idlers would gather to watch and the little hawk, with or without its quarry, would alight on a utility pole or a tree and refuse to come down for hours, while Tony cajoled it and blasphemed it and tried to shoo Spaniards away.

A luncheon party of hard-drinking expatriates on the terrace of a granite seaside villa outside Palma de Mallorca . . . After coming to the island I had made acquaintances among these gentry and in fact had joined their perennial revels for a while, but in the long run I had work I wanted to do and not that stout a thirst. Most days I would pound out words till lunchtime, hoping they'd turn out right, and in the afternoon would go to the boat club and associate with Mallorcans, who drank very little beyond wine with meals, and took their chief pleasure from sailing small craft across the lovely wide bay, and from the pursuit and occasional capture of vacationing French or Scandinavian girls who liked boats. Except in the cockney sense, they were not bird watchers and neither was I when among them, remaining content with the gulls and terns and sandpipers that belonged to the sea and its fringes.

For some reason I broke the pattern that day and went to the expatriates' party. Things got active somewhat earlier than was usual even in that set, abetted by soft-stepping domestics bearing pitchers of iced Catalan champagne laced heavily with gin. Our host and hostess quarreled loudly. A fired American television executive, nursing his wounds abroad, aimed a punch at a Dutch homosexual which missed but made the Dutchman weep. Other lusts and hatreds surfaced. A buxom young Swedish woman managed somehow to let one breast escape momentarily from her dress's neckline plunge for all the world to see—in ornithological terms a very great tit indeed. Lunch was consumed by those willing to interrupt their drinking for it, and finally an enormous yellow cake surrounded by dancing blue flames was wheeled out by the household's young Andalusian cook, a sort of friend of mine (his sister cleaned my tiny cottage twice a week; our world there was small) who aspired to become a hotel chef and was fond of concocting fancy dishes.

"Over here, everybody!" the hostess called. "Matías has a surprise!"

We gathered and watched brandy flames lick the sides of the yellow cake. Next to me Matías surreptitiously twitched a tiny wire and a trap door flipped open in the top of the cake, but nothing else happened. Pursing his mouth, he reached through the flames, poked his finger into a hole beneath the trap door, and goosed into view a small bird with black-and-yellow wings and a red face, which stood beside the hole and looked back at us, more or less, its lids half-down across its eyes. With some private smugness I was able to recognize it as a European goldfinch, but it was a sorry and draggled specimen by that point, swaying and unwell.

"Oh, my," the hostess said with doubt, and from the carefree assembly came a few cackles and snorts of the kind that some people issue when nervous.

"Fly, cabrón!" Matías muttered to the bird, and nudged it again with his finger.

The goldfinch lurched, shat, and staggered across the icing, leaving tracks. At the rim of the cake it paused for a moment while blue fire singed its feathers, then toppled forward onto the table quite dead.

Against the ensuing babel, Matías was still muttering, but now directly to me. "He was supposed to *fly!*" he said, aggrieved almost to tears.

Maybe in essence that was bird observation in Mallorca. . . . Nightingales did sing to us from the island's hillsides in moonlight, though, as they had sung to aboriginal slingsmen and to Phoenicians, Greeks, Romans, Goths, and the other waves of outlanders who had arrived there through the ages. You could hear them from a sailboat while easing along inshore under a soft night breeze from the land, with wavelets going chuck-chuck against the sliding hull.

[5]

In the world's late 1950s and my own late thirties I came back to Texas for a visit, and stayed on because my father was ill. Nothing was pulling me elsewhere just then, and home ground seemed as good a place as any for thinking over what might come next. Such pondering was in order, since I had just blown more than two years' labor on a novel that had turned out badly, and there was in my mind a large and darkish question as to whether I'd better seek out some other line of work, more standard and more gainful.

Characteristically, I guess, when the pondering turned gloomy I stuck it away somewhere and went off to do things I liked, there being plenty of things of that description in home surroundings not visited for years. Many of these involved people, mainly old friends—a philosophical rancher wanting book talk and a little help with his hay crop or calves, a lawyer who liked to sit up late over sour-mash whiskey and debate the plight of mankind, a family doctor whose joy it was to point out just where I'd gone wrong in life, a small-town merchant who collected the inscriptions from country gravestones and knew the tales of gun fights and Indian raids that lay behind them, three or four old cronies with whom I now had in common the mere but sufficient fact that we had hunted and fished together since the stage of Daisy air guns and cane poles. . . .

As often as not, though, the things I liked to do were things I did alone. Sometimes with a gun or a rod and sometimes not, driving or walking or steering an old canoe I'd salvaged and patched, I poked around parts of the countryside familiar to me from so long before that to drop down into a limestone valley or to round a river bend, and then to see an elm tree or a cliff or a deserted shack that unconscious memory had known quite well would be there, had the resonant, echoed feel of dreams. So did the touch of the dry Texas winds, and the hill-Southern vowels in country people's talk, and the calls of the region's creatures whether I could put names on them or not.

Furthermore I piled up days on days into weeks haunting libraries: dredging up swatches of regional history that I'd known as a youth mainly in scraps and distortions, sniffing out the identity of wild shrubs and weeds whose leaves and blossoms I carried around pressed between dollar bills in my wallet, poring over pictures and descriptions of birds and small beasts and even bugs.

In some part of all this I had the stimulus of volunteer research and writing for a friend's project to restore some pioneer log houses, but the bulk of it, bookishness and rural roving and all, I did simply because that was what I felt like doing at the time. What it amounted to was a homecoming, a reexploration in adult years of roots and origins, an arrival at new terms with the part of the earth's surface that was and would remain, regardless of all its flaws, more my own than any other part could ever be. The wandering years, it seemed, had served their purpose. I could now exist where I belonged, chasing echoes, without wondering if there might be better things to chase elsewhere. There weren't, not for me. I'd gone to a good many elsewheres and was glad I had, but I was back home now.

And without much dark pondering having occurred, the work that I wanted to do fell into place and began to speak in my own voice, for better or worse, of these matters and of others.

During this spell of homecoming and realization, not strangely perhaps, birds began to interest me more than they ever had before.

Bird echoes in home country were strong echoes and frequently literal ones—a fluting or a chit or a squawk that spoke to old memory, but often without my knowing what creature it came from. This ignorance had never disturbed me much, but suddenly now it did. The time seemed to have come to find out, or at least to pull together and augment the scrappy store of awareness acquired from the South Texas uncles and country doings when young, from parents with a feeder outside their breakfast room, from the Horrible Doctor and George Williams and the old Spenserian in Austin and his green Carolina highlands, and in some degree from just being around for nearly four decades with eyes that had sometimes been open and ears that had sometimes heard things.

For dim and maybe shameful reasons I am an avoider of group activities and attitudes, a shirker if you like. So it is perhaps a measure of the seriousness with which I viewed birds at that time that I not only joined the local Audubon Society but even attended meetings and tagged along on Sunday morning bird walks, Christmas counts, and other such events. Blessedly, I found that many of the Audubonites were themselves staunch group-avoiders by temperament, who tolerated that one aggregation of people for pragmatic purposes like mine. They were a heterogeneous lot with a floating fraction of fringe loners far more cemented in misanthropy than I, the latter tending to stay in the Society's ranks for only a year or so before drifting back to solitude to mull over what they had learned. Reverting to character in time, I did much the same thing myself, but with a few lasting friendships and some gratitude that has lasted too. The best of the Audubonites had wide knowledge and were wholly generous with it, as are most people who love some field of inquiry for its own sake and not for cash or status.

Nearly all of them were likable, even when idiosyncratic. Consider, for example, Mrs. Y., a small and sixtyish widow with maroon-tinted hair and the innocent face of a vireo, who clearly lacked the urge to learn very much about birds but exulted in seeing them and endowing them with human traits and ways. I recall one handsome male oriole, a migrant Bullock's I think, which a group of us watched take a splashy bath in the shallows of a creek, then preen himself in sunlight while perched on a high twig. Finally he cocked his eye at us, uttered a hypocritical alarm note (who did he think we'd been, all that time?) and flitted off into the woods, whereupon Mrs. Y. said in delight, "Oh, look! There he goes to his little wife, all nice and clean!"

Harder-nosed birders, including me, felt protective toward her and feared that one of life's rough edges might lacerate her in passing. Hence we were agreeably astonished when she snagged a rich, tough, retired real-estate man in marriage and started going off with him on farflung nature tours, anthropomorphizing glamorous fauna in habitats ranging from Malaysian rain forests to the fjords of Norway. But she managed to tempt her love into attending only one of the Society's meetings, at which they showed us some South American slides. He clearly viewed us as environmentalistic subversives in tennis shoes and refused to risk being tainted.

Or there was Mrs. P., the spouse of a subdued attorney who was seldom seen among us either, since he didn't care for birds. She was large, competitive, tweedy, and not overburdened with charity toward minds less quick and forceful than her own. If two or three of the other members knew perhaps a bit more than she did about the organization's main topic of interest, no one ever heard her admit it. The talk of gentle Mrs. Y. and other sentimentalists could set her to muttering and snuffling, and occasionally she got so fed up that she quit the Society and all its works for weeks or months on end, but always came back because she couldn't stand not competing. It was quite usual to have her desert a bird walk soon after it had started, stalking off in disgust with a military spine and her binoculars gripped in both hands. Sometimes she would rejoin us later and announce, glaring about, that she had just identified some species nobody else had seen—a blackheaded grosbeak, maybe, or a barn swallow in summertime.

I remember a few polite questions from our other experts in regard to these unusual sightings, but never any very spirited expressions of doubt. For one thing Mrs. P. did know a lot about birds, and for another there was her aspect. I liked her. Even at her most outrageous she had a spark of fierce intelligent humor, and she kept things nicely stirred up. But I never could blame her lawyer husband for being subdued, or for his want of interest in birdlife.

We had a real ornithologist too, a dedicated professional who maintained contact not only with that chapter but with some in other cities, since informed amateurs were a good source of leads and data. Though the members respected his knowledge, some were upset by certain of his practices, in particular his occasional "collection" of museum specimens with a shotgun. This feeling switched strongly toward me after I showed him a nesting population of golden-cheeked warblers in the limestone hills southwest of Fort Worth where I'd hunted and fished since youth, and where in fact I now live. The ornithologist was delighted, for the species had not been previously recorded in those parts, and he promptly shot a few to avouch their official presence. But *Dendroica chrysoparia*, shy and tiny and beautiful and rare, is a sort of totem for Texas birders, and when word of these slayings leaked back to the Audubonites, as word inevitably did, the more puristical of them seemed somehow to blame me more than they did the killer scientist, and I never did get all the damage repaired.

It was trouble that had been waiting to happen, for these folk were already darkly aware that I still went forth with a shotgun myself from time to time, and not in the interests of science. Relations between hunters and other nature enthusiasts can be complex, and they produce some odd connections. One of the brightest of the Audubon ladies, for instance, had started birding as a young bride while accompanying her husband on his forays after doves in autumn, studying more fortunate unsporting species while he blasted away at graceful gray shapes hurtling across the blue. Though in the end she had cured her mate of his blood lust, she looked back on those younger days with nostalgia and viewed my known wrongdoings lightly, sometimes teasing me about them.

Not so the true Thoreauvians, who recognized evil when they saw it, especially after the Golden-Cheek Massacre. These were mainly quiet and gentle people in whose blame there was less anger than silent or muted reproach, and with a long-familiar itch of guilt I was privileged yet once again to see myself as Mr. Hyde.

It was not guilt, however, but practicality that made it tough for old Hyde to fit birding and hunting together within the shape of his own life. Hunting usually takes place where birds abound, but watching them is another matter. Dove hunting may pose the most conflict, for it entails a lot of sitting and waiting and looking around, and it comes in September and October when many local species of birds are ganging up for migration and northern sorts bound southward have started to pass through. Armed and camouflaged and stool-seated beside a stock tank or a stubble grain field, let's say, you become aware of eight or ten kettling hawks in the sky, buteos of some sort, tailing one another in a lazy-soaring spiral while the spiral itself drifts swiftly southward with one of the season's frontal winds.

You lay your gun down and seize the field glass dangling from your neck. Three good pink-breasted doves come whistling along the wind from behind your right shoulder and you grab up the gun and fire, too late to have a chance of hitting one. By the time that disgruntlement expends itself in bad language, the hawks have become a pattern of mere dots far to the south, unidentifiable even when magnified. Further bad language ensues. . . .

[6]

My hitch of active duty with the Audubon Society lasted for a couple of years or so, and for two or three years longer I kept on birding alone or with friends whenever I had the time. As a result I turned at last into a fair-to-average student of the subject, achieving not expertise but at least a general familiarity with our local birds and their ways. That was fortunate, for soon afterward the demands of a new stretch of life, with a new set of interests, pretty much swamped ornithology. If serious birding doesn't fit well with hunting, it fits little better with building fences and barns and a house, gardening, handling livestock, tending bees, tilling and sowing and harvesting field land, and any number of other purposeful rural activities that during the next fifteen or more years were central in my mind. For the regional countryside was where that homecoming led me and mine after I married, grew used to the notion of staying in one place, and metamorphosed backward into an ostensible Texan again.

Of existence on this rock-strewn, hilly stock farm of ours, I have written in other books and I won't dwell on it here. Early along, there was much hard work with a reasonable amount of fulfillment, and a perishable if requisite illusion of restoring the place to economic use, nearly a century after the catastrophic depletion of its primeval soils by too much cotton on vulnerable slopes and too many cows on the grass. All of this required a certain earnest practicality of outlook, and not being in my heart of hearts a truly earnest or practical fellow, I am relieved and grateful in this later time to find that the best thing I've acquired in these battered, cedar-clad limestone hills has been not the mastery of yeoman skills, though I'm glad enough to have done all that, but simple awareness of natural rhythms and ways while living on the land through the seasons' cycle, year by year.

Awareness certainly of the land itself—of what it can and can't be made to yield, of what men have done to it and the revenge it has taken for this. But awareness too of wild creatures and plants, and of the ways in which they function with dirt and terrain and climate to shape a whole pattern of livingness, even in tired and diminished places. Even here. Their pattern will exist when I am gone, and with luck even when our civilization is gone. That the comfort to be found in this thought is of a brownish hue, I grant, but being of sunny disposition I see it as comfort nonetheless in an age woefully short of such reassurance. . . . In their vastly differing ways, things squabble for territory and for mates, pair, produce young, feed, and are themselves fed on in their turn, croaking and whistling and grunting and howling and singing and issuing their other noises, if any, along the way. And all life passes back to the dirt and the water for digestion and renascence, quite simply yet very complexly and without ever reaching an end, thus far at any rate.

These things I seem to comprehend best, though never entirely, here on this piece of home ground—in terms of such things as coyote versus red fox populations, or the prosperity of an individual great blue heron in relation to a specific dwindling creek pool full of minnows and sunfish, in a dry hot summer. And I guess this is why, most of the time, I remain content these days with the birds I can see and hear on my restricted rock pile, like my parents in their shady back yard long ago. Over the years I have had pleasant chances to view new species in new surroundings through one circumstance or another—writing assignments that took me elsewhere, a stint with the Interior Department in the Potomac river basin, treks to Mexico with the Horrible Doctor during a time when his chief passion was bringing back tropical species for an aviary at the Houston zoo, fishing trips to the Rockies or the Florida Keys. But home seems to be where I can discern patterns most clearly, or can best attain the illusion of discerning them, and home is where the birds have come to mean most to me.

The old, sharp, Audubon Society cognizance of detail—of wing bars, eye rings, streakings and specklings of breast, alarm notes, and so on—has blurred quite badly in my head through the years of absorption with yeoman matters, and I seem fated to spend the latter end of my days as a mere glimpser of birds. But we live our lives among them here, glimpsing many in the course of a country year, and in some ways they have more meaning for me now than when I was studying them more closely. I am most fully aware of birds while nosing around without haste or real purpose, say down a stream or along a wooded slope, conscious of winds and sounds and flitting motions. But I heed them too when performing such unhurried, ruminative tasks as patching fence, pruning fruit trees and vines, or wandering through brush in an effort to find out where some heifer has hidden herself to calve. And these days, agreeably, there seem to be more of such easygoing things to do than of the arduous, earnest ones that prevailed when energy was younger and the economic illusion still thrived.

Even indoors, unless you lead the sort of sealed-off life that is warmed and cooled all year long by machines, birds are often with you. Their songs and calls are audible during much of the year, and if you have the vice of glancing out doors and windows, you're often not really inside at all. The big metal-framed casement of my office at the rear of our barn, for instance, has a view that encompasses, near at hand, a pile of old lumber, some farm machinery and rusted junk, and a few twisted live oaks. Farther out, it widens fan-shape across ten acres of rising, grassy horse pasture with woods at the higher end. Each tree and stump and boulder and fencepost of this unspectacular vista is engraved on my mind, and many a time over the years, sitting at the typewriter, I have been lured away from composition by small natural dramas being enacted somewhere within it, easing out with a field glass to ascertain what kind of flycatcher is assaulting grasshoppers and butterflies from the top wire of a fence, or to analyze the tactics of a bullsnake in its raid on a mockingbird nest.

Hawks are perhaps the worst seducers. I've never learned them right, and when a problematic one shows up, something in me always hopes it may bring final enlightenment. So far none has done so, but some can do interesting things, like the sharp-shin that once zoomed under my office awning in hot pursuit of a junco and loudly broke his neck against the window. I felt much worse about this than I imagine the junco did, but the mishap did provide some uncommon barred feathers for use in tying trout flies.

[7]

Mr. Hyde is still on hand, I guess, though much enfeebled by time. Dedicated hunting does not seem to mesh much better with country life than does dedicated birding, not only because of yeoman preoccupations but also because various sorts of quarry are always around, and going after them becomes less a ritual occasion, planned and prepared for, than a matter of momentary whim. For a long time I did more or less adhere to a pattern of eating wild meat or fish once every week or so, shooting a deer for the freezer most years, and rambling occasionally about the place to see what the Red Gods might provide for supper, whether a widgeon or a gadwall from the weedy stock tank on the hill, a couple of squirrels, a panful of sunfish from the creek, or whatever. Increasingly, though, these deities have seen fit to provide little or nothing—in part because aging legs and eyes and reflexes have reduced the range of my outings and my ability to handle a gun as swiftly and well as fond memory claims I once did. In part too, I'm sure, it's because with the years one's quieter, gentler self gets a bit bossier than earlier in life. Even angling, though I somehow love it more than ever, is a much less intense affair than I used to make of it, for I take my time on the water, gaze about at bugs and birds, and sit down on rocks or grassy banks to ease my joints and to think and putter with tackle. As often as not nowadays I find myself releasing caught fish to the pools and riffles they came from, undamaged save for an instructive sore lip.

Quite possibly old Hyde will wither away before I do, and I'll finish my years as purely a watcher and thinker in relation to natural things. In honesty I don't find myself yearning toward such a state of being, for all my life hunting and fishing done right have been a fulfillment, and a ritual link with past generations of my people—with all predatory people, for that matter, back into times when the planet was teeming with live wild meat across its wide surface, and all of mankind had blood on its chin just like my Horrible Doctor.

But there are occasional signs. . . . One morning four or five Aprils ago, I was waked in gray light by the loud gobbling of a turkey cock close at hand. I rolled up on an elbow and looked out the window, and there he was in the little orchard below the house, not more than fifty feet away. He was blue-headed and bronze-feathered and huge, with red wattles distended and tail fanned wide to show that he craved a fight or a tumble or both, and didn't care who knew it.

It was fine to see him. They have been returning to our part of the country in recent years, aided in part by state releases of fresh stock and by a series of moist springs favorable to hatching. But the main helpful factor has been a dwindling of the region's old native human population, as high land prices have tempted them to sell out and their progeny have emigrated toward urban wages and ways. These people's gradual fading is something I've regretted, for in general they were tough, wry, enduring folk more attuned to life on this hard land than we latecomers are or can be. In terms of wildlife, though, it is hard to feel very bad about the change. If something was meat they killed it and ate it as their forebears had done forever, without a thought for effeminacies such as game laws, conservation, and the survival of breeding stock. They also liked lots of poundage in return for ammunition and effort expended, and in consequence thirty or thirty-five years ago it was hard to find sizable wild creatures anywhere in the neighborhood, except on three or four big ranches with jealously posted boundaries. Jacklighting deer was an honored tactic, as was the wholesale slaughter of turkeys on flock roosts at night. One local told me with quiet pride, in describing such an expedition, "I do believe we got the last one."

I was shaped otherwise, and despite a couple of excesses with ducks on the Houston prairie in college days I've never been much drawn toward carnage. Nor does the restricted type of hunting that I really care for—the wingshooting of small upland species with lots of firing and relatively scant results—include such things as turkeys. The only one I'd ever killed had been on a friend's luxurious deer lease, a deed carried out half-reluctantly and without great joy in the aftermath. A couple of times recently I had watched a winter flock of thirty or more forage through our yard while I sat on the porch, untempted.

Nevertheless, I wanted that big handsome tom in the orchard. If I didn't know just why, I didn't know why not, either. Taking him would be legal, the spring gobbler season being open, and moral enough in terms of the scheme of things, since any hens that he didn't breed would be bred by his polygamous rivals. His flesh would be put to use. Even his plumage would, though a good many years of my kind of fly-tying wouldn't consume it all. And there he strutted, oblivious and full of himself and more or less asking for it.

The only gun close by was an ancient Winchester twelve-gauge pump of the sort with a visible hammer, a family heirloom kept in the bedroom closet with a handful of buckshot shells. Sliding out of bed and loading this relic, I eased through the door onto an open porch and peered around the corner of the house. He was still magnificently there, and still so charged with lust and ego that there seemed to be no room left for the fabled wariness of his kind. While I watched, he drooped his wings and rattled their flight quills and did a little dance step on the dew-spangled grass, beautiful and ridiculous both, before vibrating all over as he rolled out another proud gobble upon the morning air.

I clatched the old shotgun's hammer back and laid the bead sight on his bald blue head, which at that minimal range with a full-choke twelve would shortly not exist. Except that I looked down the barrel for a moment too long, then raised it toward the sky.

"Damn you, turkey!" I said. "Get out of here!"

My voice and the movement of the gun made him swivel his head to fix on me an eye from which the glaze of self-esteem was quickly fading. He said in alarm, "Pitt! Pitt!" and deflated, his fluffed-out feathers closing down against his body and his widespread vertical tail collapsing to a streamlined wedge. Then he lowered his head and wheeled and ran like hell down the alley between two rows of trellised grape-vines, and I fired a blast in the air to speed him as he skimmed over the lower orchard fence and dashed into brush beyond.

Only at that point did I notice that the spring dawn chorus of small birds had been in full throbbing voice, because they hushed when I shot. But very soon a redbird throated chew, chew, and a Bewick's wren itch-itched and trilled, and one by one the others came in until the whole sweet, pervasive cacophony was filling the air again. Some-times half-awake in bed at that time of year and that time of day, if I'm trying, I can count ten or twelve species by the sounds they make, while hearing other familiar ones that I can't name. It is fine to listen to them, and fine to know the little that I do know about them, and fine to have them there.

It was fine to have the big tom turkey there also, and he wouldn't have been if old Hyde had had his way.

[8]

Sometimes birds impinge on our lives here in minor practical ways, as when a specific flicker goes queer for the house's plank siding and starts to chop round holes in it, or when jovial pirates of several species gang up to plunder the orchard's ripening fruit. Sometimes also, types from outside the usual pattern appear—a pair of goshawks that winter in the farthest hill pasture, a parakeet hanging around the corrals and hobnobbing with goats, a golden eagle, a Western tanager, a single night heron that arrives late one summer and for a couple of months rasps out his lonesome complaint in the small hours, or maybe he thinks it's music. . . .

In the main, however, the ones that are part of our lives are pleas-antly predictable in their ways, driven by seated instincts and by the shape of the year. The most comfortable presences, old friends some-times recognizable as individuals with quirks, are the year-long residents like mockers, wrens, cardinals, quail, titmice, buzzards, roadrunners, owls, and so on. But there is a familiar rightness too in the northern species that spend the cold months with us, ranging in kind from small, secretive, brush-loving finches of many varieties, to bluebirds, waxwings, flickers, and huge barking aggregations of robins. Spring takes these away abruptly, but in recompense brings back others that have wintered to the south, of which each sort arrives in its time, with its own sounds and rules of conduct and its own infusion of procreative fever.

Phoebes build nests beneath the house's eaves and overhangs and in the open-ended barn. Wrens stuff theirs into the fan housings of tractors and all other hollow places they can find. Bright summer tanagers set up in the elms and chittamwoods beside the apiary, snatching slow nectar-heavy bees from the air. Yellow-billed cuckoos, our "rain crows," speak no Old World words of fear but cluck prophecies of moisture that all too seldom come true, here on the fringe of West Texas. Crested flycatchers wheep and issue fartish frog calls. Scissortails start squawking loudly at the first hint of dawn and keep it up all day. Golden-cheeks pipe faint thin music on the cedar slopes across the creek, painted buntings squeak theirs in the orchard, and all over the rocky, brushy landscape dozens on dozens of additional species find their territorial niches, announce their claims melodiously or otherwise, and assume their functions of courting, begetting, eating, and being eaten.

Because our neighborhood, by and large, was too starkly despoiled in the old days to be worth much further ruinous human attention now, our resident birds do well enough most years. But those whose genes impel them toward travel face queer poisons and forest destruction and other misfortunes in distant places these days, and sometimes don't show up when they're supposed to, or at all. The rough-winged swallows that used to burrow nest holes in dirt bluffs along the creek were such a casualty a while back, and every passing year or so, whether through real subtractions of this sort or through my own ineptitude and slothfulness as an observer and listener, one or another usual species seems to be missing.

Thus there is affirmation in the continued passage northward and southward of the more spectacular migrants, dramatic in size or numbers or both, which seldom stop here even to rest. In some crystal, melancholy November spell with a new norther blowing down crisp from Canada, the yelps of geese and the grating calls of sandhill cranes may sound at intervals all day long as the big chevroned flights move across the sky, and in the sight of them there is exultation that such creatures can still exist in our people-teeming and extirpative times.

Some years thousands of gulls, startling in this dry hinterland, fly through at treetop height in raucous, disorganized waves, and watching at a lucky time you may sight white pelicans in tight, high, slow-flapping flocks, or even tall whirlpools of silent hawks, rarer now. And all the while, myriads of smaller, less conspicuous birds are also moving through, usually in darkness, bound north or south according to the season. These do often pause among us to rest and feed, and may show up colorfully at times, as when a mixed throng of warblers speckle a newly leaved pecan tree with their bright vernal plumage in May.

Of all these passers-through, the species that means most to me, even more than geese and cranes, is the upland plover, the drab plump grassland bird that used to remind my gentle hunting uncle of the way things once had been, as it still reminds me. It flies from the far northern prairies to the pampas of Argentina and then back again in spring, a miracle of navigation and a tremendous journey for six or eight ounces of flesh and feathers and entrails and hollow bones, fueled with bug meat. I see them sometimes in our pastures, standing still or dashing after prey in the grass, but mainly I know their presence through the mournful yet eager quavering whistles they cast down from the night sky in passing, and it always makes me think what the whistling must have been like when the American plains were virgin and their plover came through in millions.

To grow up among tradition-minded people leads one often into backward yearnings and regrets, unprofitable feelings of which I was granted my share in youth—not having been born in time to get killed fighting Yankees, for one, or not having ridden up the cattle trails. But the only such regret that has strongly endured is not to have known the land when it was whole and sprawling and rich and fresh, and the plover whet that one's edge every spring and every fall. In recent decades it has become customary—and right, I guess, and easy enough with hindsight—to damn the ancestral frame of mind that ravaged that world so fully and so soon. What I myself seem to damn mainly, though, is just not having seen it. Without any virtuous hindsight, I would likely have helped in the ravaging as did even most of those who loved it best. But God, to have viewed it entire, the soul and guts of what we had and gone forever now, except in books and such poignant remnants as small swift birds that journey to and from the distant Argentine and call at night in the sky.

An earlier version of "Self-Portrait, with Birds" ("Recollections of a Texas Bird Glimpser") was published as the introduction to *Of Birds and Texas,* a folio of bird paintings by Stuart and Scott Gentling (Fort Worth: Gentling Editions, 1986). The present version was published as a separate book, *Self-Portrait, with Birds: Some Semi-Ornithological Recollections* (Dallas: Chama Press, 1991).

Composed in Centaur types.

The Land

HIS CHAPTER

*A*S ALWAYS, AFTER RISING and turning on the coffee he went to stand spraddle-legged in shorts on the little concrete-floored side porch, facing the eastern horizon's pale blushful smudge of foretold daybreak. Stars still hung above it and he could see no clouds about, though wishing for them. Between him and the predawn were a honeysuckled fence that shielded the house a little from the highway, the highway itself with honkytonks and welding shops and repair garages and quick-food stands all silent now, their neon mainly dead, and then prairies dropping to a far-off wooded riverbottom and rising beyond it, specked here and there with random lighted windows in creepingjesus suburbs that had not been there three years before. At a distance to his left were the night lights of the city that had spawned the suburbs. Puked them, the Old Fart put it to himself when pondering such matters, but he was not pondering suburbs now. He was watching the promise of day, and waking up, and relieving himself on vocal absorbent flowerbed soil.

With shudderings he finished, felt suddenly the windless morning cold of March, and went inside. Beneath blankets Samantha stirred and spoke from a mouth stiff with sleep, concerning her spirea. He shoved down a flick of rage not only at what she was mumbling but at the fact of her being awake. On Sundays, when he did not work his half-day at the station out the highway, he counted on two or three hours of quiet and solitude to muse and putter before she got up for church.

"Nitrogen," he said. "Potash. Good for them bushes. I hit a different one every day."

Muffled and descending, her reply sank back into sleep. Relieved and a bit guilty because of it, he eased into pants and flannel shirt and blue peaked cap and went out to the kitchen. Into a glass of cold milk he crumbled wedges of last night's cornbread and fished them out with a spoon and ate them, then poured and sipped black coffee with honey in it. Considering the silent radio, he decided to leave it silent, not caring about the news and knowing already what the weather reports would say, weather being something he did care about and always had. Had had to care about.

Southwest dry winds off the Old Mexico desert, or maybe a dry norther with no Gulf moisture in the air for it to loose. Clear skies, as there had been mainly since early January, the autumn's rain sunk two feet deep or more by now. A winter drouth was harder to take somehow than summer ones were, unreasonable. . . . A hell of an electric bill there would be this month, for pumping from the well to the garden. She would have some things to say. Let her. It cost less than the new city water, to which so far he had refused to be connected, though they came and threatened him into hooking up to the sewer they had finally pushed out that far, despite a good septic tank that sub-irrigated his fruit trees. Creeping, crawling, surrounding-him bastards.

Nursing his coffee cup between big-knuckled hands warmed by it, the O. F. cursed creepers and crawlers and rainlessness. He was not, however, very angry. The city would come and eat him up if it wanted to, and of drouth he had a lifetime's knowledge and could accept it when it came. Nor was there any longer a problem, for him, of wide pastures needing rain. Just a vegetable garden, and it could be watered, if expensively. And a piece of bermudagrass front lawn and flowerbeds too, hers, but the longer the lawn waited for rain the less it would need to be mowed when warm weather came; the O. F., though tolerant of such foibles in others, lacked enthusiasm for lawns and flowers and other tame, growing, troublesome, pretty things that demanded water and care but couldn't be eaten or fed to animals. Wild growing pretty things, he conceded, were something else and he liked them. Besides, some of them furnished honey and others grazing and they all helped hold dirt where it belonged.

It would be time to milk if he still had a cow but he didn't. When the old one had died the females, Samantha and their married older daughter Kate who lived in the creeping city, had kicked up such a fog about his getting another that for once he had gone along with them. In secret he had not much minded, being a little tired of seeing milk go to waste or to chickens because he and Samantha could use only a little and Kate had decided raw milk was unsanitary. But for livestock now he was down to hens and bees and he missed having animals around, to worry over their quirks and needs. During practically all of his life there had been animals to think about and care for, sometimes hundreds of them.

*   *   *

For the O. F. had been a cowboy once, of sorts. Not born to it, but a fair enough hand nonetheless. He had not especially intended all that, but when he thought about such things he had not intended a hell of a lot of what had happened in his life. Except leaving Oklahoma . . . He had grown up in the southeastern corner of that state, the Little Dixie part along the Red, good farming country in its flatter parts, mild green country with most years plenty of rain. But its people had been around there for a good long while, and their ways tended to hem you in, if you were restless and ready for work that went somewhere, and part Choctaw and the part that wasn't came out of a family that had been sharecroppers since who throwed the chunk. Hemmed you in especially during a Depression that started just after you got married, having waited till things looked right. He made up his mind finally to quit being hemmed in, and afterward he supposed that had been the same thing as making up his mind to leave, though to begin with, leaving had not been what he had intended. One afternoon he cornered his boss at the barn mule pen, a man of about thirty who was also his landlord.

"I need a little more money, Josh," said the O. F., then a Y. F., twenty-seven. "Me and Laurie we're scraping bottom. You ain't paying me no more than you pay them darky mule-drivers, and me doing a good part of their work."

"But they ain't got no eighty acres to share-farm like you do," the landlord said. Country neighbors all their lives and remote kinsmen of some sort, they were easy enough with each other, the main difference between them being that he had hold of a thousand acres or so of land, most of it his wife's, and the Y. F. had hold of nothing much but a girl wife and a baby boy, and his wife had nothing but a daddy with a grocery store from whom the Y. F. would accept no help. The best land the landlord had he farmed for himself with hired labor, and the Y. F.'s job in that operation was taking care of the mules, nearly sixty of them. What he got from the sharecrop place, if anything, was extra.

"Eighty acres," he said. "We been over that. Them clay hills is plumb wore out, like they was when your papa got through with them. It takes about ten roosters to fertilize one egg, up there."

The landlord grinned and said, "Didn't I use to farm it too? I told you, whenever old Haskins makes up his mind to go ahead and die, I'll let you have that place he's got."

"Haskins is good for another twenty years," the Y. F. said. "Anybody that talks that much about how he hurts. All I want is five dollars more a month, Josh. Thirty-five measly bucks."

"Ain't nothing measly about a buck right now," the landlord said. "I can't see it."

"Well, I ain't staying."

"Sure you are," said Josh. "No place else to go, these days. Loan me a bite off your Tinsley, if you got some that ain't sweated up."

"No, I ain't staying," the Y. F. repeated without anger, fishing for his tobacco and pondering the fact that after all that was what it came to, not staying. Leaving Little Dixie. Well, by God, that was what it came to, then. . . .

The old Chalmers touring car, shot when he bought it and not much improved since, carried them as far as Sweetwater, Texas, before it blew up for good. An aging bachelor with a filling station watched it die with them, continuing to squirt his hose into the radiator even after it was clear that whatever water went in was coming right back out again through a big crack in the engine block, not that the tires would have gone much farther anyhow or the gasoline money either. Then he put them in a lean-to room back of the station and fed them pinto beans and biscuits until the Y. F. got a job carrying water in buckets to workers on a pipeline, kid work at kid pay.

Still and all, he believed it was going to work out. But then one night the baby died with a quick fever before they were even certain he was sick, and her family sent her a train ticket so she could come back home and eat groceries out of the store with them, and she left alone because he would not go with her.

"Not won't, honey," he said. "Can't. It's like I'd done swore to it. I left out for good. You go ahead if you want to, and I'll send for you later when you got your feelings straightened out."

"I don't promise nothing," Laurie said. "I just want my mama. I want to sit down and look at some trees and not think about nothing at all."

Later, divorce papers caught up with him somewhere and he signed them. He was still twenty-seven, having been doing man's labor since fourteen when his parents and sister died of the World War flu and he quit school to drive pipe-wagons in the oilfields for a while. He had now no people anywhere closer than an aunt or two and some cousins. He could not think at all about the baby for a long long time, and he felt guilty about Laurie too, all the rest of his life. But she had known about the leaving for good.

Josh wrote him also and said a lot of the mules were sick and soremouthed and he had not really known the Y. F. wanted a pay raise all that bad, and as the Y. F. read that part he grinned a little bit sourly. He wasn't going back. He might be good and messed up, but he wasn't hemmed in any more.

He did miss mules and cows and things, though, and missed farming talk and country talk, there among the rootless hard oil-field workers. They worked through country—mesquite country and grass country, sandy and rocky, rough and smooth—but they paid it no mind at all. By now he had followed work a hundred miles south, into the rolling limestone Edwards Plateau region, a full pipeliner himself with fair wages for those times. But one Saturday when he heard a dried-up old rancher talking in a café with someone about trying to hire a fence crew, he sidled three stools over and asked about it. And though the pay, besides food, was not much more than tobacco and shoeleather money he took a job, riding out the next day on the back end of a flatbed truck with fifty sacks of cottonseed cake and three Mexicans and two bleary pale winos while the rancher and a couple of slobbering border collies sat in front. He knew about post holes and barbed wire and all that tedium, but it would be country work anyhow. He had had enough of long straight ditches and of threading big pieces of iron pipe into one another, and of listening to his fellows' talk of intermeshed weekend beer and fights and poon-tang. People were the different ways they were and he had known about that for a long time and it was all right with him. But a couple of his mother's half-Indian brothers had been mean, troublesome, hard-case drunks and as a kid he had seen enough of that. It was not a way of life he hankered toward.

Nine months later when the fencing was all done the Y. F., having outlasted a succession of Anglo drifters whose thirst that limestone vastness enhanced, and several wetbacks whose homesickness finally won out over the lure that even Depression gringo wages held, went to the ranch house to draw his pay, which he had let ride till then. It was a two-story, wooden-galleried cube of limestone slabs put up in a liveoak grove by the rancher's grandfather in the late 1860s, when he had brought his clan there from the Fredericksburg German country, with Comanches still around. It sat in a pretty valley, and the barn and other outbuildings were of stone too, with hewn timbers, more solid by far than any country structures the Y. F. had ever seen before. The rancher, a widower in his late fifties named Schraeder, lived in the house with eleven border collies, sipped bootleg sotol through the day without ever getting drunk, was attended by an aged scolding Mexican cook who had her own stone cabin nearby, and for help kept a couple of married vaqueros whose children were shouting this evening down at the springfed cypress-bordered creek below the house where they swam.

He had a big nose and small sharp dark eyes and spoke nasal West Texas English tinged by the separate facts that he had grown up speaking German at home, and that during the several years since his wife had died he had had little occasion to speak anything but Tex-Mex Spanish except on visits to town. There was windmill grease on his shirt. He said, shoving a sheaf of bills toward the Y. F. across the table, in his office by the living room, "I stuck in a little extra. Shame it ain't more, the way you worked."

"I only done what there was," the Y. F. said.

"I watched you," old Schraeder said. "Getting ten hours a day out of them old rummies without even making them mad. Treating them Meskins like they was people and learning some of their talk."

"Nothing hard about that. They're pretty good folks."

"Damn right they are," said Schraeder. "One of my grandmamas was a Meskin."

"One of mine was an Indian."

"You like this country?"

"I guess I do," the Y. F. said. "It ain't what I'm used to, but a man feels like he amounts to something, sort of."

"The way you handle them wagon mules, I bet you could make out with cows and horses and goats and stuff."

"I reckon I could."

"Well, God damn, I guess we'll keep you," old Schraeder said without the subject's having been mentioned before, and kicked at a dog beneath the table that had just horribly broken wind. He said, "She always feeds them frijoles. . . . You'll have to take orders from Domingo for a while, but I don't guess you'll mind that. He knows more about the place than anybody, maybe including me."

"You got some farming that needs doing," the Y. F. said.

"*Farming?*"

"You got some flat bottomland here in this valley that ain't never been turned," the Y. F. said. "Deep black dirt, two or three hundred acres anyhow, maybe more. It don't need nothing but a little brush cleared off. You could run water on it out of that creek and raise plenty of winter oats and hay and stuff. Or anything else."

"Chingar," old Schraeder said. "All we needed around here was somebody else trying to run things. It was one reason my grand-papa moved out on them other Dutchmen way back yonder, to get away from dirt farming. That and a Meskin wife that didn't like Dutchmen and they didn't like her."

"Just the same, it makes sense. Ain't no point in buying all that hay and feed you use."

"We'll see," the rancher said. "You'll be staying here at the house; there's a room old Juana can fix up for you."

Which was the start of that.

*   *   *

He added hot coffee to his cup without sweetening it further, and carried it out the back door into the little patio space there, under a big hackberry. Gray cold dawn light had come on, with no wind still, and somewhere a redbird throated chew, chew, tentatively and did not finish the song. The space was paved with old street bricks he had hauled in from a dumpground, and had flowerbeds and chairs and a table and a grill, also made of street bricks, where sometimes he cooked meat. It was enclosed all about with fences and hedges and had evolved in the past few years as a refuge against the increasing stir of people as the neighborhood built up around them. The O. F.

liked its privacy though without usually admitting that he did, it having been Samantha's idea in the beginning.

Beyond the gate in the wood fence that walled the patio to the rear, in the bare-dirt chicken and laundry yard outside his garden, he paused to look at his bees, three trim white hives that he had broken down and rummaged through a few days before, to find that they had wintered well and were rearing young for spring. One solitary worker trundled out onto a hive porch in a little semicircle, found the air still too cool for bees, and without stopping went back inside to spread that news. Later in the day, though, they would be working oaks and things for pollen. The O. F. while sipping coffee and watching the hives reached up with his free hand and felt along a hackberry branch that dipped down across the fence, and thumbed the green flex of emerging buds. He would have to move the hives soon, probably to the orchard now that no cow grazed there to nose them over. Samantha claimed they soiled her sheets on the line and the O. F. knew it was true; a bee with a load of poot was too neat ever to drop it in the hive but even in winter would fly straight out and cut loose in the air. He liked bees and had been around them forever. At Schraeder's he had kept fifty-odd colonies, a few in good frame hives like these and the rest in tall boxes of the sort his father had once used. Here near the city they were less pleasure than they had been at first, with people planting ligustrum hedges that queered honey and spraying poisons that killed bees.

The thermometer bee, or another like it, came out and looked around again. "You better go back in there and holler up a rain dance," the O. F. told it. "Ain't going to be much flowers, the way things are."

Setting his empty cup on one of the hives, he dipped milo maize from a can in a shed and scattered it, then let the hens out of their house. They filed through the little flap-doored entrance and down the cleated board in order of their known precedence, fat big Orpingtons certain of their dignity and in no hurry, each with one wing clipped to keep her from flying over fences. He wanted to hatch some eggs this spring, and needed a rooster soon.

Beside the henhouse on the alley side his eye sensed pale movement, and when he turned and looked, it was a little red-eyed, bench-legged, white feist dog standing with some surprised belligerence not far from the hole through which he had just come under the heavy net fence, and which the O. F. had been intending for weeks now to stop up.

"Dog, what you got in mind?" the O. F. asked.

The feist replied with a low-muttered insolent growl whose purport was clearly that it was none of the O. F.'s business. But it was. The O. F. knew, from out of his long countryman's experience with wandering canines, just about what the feist had in mind, or what if not now he would soon have in mind.

Nothing having happened, the dog tried a somewhat more confident growl almost edging into a bark. The O. F., raising one shoulder and lowering the other and waggling loose hands at his sides, leered grotesquely and lurched toward him. The half-bark became a squall and the feist turned and ran for the hole under the fence, bumping his head three times against the thick bottom wire before he got it through and fled off down the alley.

You could practically always do that with little red-eyed dogs.

"That ain't a very nice way to act," someone said, and the O. F. swung guiltily toward the voice and saw a dark lean tousled girl in green standing in the alley, smiling slightly. A part of his mind recalled hearing a car door slam on the highway and then an engine's surge; someone had let her out.

"I got chickens," he said—unnecessarily, for the big hens were chortling and scratching among the feed he had strewn for them.

"We lived in a country kind of a place when I was little," the girl said. "And we had us some big white turkeys and a dog got in and killed twelve of them one night. Not even to eat, just to kill."

"Uh-huh," said the O. F., relieved to find comprehension. "Did your daddy get the dog?"

"I never had no daddy," the girl said shortly. "At least that I remember. He hauled out."

The O. F. grunted and studied her. The long black hair needed a hard combing and there were smudged pouches beneath the dark eyes, but it was a shapely enough lean face with maybe a little Indian in it, or something like that. And a lot of tiredness, years of that. Not over twenty-five or twenty-six, maybe less. The green dress was rumpled and into his head came suddenly an old jukebox tune, with fiddles. Coreen, Coreena, it said. . . .

Coreen, Coreena-a-a-ah,
Where'd you stay last night?

He said, "I got a girl that looks a little bit like you."

"I bet she looks better than me right now," the girl said. "I bet she ain't sneaking home to her kids up no damn alley at six thirty on Sunday morning."

"She could be, honey," the O. F. said. "I don't know where to God she is."

"You run her off."

"No," he said. "No, I don't think so. Maybe I ought to have known more than I did, to help her some."

The girl looked at him gently but with dismissal; she had enough troubles of her own, the look said. "Anyhow, your girl had a daddy," she said. "Good-bye, old man." And went on along the alley, teetering a little on high heels in its dry rough-rutted ground.

You're all mussed up,
And your clothes don't fit you right.

Feeling older than he had before, the O. F. brought salvaged bricks from a pile in the corner of the chicken yard and laid them in the hole beneath the fence, stamping them firm with his heel. He was not ready to think about Midge yet, Midge being one trouble with Sundays, when you did tend to think. Midge who had come to see him six months before, for the first time in nine years, and had gone away into nowhere again . . . He passed through the garden gate and closing it behind him squatted at the end of a row of young potato plants to survey the lines of early things, frost-safe or nearly so, that he had been putting in since January, each in its proper time. English peas grasping upward blindly for the fencewire trellis he had erected for them. Radishes and lettuce, already usable. Chard and beets and carrots and cabbage and collards and onions, some almost mature and others just thin green lines of recent sprouts, and in between the rows the nearly weedless, cultivated prairie earth, blacker now than when he had first turned it up from sod nine years before, mellow and sooty with humus from the manure and hay and compost he had fed it season by season, year by year. Ritually and almost without knowledge that he did it, he reached down and grasped a light clod, and felt it collapse flakily between his fingers.

By God, he might not know all he needed to know about people, and he was fairly certain now that he never would. But he knew dirt, and dirt knew him, and dirt mattered. The feel of it light and right in his hand or the smell and look of it turning up and over from a plow or slicing beneath a hoe or churning under the tines of a tiller took away from feeling old and set worry to one side. He knew it was not so for everyone. . . . Of boys he had known in childhood, raised on the same tired red hill land his father and he had had to work and live from, many had taken off for towns and factories and filling stations and railroad jobs as soon as they were big enough, bitter against the soil for the rest of their lives. Others less rebellious had stayed on to hate it and fight with it where they were, as their fathers had done, maybe with tractors now, maybe forcing a little more production from the sour clay with what bagged fertilizer they could afford or their landlords were willing to furnish. Or maybe doing it better now; he did not know. He had not gone back to see, ever. Nor felt the need to go.

There were bound to have been some, he knew, who like himself knew about good dirt from seeing it in the bottoms that richer farmers owned, and on the high hillsides too steep to plow, where trees grew from it and grasses held it firm. Some even who understood that by caring and by work you could make sorry tired old dirt over again into good, if you had time and the stuff to do it with. His mother had shown him that in the little garden she kept, red rain-eaten clay in the beginning, with a little sand to it, like everything else around that farm. He had watched and helped from babyhood as she hauled to it pitiful interminable buckets and barrows full of chicken and mule and milk cow poot and forest leaves and pea hulls and hogpen muck and dead dogs and snakes and poultry-plant guts and heads and feathers and anything else she could get hold of, and dug them all in with a hoe, and sowed year after year in the darkening loosening soil her queer Choctaw jumbles of corn and tomatoes and beans and squash and things not even in proper rows, but always lush.

You could only own land in your head, his mother said, the way she owned that garden. They had never had title to it or to anything else worth having, but they had eaten well just about always. It was God that did it, she said, God in the dirt. You fed God and He fed you. He supposed she had been about half-crazy, his mother, raised

among the sad, beaten, uprooted, preacher-hating Indians that were
her own mother's people, with a white sot father who showed up
from time to time to make another baby. Other people had thought
her crazy. He did not even know how she had worked out that business about God, or where the seed of it had come from; some full-
Indian farmers he had known had been as iron-headed and brutal
toward the land as anyone else.

But he was glad enough to have had her for a mother, crazy or
not, for what she had shown him about dirt. Dirt was, if truth were
told, a big part of his own religion too.

*   *   *

And despite old Schraeder's voiced distaste for farming, he had
had a streak of that religion inside him. It was the damned Dutch
blood, he said. Mainly he had it in terms of grass and rain and animals, and keeping cows off a hilly range that was starting to wash,
and refusing to put out poison bait for coyotes till they had eaten up
two or three dozen goats, and things like that. But long before the
Y. F. turned up at the ranch, Schraeder had been aware of that good
bottomland and had thought over its possible use. Now, with someone else who cared, he found a contractor with a big crew of wetbacks and set them to grubbing out mesquite and pear, and months
later when they were through they had uncovered nearly four hundred acres of flat plowland in six fields along the creek.

It was too much farming for mules and a man or two or three,
though the Y. F. said it wasn't, not if they concentrated on getting one
or two of the fields in shape each year. He started in stubbornly with
a team and a rusty double sulky plow traded from a neighboring
ranch, but a couple of Saturdays later old Schraeder rattled home
from town with a new green tractor and a one-way disk plow chained
down to the big bed of his truck, and told the Y. F. to go in and charge
any other implements he needed.

"A field a year ain't enough," he said. "I want to get a look at
the whole shittaroo all green and pretty before I die."

The climate with its long dry spells and its searing winds and its
short wet stormy times whose moisture you had to save and use just
right was new to the Y. F., and Schraeder knew nothing about farming at all. Their first winter oats were sparse and nearly worthless for

grazing because the Y. F. had not allowed for moisture and time enough to rot the turned-under sod before he sowed. But a wet spring followed and in the summer they made enough sudan hay that Schraeder sold five thousand bales over and above what his animals could possibly eat in the four dead months of the winter to come. In time they got the feel of it, aided by the virgin land.

The fifth year, the Y. F. ditched and bordered for irrigation in two of the flattest, largest fields and sowed them to permanent alfalfa, and before long the farming and the haying were an easy part of the ranch's functioning, along with calf work in spring and fall, and doctoring through the year, and shearing mohair goats, and fencing and fixing windmills, and the other things there were to do on eleven thousand rough acres with three hundred cows and six to eight hundred goats and assorted horses and mules and machines. By then the little colony of ranch Mexicans saw him as a part of things, and liked him. He was into his thirties and therefore, I suppose, no longer a Y. F. but just a lean tough-fibered F. The hard, dusty, pleasant work suited him well, even horses, for he had always been quick with his hands and with beasts. And if he remained clumsy with a lariat rope, a tool you needed to come to young, the fact was that with Domingo and Tomás around, nobody else got to do much roping anyhow. . . .

In the town he found a library with a section of farming and livestock books, and he took to deviling old Schraeder about new and better ways to do things, sometimes with success. They built working chutes and headgates in the corrals, which disgusted Domingo and Tomás but got cow work done faster and less roughly, and cross-fenced some of the pastures to manage the grass better, and rotated crops on the farmland, and began to put bulls with the cows for only a couple of months a year, to make calves drop together in the spring before screw-worms made a start. From books, most of it . . . Sometimes, though, Schraeder balked.

"I don't want no part of it," he said of a hog-raising scheme the F. proposed. "No more than I did with them snotty-nosed sheep I finally got shut of. If you like hogs, you build you a pen out of sight down the creek somewhere so they can't get in my water or eat my grass or stink up my air, and I'll sell you grain and hay for what it costs to raise, and you sell them fat nasty bastards for what you can get, and keep it. I ain't no hog man."

Later on, out of hogs and other things that Schraeder didn't mind his doing but wanted no part of, the F. made some years as much as four thousand dollars besides his pay, but that too suited the old man fine. If you did your work for him he was for your getting whatever else you could, and for that matter some of the F.'s random projects, like the bees and the big vegetable patch by the creek, had side benefits for everyone.

At thirty-six he married the librarian in the town, a spinster of thirty-three. It was perhaps inevitable, since she was one of the only unmarried women he ever saw, and Samantha saw few men who cared for books. The ones he liked were only one kind of books and no Hawthorne or Poe, but books. It was his energy too, she said later when things had gone a bit sour and she was wondering aloud what had inflicted them on each other, a habit perhaps developed by reading Poe, or someone. "Like something was about to break out through your skin," she said. "Like you were going to start running, or jump up in the air and yell."

"I still got it," the F. said. "You just don't like where it goes to any more."

"I don't care where it goes," she said. "I just want a house in a town and some neighbors the girls can learn to talk to in English. What you like is doing things. What I want is to be somebody."

Though without saying so, the F. could not see the difference. What you did you were.

Of the way he was in those early years at Schraeder's, he later remembered mainly a feeling like leaning forward on his toes, straining to get on into what came next to do. All the hemmed-in Little Dixie thing was gone, along with red clay and Laurie and Josh and the rest. So God-awful many things to do now, good things worth doing, and the days and years so short . . . After they married they lived in a rock house by the creek where one of Schraeder's uncles had once lived, and a baby came, Kate, and a war too but they did not want him at his age with a mule-kicked knee, and still there was more to do than there were days. When Midge was born in the last year of the war and Samantha started tugging toward the town, he was forty-two and had been at Schraeder's, he counted up without believing it, for fourteen years. He wished to hell the young bad years had gone that fast, and the good ones had slowed down.

Not that they were finished, just changed a little. He did not have the habit of introspection, but he knew he was not built for fighting with a woman. As far as he knew, she was right, and that possibility made him guilty. Women, he recognized by now, made him guilty. With money he had saved from pay and hogs and things he bought a little white frame house in the town an hour away from the ranch, and she moved there with the girls. The arrangement had worked as well as anything could have worked for them, he guessed. He stayed there in town sometimes, driving out to work, but less and less with the years. Mainly he used his old room at Schraeder's house and moved out to the cottage by the creek when Samantha brought the kids down for weekends, and always for the summer. Summers were good, the girls at the creek or on ponies, yelling Spanish with Tomás's kids, Samantha soft and easy with him now that she could get away when she wanted.

Old Schraeder said little about other people's business, but observed one winter night at supper, "A man like you and me, he don't want to expect too much of a woman and kids. It's like he ain't got room to give them what they want."

He had two children in their forties, the F. knew, neither of whom ever came to the ranch. The daughter was a hard drinker working on a fourth rich husband in San Antonio and the son was an executive of some sort.

He said, "I reckon you're right. The trouble is, there's Midge."

"Midge," Schraeder said, and grinned. Kate at fifteen was the head of her class at the town's high school, but Midge at ten was another thing. "The trouble ain't Midge," he said. "The trouble is you and the way you're so damn crazy on her. Why don't you bring her on out here and make a tomboy Meskin cowgirl out of her, like you want to? She could ride the bus to school."

The F. shook his head. "Samantha don't like that notion," he said. "And I guess she's right. They fight all the time, but a little girl needs her mother."

(He had told Midge that too, after she had brought up the same idea one evening and there had been loudness and Samantha had left the room about to cry. Midge looked at him with hazel eyes out of a dark Indian-jawed face in which he could see his own. "I don't need her," she said. "I don't need her ever. I need you and Concepción and Paint and the creek."

"Honey, it won't work," he said. "We got to think about your mama." And she had turned and run out of the house, after which he had been obliged to feel guilty about her and her mother both.

Schraeder said, "Uh-huh. Did you all bring in that old cancer-eye cow this morning?"

He died that year at eighty, not frailly diseased but hacked up in a wreck of the new car he drove between the ranch and town with the pedal on the floor. He lived through whatever they did to him at the hospital, and the F. with Domingo and Tomás was let in to see him. Old Schraeder with tubes running in and out of him breathed hard and looked at the F. through half-closed small dark eyes and blinked in recognition.

The F. said, "We're here."

"Hola, Don Gus," said Domingo softly. "Man, horses are not that bad."

Schraeder blinked again, then closed his eyes. They went out and sat in the corridor with a priest whom Schraeder, a thoroughly apostate Catholic, had refused even to look at, until a nurse came to say that the old man was dead, and the F. felt somehow that it had not ended right. They had been together for twenty-four years, he and Schraeder, and there were things he would have liked to say, though he did not have the words and perhaps they hadn't needed saying.

He stayed on at the ranch as manager for seven years after that, hardly ever seeing Schraeder's son to whom he sent accounts, running things as they had been run, though without any longer the push to find new things to do and new ways to do the old ones. Then in 1962, with Kate through nurse training and married to a young intern in Dallas and Midge just finishing high school God knew how, the ranch was sold to an Abilene oilman who had ideas of his own about how to run it and a manager of his own to carry them through. Domingo and Tomás stayed on with their wives and what children were still there, but the F. moved out with little regret except over leaving them; he was fifty-nine and had money saved besides a lump that Schraeder had willed to him. He walked down and kicked at the dark moist earth of one of the alfalfa fields, and that was good-bye enough between him and the place. He would own it in his head, if he never saw it again. Schraeder had understood about that. He had owned the ranch himself, in his head and on paper both, but he had known that the F. and Domingo and Tomás owned some of it too. The F. guessed the oilman and his manager would own it that way in their turn. He hoped for the sake of the land that they would.

Midge was supposed to go to college that fall and Samantha said she wanted to, beneath the sullen silence that had come to be her way toward them. In between spells of running off to New Mexico with a girl friend and getting expelled from school for smoking or squabbling with teachers or something else, she had always been good with English and math and things she cared about. But one Saturday night in August she went out to a movie with a local good-looking dreamer who had had a couple of years at the University, and on Monday she telephoned from Austin to say that they were married.

"That's what you want, is it?" the O. F. said against Samantha's sobbing from the sofa. For an O. F. he felt himself to be by now.

"I guess so, Papa," she said. "It's time I did something on my own."

"Well, see if you can do it right."

"I will," she said. "Tell Mama . . ."

"What?"

"Nothing," Midge said. "Don't tell her anything. I love you." And hung up, having said that last thing for the first time in years. The trouble was, he saw, that she was the way he had been, dark and quick and restless and hemmed in, and he had not been able to help. There had been a time when he might have helped, but he hadn't.

He made a try, too late. She wrote them once and then no more, and after four months he drove to Austin to look for her. The address was in an old unpainted district near the river, with used-car lots, and there was a hard fat woman who said yes, they had lived over her garage for a time and had left owing rent. "He growed a big mustache," she said. "All he done was monkey with that God damn motorsackle he traded his car in on. Took it apart and put it back together. They come to repossess it but he had done lit a shuck out of here."

"Midge said he was writing on a book."

"Some book," the fat woman said. "All them God damn gears and wheels and nuts and bolts and things drooling grease on my driveway. I think she was pregnant when they left. In fact, I ain't real sure they left together; he might of took out first. . . ."

*   *   *

After that, the O. F. considered, things had mainly just happened to him, more or less hemming him in again, though it did not matter as it had when he was young. Old, having known something different for a while, you went ahead and let things happen and said the hell with them. Most things.

Anyhow he had put this place together; whatever it was was mainly his doing. When Kate had had her first baby in the city where her husband was a resident surgeon and was going to practice later, there had been no good reason to resist moving there as Samantha wanted to do, to be near. Not into the city itself—he had had the sense to balk at that. But onto a bought half-acre of nearly open prairie by the highway well outside of town, with some hackberry trees and a little house that he braced and re-sided and re-roofed and added onto that first year, besides starting his garden and orchard. Scrawny though it was, in shaping it up with fences and pens and sheds, in turning new earth and nurturing trees, there was some of the feeling he remembered from the good years with old Schraeder. Sometimes in his mind as he worked he talked to Schraeder, arguing with him usually as they had so often argued, for Schraeder even dead was very stubborn, and so was the live O. F. Their worst disagreement had been over whether or not to stretch expensive non-climbable Ellwood V-mesh fencing around the rear of the place, Schraeder saying it was a waste of money. But the O. F., who won the argument, was proved right later on when the neighborhood grew and small boys proliferated.

She had showed up at the filling station one day in early fall, having found out somehow that he worked there. It was a big messy friendly station and garage with a café next to it, out beyond the edge of things, and was much favored by truckers and by countrymen hauling trailerloads of animals to or from the city's auction yards, and people like that. They were one reason the O. F. had taken part-time work there five years before—they and the fact, which he cited obdurately to Samantha and Kate, that he had always earned some sort of a living and wasn't going to stop doing so till he had to. He understood their objections, as mother-in-law and wife of a sharp young doctor on his way up, to greasy-handed garage work and banter with the profane owners of small ranches two counties out from the city; he was even willing to feel a little guilty about it. But the people Kate and the doctor knew did not hang around that station, and the O. F. kept on with his work.

He was at the grease rack that morning when the station's owner, a hardworking nervous man of fifty, came to get him. "You got a personal customer," he said.

"Quit it," said the O. F. "I ain't got time to kid. That fellow wants this pickup by eleven."

"I'll finish it," the owner said. "She wants you, asked for you. Wish some that looked like that would come around asking for me."

She was parked beside the station in a big maroon hardtop, and the O. F. when he saw her said, "Lord God."

"Hey, Papa," she said, a woman, with made-up eyes and lips and tended dark hair and a yellow open-throated dress that looked expensive. She said, "I wanted to say hello."

"Get out of the car," the O. F. said. "No, wait. I'll tell them I'm leaving and we can go someplace and talk."

"I don't want to talk," she said. "I'm not going to stay. I just wanted to get a look at you."

"Something to look at, ain't I?" the O. F. said, seeing through her eyes old peaked cap, stained green khaki uniform, seamed sagging bespectacled face, callused grease-marked hands, all.

"Damn right," said Midge. "You're beautiful."

"You won't . . ." he said, and stopped, knowing her as stubborn as himself, and no longer a child. He said, "What are you doing, honey?"

"Dancing," she said.

"I'm talking about every day. What do you *do?*"

"I dance," Midge said, and grinned. "They call it exotic. . . . I make out all right, I guess."

"Here? This town?"

"No. I move around. Papa, don't ask questions."

"Still married?"

"Just don't," Midge said. "Some of the answers you might like all right, and some of the others you wouldn't, and there isn't any point."

"All right," he said, for she had always been able to make sense to him when she wanted to. "I missed you."

"God, I missed you too," she said, and looked down at her lap. When she looked back up again her eyes were shiny but she said, "Good-bye. Tell Mama and Kate I said hello, if you want to."

"I probably won't," the O. F. said. "Could you send a postcard once a year? It'd help."

"Maybe. There isn't much point, though. I left, Papa."

"Yes, you did," he said. "I guess you had to."

"Good-bye," Midge said.

"Don't let them get you down," said the O. F.

"They already did," Midge said, and started the big engine, and drove out into traffic, not looking back.

He supposed it was something just to have seen her, to know she had survived. Even if it did wake the whole thing up again, inside you . . . It *was* going to rain, some time soon. Rising from his squat at the end of the potato row, he felt it in his mule-kicked left knee, and gripped the kneecap with his hand as he straightened up. Toward the southeast when he looked, a long dome of misty cloud showed above the horizon, blowing in fast from the faraway sea and obscuring the risen sun. With certainty he knew that the land would get rain out of this one, and high time, too.

"Hello, Grummer," the boy said behind him.

"Don't let them chickens in," said the O. F., shooing with his hand. The big yellow hen squawked and ran back out through the garden's gate, and the boy in Sunday clothes and tie closed it behind him. "Hello, boy," the O. F. said. "You and your mother come to get Grummy for early church?"

"Yeah, but she's not ready. What you doing out here?"

"Watching things grow," said the O. F. "If you lean down and listen right close, you can hear them squeak, coming up out of the ground."

"Go on," the boy said. "Mama says it's nasty, that junk you put in the garden. All that ganure and stuff I helped you with."

"The nastier the better," his grandfather told him, bending to yank at an early sprig of johnsongrass. "And after you feed it to the dirt and the dirt eats it up, it ain't nasty any more. It's beans and potatoes and such."

The boy looked dubious, but he would think it over; he had that kind of mind. They got along well enough, he and the boy, considering that they only saw each other once a week or so these days. But the rest of the time it was Kate and her ideas about how things were or ought to be, and the doctor father, and school, and TV, and God knew what all else, and before very long there wouldn't be much he'd want to hear from a beat-up sort of country grandfather that chewed Tinsley Natural Leaf. There were signs already. It was all right; the boy would have to live in that city world of which the O. F. stubbornly knew as little as he could manage to know. He wondered for maybe the thousandth time if Midge had had a child or children, and if so what they were like. He saw them as like her. Briefly and with a foreknown ache of longing, he indulged in a vision of himself in a rock house in a creek-watered green valley like Schraeder's, but his own, with dark and quick and restless grandchildren all around, learning country things. At night sometimes he went to sleep with that vision in his mind.

The boy said, "Man, those Lions really clobbered them last night."

"Did they?" said the O. F., and tousled the boy's combed head, feeling it lean gladly into his touch.

"Grummer," the boy said frowning.

"Ho," the O. F. said.

"Grummer, say you had like a dog and he died, and you buried him in the ground. . . . And then something green grows up there and you eat it. Would you be eating that dog?"

"In a way you would," the O. F. said. "I reckon we eat just about everything that ever lived, every time we eat."

After thought, the boy looked up. "I don't care," he said. "It's not nasty. It's like eating Jesus in church."

"Maybe it is, at that," said his grandfather, nudging dark loose earth with his toe and feeling in old hurts the certainty of rain. "We feed the dirt, and the dirt feeds us."

"His Chapter" is from *Hard Scrabble: Observations on a Patch of Land* (New York: Knopf, 1974; Austin: Texas Monthly Press, 1985; Houston: Gulf Publishing Company, 1993). Reprinted by permission of Alfred A. Knopf, Inc.

Composed in Baskerville types with Rhapsodie Special initial.

NINETEEN COWS

STANDARD AGRICULTURAL publications and the farm-ranch pages of our Sunday newspapers tend to be condescending toward small-scale cattle raisers, as indeed they are toward small-scale anybody else in this age of agribusiness, or agri-bigness as someone has called it. Only the other day I ran across a slighting reference, in an interview with a Texas A&M professor who was touting the recycling of used Baggies into feedlot rations or something on that order, to "people that have nineteen cows." It stung a bit, for I usually have only a few more cows than that myself—rarely in excess of about thirty-five, with a bull and varying numbers of attendant offspring from year to year. But it didn't sting very much, because no learned Aggie could possibly wax more brilliantly caustic about my relationship to bovines than I have waxed about it myself when a bad winter or a drouthy summer has made tending them an onerous daily concern, or when the market for calves, as frequently, is so miserable that any owner who can count on his fingers can see clearly that they're costing him more to raise than there's any chance of recouping when he sells them as his land's major product.

And yet, despite occasional resolves to get rid of the whole herd and to let the land revert to brushy wildlife habitat where I might stroll unconcerned bearing gun or fieldglass or just a set of appreciative feelings toward nature in her magnificence, such as it is around here, I'm still saddled with my quota of these large and fairly stupid beasts about a decade and a half after buying the eight weanling Angus heifers that were the mothers and grandmothers of my present bunch. Nor does it seem too likely that I'll break loose from them unless I manage to break loose from the land itself, a possibility that I think about fondly from time to time when country life grows cluttered and demanding. For the cattle, unnumerous and marginally economic though they may be, constitute the place's reason for being, in a way. It has been "improved" with them in mind. Together with some goats and a couple of horses they make it a "stock farm," a designation that usually serves to convince the mercenary outside world, including the Internal Revenue Service, that I'm not hopelessly impractical in my possession of the better part of a square mile of rough country most of which is suitable for nothing but herbivores and wild things.

Another trouble is that for foggy and complex reasons I like cows, stupid or not, and like the simple, only occasionally arduous, annual routine of working with them. Beef cattle take care of themselves during a good part of a normal year if given enough pasture to graze—what constitutes "enough" varying quite a bit from region to region. In my neighborhood the carrying capacity of average unimproved grassland is usually stated as about twenty acres per animal unit: i.e., one grown cow with or without a calf, or equivalent numbers or fractions of other beasts depending on size and appetite. Elsewhere the requisite acreage may be considerably less or a great deal more, according to rainfall and the richness of the land. Whatever it is, if you stay within it, most years your cattle will be all right with only a little labor on your part. If you don't you'll run out of grass, have to buy and haul in a lot of feed, and get to watch your denuded topsoil escape as silt or dust under rains and winds, but of course you'll be in good historic company. Overstocking has long been the rule in most of the West and elsewhere, and it still is among some operators. Of one rancher in Bosque County just south of me, they used to say that every morning he'd go to a slope in his pasture and lie down on his belly, and if by looking up toward the hilltop and the sky he could see a sprig of anything growing, he'd go out and buy another ten cows.

Much of the work with cattle lies in making sure they've got enough to eat during the hard parts of the year, chiefly winter, and that what they eat has all they need in it. This means storing up hay in spring and summer for the dead months and hauling it to them in a pickup when needed, sowing wheat or oats or rye on patches of arable land in fall for green high-protein grazing while regular grasses are dormant, and buying supplements and processed feed for use when rains fail or extreme cold keeps the green stuff from growing. Dry summers mean some extra feeding too. Otherwise, except for such general rancherly activities as doctoring occasional injuries and ailments, keeping an eye on first-calf heifers in case they need obstetrical help, segregating the younger ones against rape before their time, spraying or dusting the herd against flies, and fighting back brush in pastures to keep it from crowding out grass, the main work has to do with the production and nurture and management of calves, which are your stock farm's primary crop and the chief source of such cash profit, if any, as you will enjoy from it.

In the days when the horrific screw-worm was bad in Texas one of its favorite points of attack was the navels of newborn calves, where an infection could quickly prove fatal. Sensible owners therefore tried to restrict calving to winter and early spring before the flies that bred these gnawing maggots appeared—which, gestation being a little over nine months, meant running a bull with the cows from about February until midsummer and then taking him away to dwell lovelessly in solitude or with some steers or horses. Nowadays, with the problem largely eliminated by annual releases of sterile male flies along the border and in northern Mexico, some of us still more or less follow the old schedule either because we're hidebound or because we pessimistically expect the flies to bypass the control program one of these years and come down in swarms again. Others avail themselves of new freedom by arranging to calve in spring and early summer when grasses are usually lush and cows' production of milk is highest.

Most range calves manage to get born without trouble at whatever time of year, and if they have good mothers grow healthily to the age of four or five months before you need to worry much about doing anything to them, though some graziers put out creep feeders to promote growth—roofed bins full of rich stuff that the calves can reach but larger stock can't. But at some point they need to be "worked," a process which I've found sometimes inflicts a bit of trauma on visiting non-enthusiasts but which, despite a component of casual brutality, is for cowmen a rather exhilarating task that has in it not only a lot of fine dust and bellowing and kicking and uproar but also the solid satisfaction of bringing order out of chaos. The main operations are inoculation of the calves against two or three common diseases (more in humid regions), marking them with a brand and/or earmarks and/or numbered eartags, worming where intestinal worms are a problem, dehorning horned breeds if you dislike horns, and castrating the males.

Except on some big ranches and among people who just like cowboying, few calves these days are worked in the old colorful way with ropers on horseback and other people who throw the beasts and hold them down while still others utilize knives and syringes and branding irons. Skilled help in this as in other realms is short, so instead nearly all small operators and most big ones do the job with a minimum of assistants by driving or tolling the herd into a set of pens, separating the calves, and shunting them through alleys and chutes to some device that catches them and holds them more or less firmly. This can be a simple headgate that grabs the neck or, more efficiently and expensively, a squeeze chute that clamps on the whole creature or a "calf cradle" that not only clamps but then swings up and presents him to the attentions of his nurturers like, in the poet's phrase, a patient etherized upon a table. Except that anesthesia is not a part of the process.

Anthropomorphism being what it is, castration is the part that fascinates and bothers unaccustomed spectators most, especially male ones. It needs to be done in part because the market usually pays better for steers than for bulls, though many will argue with you that there is no difference in their meat. But the chief reason for it is convenience in handling cattle. Steers are docile, they can be put into a pasture with big nubile heifers without fear the latter will be bred too young, and above all they lack the sexual smolder that sends even young bulls on patrol along fencelines, looking for a way out and often finding it.

On very young calves castration can be accomplished with practically no shock to either subject or witness by using a tool that places a heavy tight rubber band around the upper part of the scrotum, which subsequently atrophies and falls off. But in older animals this poses some danger of tetanus, and they have to be done with the ancient and very efficient knife or some other cutting instrument, or with bloodless emasculators like the Burdizzo, a heavy set of compound-leverage pincers that crush the spermatic cord without breaking skin. This implement was invented many years ago by an old Italian vet, whose name it bears and whom it made rich, and is still manufactured painstakingly in Milan for use throughout the world's warm regions where fresh wounds are subject to quick infection and to parasites. The instructions that come with it bear the doctor's mustached, starch-collared likeness and a rather hilarious photograph of a calf that must have been tranquilized to the gills, since he is shown submitting to the operation without a surge or a kick or, as far as can be told, a bellow of indignation. . . . Here in the Southwest the Burdizzo had its heyday when the screw-worms were having theirs, but even now a good many people, myself among them, still like it for its cleanness and lessened shock effect, though it's more trouble than a knife and can hardly be called humane.

Having worked your calves, the main thing you do with them is sell them at weaning age, six months or so, or maybe a bit earlier or later according to rises and falls in the market and the state of your own pastures for sustaining some extra eaters over a period of time. After perhaps setting aside a steer to keep for fattening and slaughter and a few good heifers to raise as replacements for cows that need to be culled, you load the rest of the calves into a trailer and haul them to a weekly auction at some county seat not far away or maybe, if prices are rumored to be better there, to a city sale like the one on Fort Worth's North Side.

To confess a weakness, I find culling cows harder than almost anything to do with cattle except the worst kind of bloody obstetrics. With a small herd you come to know your animals as individuals and even if you don't view them sentimentally you have favorites among them and a relationship with the whole bunch based on what they have done for you and the longstanding responsibility you've exercised toward them. Hence it weighs a bit on the conscience when one of them has to go the hamburger route, which is where most cull cows do go, because she's started having sorry calves or no calves at all, and it weighs still more when drouth or a hard winter strikes, or cash is requisite, or the herd simply grows too large for the land you've got, and you have to cut back by selling several and need to decide which ones. Records help if you keep them, scribbled notebook pages that detail cows' lineage, birth, quirks, achievements, and imperfections, much in the manner of military service record books or a nosy government's dossiers on its citizens. If, for instance, a bright, large-eyed, trusting, shapely little cow named Pet, who will take feed cubes from your hand and will suffer her ears to be scratched, has been producing tiny calves that never get very big and are prone to things like warts, and an ill-tempered, ungainly, suspicious creature known only as Number Thirty-nine has been rearing one after another a succession of large, thrifty sons and daughters, the records will show it and you know what you have to do. Pet goes, even if the innocent confusion you think to read in her face, as she's hustled through the ring to the music of cracking whips and shouts and the auctioneer's amplified gabble, does cause twinges in your breast.

Not that cold reason always prevails, even with tougher types than me. I once saw an ancient scrub brindle rack of bones, with one horn up and the other down, in the sleek Beefmaster herd of a rancher reputed to be hard-nosed and practical, and asked what she was doing there.

"Oh, Rosie," he said with a shake of his grizzled head, evading the question. "Seventeen years old."

"But why?"

"Guess I like her," he answered with finality and I did not press, for it is unwise to tread on hard people's softnesses.

There are lots of us miniature ranchers across the continent. The scorn expressed by that expert Aggie and by others like him is not at all disinterested but sprouts, I think, from an uneasiness that afflicts agri-bigness types when they're brought eyeball to eyeball with the fact that a goodly percentage of the cattle marketed in the nation these days comes out of small to middlesized herds more or less like mine. This uneasiness afflicts others too, including old-line ranchers, who rather bitterly circulate among themselves such statistical gems as the one that ninety percent of the cattle in the fabulous feedlots of the Texas Panhandle come from the herds of people who own ten cows or less. That figure is hostile hyperbole, but the real ones are impressive enough. A Texas agricultural census shows that in 1974 people with fewer than fifty calving beef cows owned eighteen percent of well over five million such cows in the state, and people with fewer than one hundred cows—still relative small-timers in economic terms—owned thirty-eight percent.

What probably bothers our friend the Aggie most is that we're unpredictable, that the unexpectedly large or small number of beasts that whim or panic causes us to trailer to sales from year to year are a large factor in the market and can mean the loss or gain of millions by feedlots and commodity speculators and other would-be beneficiaries, according to whether they have second-guessed us well or badly. And what understandably gravels full-scale ranchers is that after decades of hardship based on generally poor cattle prices, inflation, rising land and inheritance taxes, and whatnot, they are losing much of what little control they had over their own product to a rabble of johnny-come-latelies. This irritation is heightened by a deterioration of old ranching standards, especially a loss of prestige by the stalwart British breeds of cattle and a new demand for crossbred stuff which is favored by the feedlots, and therefore by the whole market, because its "hybrid vigor" enables it to gain weight faster at less cost—even if, as some ranchers claim and I tend to believe, the meat is not quite so good.

"People like you are just messing things up," one rancher said amiably to me a few years back, when the dimensions of all this were growing visible. His ancestral land was measured in quite a few square-mile sections instead of acres and stocked with several hundred big handsome whitefaces whose careful improvement, through selective breeding and the introduction of bulls from new bloodlines, had begun in his grandfather's time. "You can't make a living out of a little herd like that, and nothing that you do with them is ever done quite right. But there are so damn many of you that you're interfering with the way things are supposed to be. The other day I shipped a truckload of nice prime calves to Fort Worth, and I got six or eight cents a pound less for them than the buyers were bidding for little bunches of raunchy speckled stuff raised by weekend amateurs in the Blacklands and East Texas and Arkansas and God knows where else."

"I've got Angus," I said a bit defensively. "I didn't invent hybrid vigor either."

"Scrub vigor," he said with contempt. But the last time I saw him, a year or so ago, he spoke with enthusiasm about the crossbred calves he was getting from running Charolais bulls with his Hereford cows. Things change, and on the list of proud traditional ranching's troubles we stock-farm types are only a single item—another and more hurtful one being agribusiness itself and the sophisticated activities of "cattlemen" more at home with pocket calculators than saddles and with steer-futures hedging than the identification of range grasses.

There is nothing new about owning a few beef cows, especially in places like Texas where social cachet of a sort has always attached to their possession and the ability to jaw about them. But the emergence of smallish grazing operations as a major sort of land use, from the upper-middle Atlantic coast down through and across the South and in parts of the Midwest as well, has taken place mainly since World War II, I believe, for various reasons of which the strongest are not social and may not even be economic. In part it grew out of the agricultural desolation of the Thirties, when farming was a dead end, and out of government emphasis since that time on taking marginal and tired or wornout country out of cultivation and sowing it to improved permanent grasses to let it rest and to stop erosion. In high-rainfall areas with deep soil, properly managed and fertilized grassland of this sort can be astoundingly productive of beef. Not uncommonly it will sustain a cow on every two or three acres or so, though in time, as world hunger swells, most places with such potential will likely be put back into crops. In less rich terrain, including places like my beat-up patch of rocky hills, the land's carrying capacity is skimpier, but on the other hand grazing is about all it's good for these days anyhow.

One element in beef cattle's appeal is the fact, already intimated, that they represent a lot less work than farming or horticulture, taking care of their own needs much of the time if given half a chance. This has weight with many owners who want their land to pay its way, but who make their main living in towns and cities, and on weekends either don't have time for agriculture or possess an immunity to the sentimental pull of plow and harrow. During market upsurges cattle can also bring in a fair amount of money, and such is human nature that upsurge prices are what cattlemen like to view as the norm, just as farmers are in love with the boom-based reference point of "parity." We are still in an upsurge just now, but unfortunately these joyous intervals have seldom lasted long, for when they begin large numbers of erstwhile spectators jump in, buy overpriced breeding stock of whatever description with borrowed money, throw them onto leased pasture, and flood the market with calves as promptly as biology permits, driving prices back down again. Thus a sleek, staggering, moony-eyed, newborn bullcalf, which your doting mind's eye sees as being worth, say, three hundred dollars or more as a weaned steer a few months later, may turn out to bring half that sum, a crucial difference considering steady inflation and the feed and hay and other things you will have invested in his mama during the long months of pregnancy and nursing. Sad to say, hardship ensues, whether small-scale or large and whether to high flyers or to the rest of us.

Nothing illustrates better the main reason, the irrational one, for the nineteen-cow phenomenon than the fact that so many of us stay with cattle despite such setbacks. We like the damned things, and our real motivation has little to do with money or labor but I suppose must be called romantic. Possibly the pull of the legendary Old West has something to do with it, for in the arteries of the purest romantics among us cowboy blood pumps hot and strong. Big hats and sharp-toed boots are common attire in regions where forty years ago their wearers would have been laughed back into brogans and farmer-style caps, and on full many a hundred-and-sixty-acre spread, on Saturdays, lariats of nylon hiss through the air and traildrivers born too late for the trail whoop yee-haw as they pound along on horseback behind high-tailed fleeing kine, making them wild as deer.

But the majority of us, Old Westerners at heart or no, do things with less flamboyance, mainly because this is easier on both the cattle and us. Some are highly progressive and thoughtful about the matter of management, perhaps lately graduated from some evening-college course in animal husbandry and loaded with data on the protein content of various feeds, artificial insemination, calf "gainability," and pregnancy testing. Others, maybe most, have read a few books and watched the way other folks do things and get along on that, and still others cling to casual methods, right or wrong, picked up in rural youth. A few happy-go-luckies engage in hardly any management at all, letting the beasts run nearly wild within their boundary fences to multiply or die and every once in a while, by one means or another, gathering up calves and selling them. And another contingent, gamblers at heart, keep no breeding stock but buy steers and heifers small and sell them large, at a profit if they're lucky.

Thus, clearly, unless a nineteen-cowman's proclivities get him slantwise with some local SPCA chapter or cause him to lose so much money that he goes broke, there is wide flexibility as to how much he needs to know and what he does with his cattle. There is also a rich variety of breeds from which he may choose—the old Herefords and Shorthorns and Anguses, Brahmans and genetically stabilized Brahman crosses like Branguses and Santa Gertrudis and Beefmasters, modish newer "exotics" such as Charolais and Simmentals and Chianinas and Limousins, and quite a few other sorts ranging from Devons and High-lands to tiny Dexters. And in a day when "hybrid vigor" is a magic phrase, unstabilized crosses of every sort abound, whether planned with care by breeders who know what they're after in terms of shape and size, or achieved less studiously by someone who just dumps a bunch of varied cows into a pasture with some sort of bull and occasionally comes up with results that would appear to have been flown in by jet cargo plane from Masai-land. The ancient and tough and wily Longhorn has its partisans, and some owners even edge away from the genus *Bos* into things like buffaloes and Beefaloes and exotic game animals. And each and every kind of creature that I've named and a good many that I haven't possess distinctive qualities of physique and psyche which some human beings will admire and swear by and others will just swear at.

Small-scale beginners are often advised that they will do best to specialize in costly purebred registered beasts of whatever ilk, since the calves will be salable at premium prices, as heifers or bulls, to other breeders—who, the theory implies, will come flocking around checkbook in hand without even being asked. This can be true enough in time if the beginner in question knows or quickly learns a good bit about genetics and conformation and artificial insemination and such things, maybe wins some prizes at livestock shows to build his herd's reputation, and builds his own by scrupulous attention to records and frank dealing with buyers. But not all of us are that fond of intricate record keeping, fuss and feathers, and the very special perfectionism and politics of the show ring, and there are some other difficulties with purebreds as well, especially in the rough country where some of us run our herds. Living on one end of your place you often find it hard to know precisely what's going on at the other ends, and hard also to keep fences in perfect repair at places where they cross streams and gullies. One visit from a neighbor's offbreed bull can wreck a purebred operation's purity for a year and reduce the calf crop's value to whatever a country auction ring determines it to be, and the young bulls you're keeping for sale to those eager buyers can wander too, messing up lineage records.

Hence registered stock is not for everyone, and most of us settle for something less expensive and less prestigious like my "grade" Anguses, maybe keeping purebred bulls with them year after year so that quality steadily improves even if pedigree doesn't. We find them good to look at, though increasingly with time we are nagged by an impulse to get a bull of another color and produce some of those bouncing, hybridly vigorous mongrels that consistently bring up to a dime or fifteen cents a pound more at sales than good calves of straight British breed. Even if we don't like their looks . . .

Having made a little money on cattle in certain years and lost some of it back in others, having worried over an uneconomic small herd through drouths and bad winters with an intensity that would have been more wisely saved for life's main problems, having been kicked, butted, stomped, and run up corral fences countless times by Number Thirty-nine and others of like temperament, having pounded large quantities of time down a rat hole over the years in the maintenance of this grudging place for bovine use, and having liked just about all of it at least in retrospect, I am still fond of cows and of tending them and am sometimes puzzled, along with other devotees, to find that everyone everywhere doesn't feel the same way. My original eight heifers have all now gone down the long trail to McDonald's, the last of them just this year at a quite advanced age, but I remember them well by looks and traits and names—Roy's Mother, Nutty Johnson, White Tits, Big Navel, and the others—and take simpleminded pleasure in recognizing among members of the present group some cast of eye, some set of neck, some belligerence or timidity, some tone of bellow that traces back to one of those founding mothers.

I can't even work up any shame about the fact that such things matter to me, nor do I really much care what it was that caused them to matter to me in the first place, whether the romance of the West, or osmotic absorption in youth of the basic Texas myth of ranches and ranching, or a memory derived from the collective unconscious of some Neolithic herding time when human life was pretty carefree. And while I still may manage to break loose from cows one of these years, I know already that if I do I won't regret having expended time and energy on them. Because it seems they are something I needed to know about, and in a day when knowledge that you don't need comes washing in on your brain in waves like surf, it is good to have a little that you do.

I'm not talking about practical needs, any more than most other cow people are even when they think otherwise. Few of them, at any rate, have trouble in getting the point of an aged joke, maybe Neolithic itself, that is reshaped and recirculated from time to time. In one version it tells of a leathery West Texan who has fought all his life for a minimal living on a few sections of caliche and stones, but has now been blessed with a couple of million dollars of unexpected oil money. When queried as to what he intends to do he reflects for a moment and says, "No, I ain't heading for Las Vegas and all them naked floozies. I ain't going to buy me no Cadillacs either. I figure to do something different."

"You do?" say his questioners.

"Hell, yes," he says. "What I figure to do is just ranch and ranch and ranch and ranch and ranch, till every damn last cent of that money is all used up."

First published as "Sacred Cows" in *Texas Monthly* (December 1978), "Nineteen Cows" is included in *From a Limestone Ledge: Some Essays and Other Ruminations about Country Life in Texas* (New York: Knopf, 1980; Austin: Texas Monthly Press, 1985; Houston: Gulf Publishing Company, 1991). Reprinted by permission of Alfred A. Knopf, Inc.

Composed in Helvetica types with Prisma initial.

COWBOYS: A FEW THOUGHTS
FROM THE SIDELINES

T HERE ARE a couple of main troubles with trying to say in print anything worth saying about cowboys at this belated point, though people keep trying anyhow. One is that an astounding lot has already been said about them, both by old cowboys themselves in reminiscences written or dictated late in life, and by observers of whom quite a few have been thoughtful persons with a good knowledge of the subject.

The other trouble, worse, is that the very word *cowboy*, let alone the concept, is freighted with such a load of extraneous meaning and connotation these days that any effort to furnish a new legitimate glimpse of the basic rural laborer, the "hired man on horseback" with whom the furor started, is forced to squeeze and edge and tiptoe its way around them. It is easy enough to declare at the outset that you want to consider cowboys who work with cows, not the movie-TV kind with barking pistols, or the country-music kind with longnecked beerbottles, or the currently chic designer-clad kind with styled hair, or the Dallas-football-team kind, or even the strictly rodeo kind. It's *not* easy, however, to set distance between working cowboys and the famous myth engendered from them, out of which have grown by one strange route or another all those Panavision epics, Waylon-and-Willie songs, bumper stickers extolling snuff, nine-hundred-dollar ostrich boots, and such. Nor is it easy either to separate your own thinking about working cowboys from your thinking—feeling, rather—about the myth itself, which in one or another form has a good tight sentimental grab-hold on some part of most Americans' minds, and especially on those of Westerners.

For such reasons, I think, a good many writers, myself among them, with a Western background and an inevitable strong interest in cowboys and their world, have tended to shy away from them as a subject. There is so damned much quicksand. . . . Nevertheless, possibly spurred by an inner need to resolve the confusion for themselves, most sooner or later seem to decide they have a few words to say, a few insights to impart.

Maybe these are mine.

Even if we narrow things down to working cowboys and elbow the myth aside, at least for now, we have the initial problem of saying what a working cowboy is, and for that matter if he still exists. Obviously somebody has to brand and castrate and vaccinate and otherwise manage all those animals you still see in West Texas pastures, but if we call the ones who do it cowboys, as in the main we do, what sense can we make of the fact that during the better part of this present century, Western-minded scholars and nostalgics—and some anti-nostalgics too—have been bidding a firm farewell to the American cowboy, relegating him to history? Clearly they've been talking about something different. What they've been saying goodbye to all these years is the original model, the kind of working cowboy who participated fully in what has been called, professorially, "cowboy culture," and there is no doubt at all that he and his world are no longer with us.

That cow-camp and bunkhouse way of labor and life, with its own wry language and its values and taboos and style that have been pored over by many commentators, involved organized full crews of hired horseback professionals, men who were cowhands pure and simple. In its full-blown form it existed chiefly in connection with large cattle operations, whether owned by individual ranchers or, as frequently, by corporate bodies. Cowboying was primary, of course, on ranches of whatever size, but the bigger ones in their old shape were that life's real matrix, its framework. When the framework started to creak and sag and change, so too did the absolute cowboy way of being. It seems to me to have ended not so much with a bang as with a waning, but end it more or less did at some point within each of the varied regions of the West.

The earliest goodbye-sayers, including many old-time cow people who set down their recollections, did see it as ending with a sort of bang. In general they shared a feeling that the flavor of authentic range life had vanished with the changes barbed wire brought. Real cowboying had been knocked in the head, they were convinced, by the disappearance of the open range, the end of long trail drives and of huge roundups carried out by numbers of outfits working great tracts of unfenced country together while sorting and claiming their beasts, the heavy incursions of farmers on grassland, the replacement of half-wild longhorns with more tractable breeds of cattle, the inclusion in ranch work of unequestrian jobs like patching fences and greasing windmills, and so on.

Many who write on the subject still see its history thus. I guess it depends on definitions. . . . Certainly the waning commenced back there when wire fences started doing away with the frontier concept of grass as anyone's property who had some cows to eat it. Plenty of big operations collapsed at that time, a full century ago, and in the decades that ensued, bigness and its ways stayed under siege as generations of new owners and investors found out for themselves what stubborn family-scale ranchers have forever known to be true: that ranching most of the time, in terms of return against the value of holdings, is a tricky and often comical business proposition. Huge expanses of the best parts of the prairies and plains did go under the plow, and the cattle empire did for the most part dwindle back rather soon to the sort of country the Old World in its hard-won wisdom had always assigned to grazing use—wasteland in farmers' eyes, rough or rocky or arid or otherwise unfit for cultivation. Graziers would never again on this planet have so wide and rich a realm to exploit as they had known on the American plains before the coming of wire, nor would their cowboys ever again lead so pure and untrammeled a herding life.

Nevertheless the West has an enormous lot of rough and rocky and arid land in it, and any Westerner past fifty or sixty, with an eye for rural things, knows that full-plumage cultural cowboys, while diminishing in numbers and prominence, were with us for a good while after that main change occurred. From my own obser-

vations, which have been neither intimate nor learned nor steadily
sustained, I'd put their demise at the approximate point when
good-sized ranches starting finding cowboy culture uneconomic,
and I think that point was reached here in Texas at about the wa-
tershed time of the Second World War, which, like the First one
before it and the Civil one before that, brought an end to many
things.

      That old range life in its wholeness was masculine and bache-
lor and physical in tone, shaped around the work done together—
or alone, for that matter, in many of the tasks—by skilled men
without much property beyond clothes and bedding and saddles. It
was in truth rather monastic within the work itself, incongruous
though the word may be in relation to the majority of such men.
Many were drifters from job to job as personal whim or seasonal
layoffs dictated, while others—more, probably, as time went on—
might stay on at one outfit for years or for life and acquire such
accouterments as wives and kids. Some, in fact, like the black hands
found on the upper Texas coastal prairies and the brown ones at
home in the South Texas brush and through much of the border
country to the Pacific, were often tied in place by social forces or
feudal preference and might well have been born on the land where
they cowboyed all their lives. Whoever and wherever they were,
though, and whatever they were like as individuals or ethnic en-
claves, the abilities they were required to have were similar, and it
was basic to the values they held in common, their culture if you
like, that on a given range at a given time their responsibilities were
toward the work's aims and toward one another, and not toward too
much else.

      These traditional crews laboring in traditional ways could do
all that needed to be done each year with an operation's livestock,
using ropes, horses, muscles, and an intricate accumulation of
adeptness and cow lore that had come down to them in large part
from colonial Mexico. Anybody who got to see them functioning,
as I and a good many other youngsters of my generation were sometimes privileged to do, knows that barbed wire had not changed
them radically. Long after fenced ranges became the rule, their

working life still often revolved around such Old West institutions as remudas, camps and chuckwagons and crusty cooks, personal honor feistily maintained, rawhide horseplay, roundups, and in some sections even occasional trail drives across country to a rail-road shipping point or another ranch.

Thus a top hand from the open-range 1870s, transplanted by time machine to a West Texas roundup cow camp in, say, 1930, might have found himself somewhat cramped by the scale of things but not too badly off base. He would have noted fashion changes in the way men's hair was cut and the slang they used and the shape of their hats and saddletrees. In gentle country he might have been startled by the arrival of automobiles bearing ranch bigwigs and spectators, sometimes female. He would have observed that the horses were bigger and better-looking than most he'd gotten to ride, and the cattle mainly less snuffy and in consequence easier to handle. His eye accustomed to virgin country would have seen clearly that six decades of heavy grazing and erosion had played much hell with the grass, bringing in more brush and weeds and baring more rocks and gouging gullies. He would have been fed and paid a little better, most likely, though cowhands' wages were still unimpressive for the abilities and labor involved.

But the job itself and the men would have been the job and men he knew. On ranches where a pasture to be worked might be fifteen or twenty thousand acres in size and a day's ride away from headquarters, what there was to do and how it was accomplished had not altered much. If here in Texas—and I suspect in most other parts of the West—World War II tolled the final knell of this way of living and working in its typical big-ranch form, the remarkable thing to a sidelines observer like me is not its ending but its long survival, a proud, dexterous, manual and horseback manner of do-ing things, spread around a great region, that endured in places where conditions were right, through at least the fourth decade of this most technological of centuries. That is pretty fair cultural du-rability in a changeful country like ours. The antebellum cotton South in all its cherished new-rich glory did not last any longer, though of course it did end with a very definitive bang.

The main things that relegated this kind of cowboying to the picturesque past are clear enough. One was harder times than usual for ranches big or little during the drouthy Depression years and after, leading to the breakup or shrinkage of many and heavy retrenchment on others, unless, as sometimes in Texas, the discovery of petroleum bailed them out. Another was a general national postwar emphasis on doing away with old labor-intensive methods, stimulated in part by rising expectations as to pay and hours and work conditions on the part of labor itself, even including cowboys. There was, in addition, the vast rapid growth of cities and the drift toward them of all kinds of country people, though in terms of the cattle country it's hard to say whether this was a cause or an effect of the general push toward change.

The practices that began supplanting the old way were rather simple ones, most of them in some use in the 1920s and '30s, that got a better toehold when the war made good cheap hired help scarce, then spread and became standard procedure in the years that followed. This was because they were now less costly than camps and big crews and chuckwagons and numerous horses, in a time during which the cattle trade found itself sharing meagerly, when at all, in the frenetic extended national boom, and for survival its practitioners had to seek out ways to whittle expenses.

In essence the new way consisted of efficient corrals, smaller pastures, and the motorized transport of men and animals. Not much, it would seem, but enough to sound that knell. . . . If, at strategic spots on your ranch—how many spots depending on its size—you build well-designed sets of pens with holding areas, working chutes and alleys, and cutting gates, and you equip them with patent headgates or squeeze chutes or calf-tables to immobilize animals for branding, dehorning, castration, inoculation, and treatment of their ills, you will have wrought a fundamental change. You have established in each such set of pens a sort of assembly-line theater of cattle management where three to five fairly capable men, most of them on foot, can do in a day the work that may formerly have needed three or four times that number of highly trained hands and a good many first-rate horses, cutting out and roping and flanking and throwing beasts and holding them down in the good old-fashioned way. You've also done away with a whole slew of lovely complex activity, and have disgruntled all true cowboys. But you've saved a slew of money, too, even considering the cost of the pens and chutes and the new fences that feed cattle to them without half the rounding up and driving that used to have to be done.

I had a good friend, a redheaded rancher now dead, who was manager and through inheritance part-owner of an eleven- or twelve-hundred-cow operation, not big as big used to go in the West but sizable enough to have maintained a smallish crew of pure cultural cowboys in the times when that way prevailed. He was not entirely typical of his breed, being one of the best-read and most restlessly inquiring people I've known, but he took cattle seriously enough. On occasion he would maintain stoutly, and in his drinking days rather fiercely, that the old way when practiced with art and restraint was far easier on animals, inflicting less trauma and loss of weight—the latter a stud bugaboo of ranchers from early times onward, because weight is what they get paid for. Since he'd had experience with both ways and was not a very sentimental sort, I assume that he was right. But even he had long since gone over to working his beasts in chutes, through sordid economics.

Pickups and trailers to carry hands with their mounts to the work after breakfast, returning them home to warm beds and wives at night, have pretty much done away with long rides, camps, and the monastic bachelor tone of cow work, even where cowboy skills still get a good bit of use. A changeover from railroads to big trailer trucks for hauling large numbers of cattle, straight from corrals to wherever they're being sent, has subtracted its measure of colorful action also. Both, along with the use of chute-equipped pens, have greatly reduced the number of men and horses a ranch has to keep and pay and feed and the amount of riding that surviving hands find it needful to do, at least outside of the roughest mountain sections. I haven't in many years, for instance, noticed in this region a young or middle-aged man with true bandy legs of the sort that some older cowboys used to roll around on when afoot, a proud deformity acquired from years of spending most daylight hours, besides a good many at night, astraddle a round-barreled four-legged friend or sometimes enemy. I've seen young, goat-roping, snuff-dipping, rodeo-aspirant types walking with legs bowed out on purpose, and very prettily traditional it is, but that is somehow different.

The few real cowboys of the old stamp whom I've known fairly well, I've known mainly as individual older men here and there over a period of decades, coming on them dehorsed in jobs at filling stations or grocery stores or boarding stables, or retired, or sometimes elevated to the economy's more respected strata. They were a varied lot, and nearly all I've kept track of have died by now. Only a couple of them had spent their whole working lives with horses and cattle, the rest having cowboyed for a few years or maybe a decade or more in youth before something—changing times, restlessness, ambition, an accumulation of stiffnesses and injuries, marriage to some girl aspiring to fancier things than life in a ranch hand's stark cottage—had led them into other paths.

Some would let you know about that background right away, while with others you learned of it accidentally, perhaps from somebody else. Even so, having been cowboys tended to loom as a central fact in their recollections, and they spoke most easily and humorously concerning its details with others who had that central memory also and a right to talk about it. On the infrequent occasions when I heard such talk I was reminded of the way old marines talk together, or old fighter pilots, or others sharing a past young-bachelor swatch of life they see as proud and special.

If these aging types had a few qualities in common besides just human nature, the qualities probably did have some relation to the thing they had all once been, unless I've read that connection into my remembrance of them. Most salient, I believe, was that none was truly a slob. One or two were pretty alcoholic by the time I got to know them, and a couple had some seized-up neurons and arterioles beneath their skulls, but those are other matters. . . . Whatever they did for pleasure or gain, most tended to do it deftly and with flair, caring about getting it right and making it look easy, in the way that a good roper's throws with a lariat may look easy to unversed onlookers. It was a sort of athlete's attitude, and I believe they'd all have made good to excellent game-players in their time if chasing various kinds of balls had mattered as much back then as it seems to now.

Born in rural times and mostly in rural places, they were fairly unanimous in a queasiness concerning remembered cotton patches, milk cows, flatulent mules, and iron-handed fathers. Only one had grown up in real ranch country, though others, raised on mixed farming-and-stockraising family places of the sort that used to characterize much of central and near-west Texas, had carried some basic cowboy knowledge with them when they'd decamped toward wider horizons. The rest seemed to have carried mainly a sour resolve to put miles between themselves and plows and cotton sacks as they moved toward that looser and freer Western life whose legend they'd already absorbed.

Seldom rooted in the places where they now lived, deficient for the most part in institutional loyalties, they valued friendship and tended to judge met strangers swiftly and directly and permanently—and often, for that matter, unfairly. I don't think many of them cared much about money and position, and in consequence they usually had little of either, though on the other hand some had adapted to current reality and had learned to care very much.

The bulk of those whom I knew were Texans by birth and had done their cowboying chiefly in the state, some having worked on the Matadors or the Swensons or others of the old, large, established outfits in the Rolling Plains and beyond, but most on more modest if still substantial spreads. A few had wandered farther. My favorite of the lot, a real friend who died in his eighties some years ago, had left his family's place south of Waco at eighteen and had cowboyed his way to Montana where he worked on several ranches, got drunk more than once with Charles M. Russell, and joined the Buffalo Bill Wild West Show in its latter years. He could deliver verbatim the speech that Colonel Cody, as he always called him, had made to introduce the Pony Express act in which he himself had ridden, and he had performed in the Roman Relays, one foot on each of two running horses, in Madison Square Garden in New York. Later he'd worked on a California ranch that furnished livestock for early Western movies, and had done stunt work there with Yakima Canutt and played on Will Rogers' cowboy polo team. He had, in short, heard the owl hoot in a good many different places and had led a hell of a life for a country boy from the Blacklands. And though by habit he spoke little of himself, he knew it had all been fine and if he liked you he'd tell you about it, in the little shotgun rent house where he lived in his last years, raising large perfect tomatoes in five-gallon cans half full of horse manure.

The joy that was still in him—and in most cowboys, I think, even when you couldn't see it—was somehow epitomized in a browned, creased, Kodak snapshot he once showed me of himself when young on a big black horse by a spruce-bordered mountain lake, wearing a high-crowned Stetson and bearskin chaps, grinning like a possum, and clearly on top of his world. The picture had in it the springtime feel of a passage I love in that most lightheartedly honest of cowboy books, E. C. Abbott's *We Pointed Them North*: "And besides, I never had time to gamble; I couldn't sit still long enough; I always had to be up, talking, singing, drinking at the bar. I was so happy and full of life, I used to feel, when I got a little whiskey inside me, that I could jump twenty feet in the air. I'd like to go back and feel that way once more. If I could go back I wouldn't change any of it."

Abbott's career dated back to open-range days, and the old ones with whom I was friendly had all functioned quite a bit later than that. But I don't believe many of them would have changed "it" very much either, any of it outside of some ill-knit bones and hernias and mashed prostates and such, and even those some were proud of in a perverse and stove-up way.

So I suppose that what my own personal perception of generalized cowboy character comes down to, as manifested in those few old-timers I've known, is mainly its strong flavor of dexterity and joy and pride. Cowboys of this original breed were genuinely competent at horsemanship and roping and the other elements of their trade, because they had to be competent in order merely to get jobs and keep them, and to gain the acceptance of the men they worked with. Some had extra-special talent with ropes or rough horses or whatnot—tales about such were legion—but all had basic skill and knowledge. Most for that matter had probably been to some degree "naturals" to begin with, because if they hadn't been the sort of youths who learned physical things rapidly and well, and hadn't had a capacity for making the varied snap decisions that range cow work entails, they wouldn't have been allowed to become the thing they were. Instead they would most likely have joined the swarms of other young would-be buckaroos for whom the legend had not jelled, and who'd drifted back home to the cotton patch or ended in strange cities somewhere, not having made the grade. It was, as

Walter Prescott Webb once noted, a process of natural selection, based not only on physical deftness and quickly acquisitive brains but also on such ancient virtues as guts and reliability.

Cowhands were thus an elite, and like all elites were proud. And being proud and mainly young, most derived a lot of sheer fun from the life they led, as if it had been play. Work *is* play, in truth, if you like it and do it well, though I expect a majority of cowboys would have been ready for a fistfight if they'd heard described as play their customary labor. Nevertheless it's clear they took exultant pleasure and pride not only in its dexterous good parts but even in its worst ones. Pride in staying begrimed and sweaty and whiskeyless and womanless for however long a piece of work took, through days on days of twelve or fifteen hours or more devoted to the pursuit and management of the dim-witted recalcitrant creatures from which they took their name. Pride in the quantity of dust they breathed, in not only riding but making good use of horses that were sometimes only half broken to the work, in getting front teeth kicked out by calves, in the coarse heavy food they gulped down at intervals, in enduring such weather as presented itself with a minimum of raiment and shelter, in flopping down at night on the ground for a few hours of itchy, coughing sleep before being waked in the dark to start again. Less pride, maybe, in ripping up hands and forearms while stretching fence wire, in getting dizzy forty feet up in the air while messing with a windmill's gear box, or in doctoring cattle's foul wounds in a bad screw-worm year, but those were parts of the whole.

The work had to give such pride and pleasure, I think. If it hadn't, why else would quick and capable young men have stuck with it, for range-cook grub and wages of thirty or forty or fifty dollars a month or whatever the times were paying? In point of fact, I suspect these men's delight in doing what they did for a living, with their resultant willingness to do it for peanut pay, probably was a main reason the old way of working cattle survived past its logical time. It kept that way economic. Up through the 1930s, in much of the West, it furnished ranches with a steady supply of what were in a sense trained young slave workers, slaves not to the ranches themselves but to their own happy satisfaction in being good at what they did, and to their love for it. And if very often they hid all that behind a dry, laconic manner with which, like many elites, they sought to convey an impression that they didn't give a damn, this was practically all front. They gave a damn, all right. It was why they were there.

Cowboys, then, were all noble fellows? It would be nice to think so. Guts and reliability and happy proud competence, after all, are powerfully attractive attributes in the eyes of most of us, especially when possessed by a horseback figure at home in big country who reminds us, not wrongly, of a time on this continent when freedom could be a literal and physical thing. So attractive in fact that the simplest, most popular form of the cowboy myth, which started abuilding almost as soon as the plains cattle industry itself, did decree very early that cowboys indeed *were* noble, endowed as a class with more or less of those virtues listed in the Boy Scout Code. Quaint in aspect and language, yes, and varied enough in personality to merit salty nicknames and provide color in pulp-magazine stories and dime novels and—later on—films, but clean-minded, true, good-hearted types, every one. If they went bad they did it whole hog and stopped being cowboys, turning instead into rustlers or stagecoach robbers or hired gunfighters or other typified miscreants within the myth.

I believe my own earliest and perhaps healthiest intimation that there was something wrong with this premise, that cowboys were human along with the rest of us, came when I was about ten and saw a particular cowboy on a Fort Worth street. I was in a car with some adults, passing small ratty hotels and cafés near the intersection of North Main and Exchange Avenue. It was a period when the stockyards and auctions and packing plants of that neighborhood were operating full tilt, and nearly all the people you saw there made their livings from cattle or swine or horses or mules— buying them, selling them, sledge-hammering them in the head, cutting them into pieces, bringing them to town for sale or slaughter, or shipping bought ones back to ranches and farms. Since the area was permanently overhung by an intense odor compounded of manure and urine and packing-house offal, people from other parts of Fort Worth usually went there only on business, though when big winds blew out of Canada in winter the North Side smell permeated the whole city and reminded us of our heritage. In itself that aroma should have served as a sound defense against the cowboy myth's effects, nobility and romance being very hard to associate with it.

Nonetheless most of us kids of that time and place did participate in the national fondness for the myth, our primary enthusiasm at the moment being directed toward a rock-jawed, straight-shooting cowboy movie star called Tom Mix. He had a horse known as Tony in whose honor, I would judge, about a quarter of the Shetland ponies in the state of Texas were then named. Nor did we usually have much trouble in squaring our feeling about this sterling figure with the fact that we lived close to cattle country, knowing or being kin to people with cowboy pasts or other cow-business connections. The city's annual rodeo was a good one, and while I suppose there were some full-time professional contestants even then, most came from the ranks of plain ranch cowhands. If fortunate, we'd been taken to visit ranches and we knew already that what was most special about real cowboys was the beautiful, violent, skillful work that they and their horses performed. But we awarded them their full share of Tom Mix's romance and nobility too, and if we spent about as much time trying to lay a loop on dogs, one another, and passing cars' headlights with lengths of clothesline rope as we did in cap-gun duels and wars, it all fitted together comfortably in our minds.

The cowboy I saw on the curb of North Main Street that day looked remarkably like Tom Mix, with a good big jaw and an aquiline nose and even a hank of dark hair falling across his forehead from beneath a pushed-back Stetson. I knew what he was because in those departed, naïve days practically nobody but ranch hands and their employers wore boots and big hats in town, where it was generally felt that only they had the right. This cowboy was not, however, acting like the Tom Mix I'd known. He was unmistakably hog drunk, and was hanging onto an iron street-sign post with both hands while he vomited partly in the gutter and partly on himself, having recently, it appeared, ingested some chili with beans.

I had seen drunks before and found them mainly comic, as children often do. This one wasn't funny to me, though. Shuddering, miserably pale and lorn and alone in that miasmal North Side air to which he'd just contributed his mite, he stared up toward our slow-moving car out of bloodshot eyes from which retch-tears coursed down his cheeks. I stared back and felt reality squirm in my mind. The myth didn't perish for me in that moment of comprehension, and if the poor devil hadn't looked like Tom Mix it might not have mattered at all. But I somehow never afterward felt quite so smitten by old Tom and his Tony, or indeed by any other members of the movie-cowboy species who showed up over the years.

That desolated reveller, I suppose, was the obverse side of Teddy Blue Abbott's thinking he could jump twenty feet in the air. Maybe he himself had felt that way a couple of hours before. Farther along in life I was to find out for myself that blowoff fun, which seeks to exaggerate joy, is more frequently obverse than not, though if you're young and male and full of yourself in a certain raunchy and innocent way you go back to it time and again, hoping for one of the occasions when it does turn out right. And if you were a young cowhand, blowoff fun was likely to be where you sought, when you could, surcease from all that happy, grueling cow work. There was nothing surprising in this, but little that was noble, either. Distant for the most part from bright lights and liquor and compliant females, locked into a system of labor that furnished no vacations and not even many days off, you tried to make the most of what free time you got, and—I judge from observation and from unproud personal remembrance—very often flubbed it in the execution and ended up like that Tom Mix cowboy, sickly plastered and clutching a signpost or a tree somewhere. Or clutching a barroom antagonist who'd just fisted your face to red mush. Or clutching, more fondly but not more romantically or nobly, one of the sagging, foulmouthed, perhaps golden-hearted women I used to see cowboys with, later when I knew what the women were, in that same stockyards section.

Not being one who gets much thrill from fulmination, I see little point in waxing censorious over other disparities between cowboy reality and the more high-flown claims of the myth, though a couple might be pointed out. Like most other physically excellent, elite-minded young men found in groups—marines, athletes, whatever—cowboys were intolerant of difference and seem to have been fairly often unbearable in relation to people from outside their own little world, at any rate when there were enough of them around to keep their group-feeling fueled and to make the unbearableness stick. In the old accounts the results usually pass as humor, and I guess they were, though somewhere along the path of later life I myself seem to have lost a sense of the full hilarity of such antics as yanking off a timorous stranger's small urban hat on the street and shooting it full of holes on the pretext that it was dangerous, while cawing laughter rang all around.

As for the myth's usual rigid moral separation of the good guys from the bad, I have more than once or twice heard old hands speak with humorous affection, approaching admiration, about certain cattle thieves they'd known, cowboys like themselves who had decided to better their lot by the direct and simple method of abstracting riches from the rich, and who may have gone back to competent cowboying afterward if their efforts led to neither affluence nor durance vile. It's worth noting also that the popularity of some desperadoes and hard-riding bank and train robbers was at its stoutest around range cookfires. For cowboys—tough, skillful, elite brotherhood though they may have been—were among the world's exploited have-nots, and have-nots on the whole, alas, have ever relished lawless heroes who disgruntle staid and moneyed folk, even if few of them may choose to disgruntle such folk themselves.

A larger quibble about the mythic nobility of cowboys and ranchers and their world and its ways has been surfacing now and then in recent years and has to do with current awareness of ecological values. It is based, of course, on hindsight. Illustrative of it, perhaps, is a complaint I saw leveled not long ago at Andy Adams' well-known *The Log of a Cowboy*, published early in this century as the fictional account of a five-month trail drive from the Mexican border to Montana in 1882, and based closely on the author's own working experience. Though without literary pretension, this is an immensely authentic piece of work, probably the most authentic on its subject, and the writer of the essay I read recognizes its worth. This serves, however, to swell his irritation that it is, in his view, needlessly marred by the inclusion near its end of an extended brutal scene involving a female bear. Adams' trailhands happen on this animal eating berries with her two cubs, rope her into snarling helplessness, and proceed happily to shoot her to pieces as well as killing the cubs, not to eat or for self-protection but just for the high hell of it. "When we met at the wagon for dinner," says the narrator, ". . . the hunt was unanimously voted the most exciting bit of sport and powder burning we had experienced on our trip."

Probably most people nowadays with any sense of how natural things mesh and link and dovetail, and any knowledge of how those patterns have been savaged on this continent—as well as on all the others—would read that episode with something of an inward wince. Yet if Adams had left it out of the picture he was painting of cowboy life, there would have been a big hole in the fabric of truth he was trying to weave. Spawned of the frontier that saw nature less as mother than as enemy when not source of wealth, cowboys in general (yes, we're still generalizing, maybe a hair too hard) were unecological exemplars of what Wallace Stegner has described as the West's curious urge to destroy itself. They stayed that way too, for about as long as they were around in anything resembling the old form, despite their affection for the kind of wide country they knew and their nostalgia for its lost virginity. For many of them, if something moved and didn't moo or neigh or carry a brand, you shot it, or pulped it with a rock or a stick, or strychnined it, or roped it and dragged it to death, and afterward maybe you felt so good about this that you hung it up on a fence by a road. Edible carcasses were most often hauled in for consumption, but edibility wasn't the point. The point was raising cattle and imposing human purpose on the land, and the traditional and easy way to view wildlife was either as irrelevant to that point or else as a threat to it, preferably the latter since it lent virtue to killing.

One of my best and brightest friends, though we live far apart these days and see each other seldom, absconded from a city home at the age of thirteen in the mid–late 1930s and made his way to Wyoming, where against the odds he earned acceptance as a "button" on a good ranch and was well on his way to full cowhand status when World War II began and he joined up. He told me once about a thing that happened after he was discharged from the service and went back to those haunts, finding old cowboy compadres there with a war behind them too and an itch for simple pleasures. They got hold of a war-surplus jeep and a jug of something corrosive and went cruising about the sagebrush, looking for things to shoot. Spotting a fleeing herd of antelope on fairly even ground, they charged and got among them at thirty-five or forty miles an hour and started firing at random. By the time I knew him he'd moved around in the world quite a lot and had started using his first-rate mind, and he felt some slight shame about the memory. But there'd been no shame in that jeep, only exhilaration. "You wouldn't believe what a time we had," he said. "We slaughtered those fast bastards right and left."

Cowboys, then, were all ignoble fellows? You might think so if you looked only at their less sterling traits. But you might yet more easily think the same thing about humanity in general if you looked at it in the same way. I fear the main point to bear in mind is—still and again—that cowboys *were* ineluctably human like the rest of us, in view of which slightly unsavory fact their commonly held virtues, quite real ones, may have been perhaps the more impressive. Even that gaily lethal attitude they so often demonstrated toward wild and natural things is flatly human, I believe, emphasized though it may have been in frontiersmen and cowboys by the opportunities furnished them by their times, their surroundings, and the tools and weapons at hand. But to follow out the ramifications of that thought would lead us into avenues distant from the subject of happy cowboys. . . . Let us note in dismissal of the topic that a good bit of this cowboy destructiveness derived less from murderous whim than from what had to be done, at least if animal husbandry of the Western sort was going to become the main use of all that land not suited for farming, which history decreed should be so. Livestock do not thrive, for instance, in the presence of such predators as lobo wolves and cougars and grizzly bears, nor did the cow crowd have an appreciative view of rattlesnakes or even such timorous beasties as prairie dogs, with their multitudinous burrows that fractured running horses' legs and cartwheeled riders through the sunlit air to collision with earth and stone. And if a lot of us now think we might have been less harsh on the scheme of things, the fact is that environmental hindsight has its own myth of nobility.

I confess to a sneaking, lingering, personal fondness for the cowboy myth, and to an ambivalence concerning it. For those of us who grew up knowing a little about cattle and real ranches, the myth came in at least two flavors. One was the widely popular, usually puerile, dime-thriller-and-Tom-Mix thing based on derring-do, while the other, less commercialized and closer to reality though just about as simpleminded at times, involved an exaggeration of the virtues and skills displayed by cowboys at work. As I've noted, youngsters of my time here in Texas had little trouble in mixing the two and thus fabricating for themselves a somewhat more entire myth, compounded of cap guns and Shetland ponies and cotton clothesline lariats. And if a really powerful use of the myth in the form of a book or a film is ever achieved, I expect it will do very much the same thing in adult terms.

I haven't seen it done yet, but neither have I seen everything that's been done. It does seem clear that rendition of the wide or popular myth of Colt pistols and fair ladies has much improved in quality in recent years as it has gained in complexity, with, for instance, occasional noble farmers or noble Indians being awarded as much heroic stature as cowboys and cavalrymen and such, sometimes more. On a more elevated level the pop myth has been subjected to some quite good high-comic spoofs, and now and again also, writers and moviemakers have been coming up with work, still discernibly mythic in point and framework, that has legitimate force and sometimes comes close to getting hold of the feel of things as they probably were, even while usually continuing to evade or ignore the real cowboy reason for being, the hard, graceful, constant work.

Maybe a case could be made for rodeo in its present professional manifestation as a supplementary pop myth that takes care of that side of things. A much sounder case, however, and in terms of more genuine myth, could be made for the painting and sculpture of the better Western artists from Remington and Russell on, where range labor in all its varied, violent color, the physical interplay of men and horses and cattle and country, is very often a main focus, dealt with for its own sake. Artists like that, whether or not they've had a whole vision of the West as it was, have known quite well what cowboys consisted of.

Valid artistic presentation of either side of the myth brings in another dimension, of course, and it may be objected that when something becomes art—i.e., truth powerfully rendered—it ceases to be myth. But that comfortable separation only works if you define myth in its cheapest sense, that of pure falsification, which isn't real myth at all. I possess neither the scholarship nor the desire to go deeply into this subject, but it's something that anyone who tries to set things down right, on paper or canvas or wherever, has had to think about. Art and myth and truth and life are snakishly entangled. Art does deal essentially with the true, myth with the ideal—and behind even the ingrained commercial purpose, the constant idiotic mayhem, the misapprehension of fact, the childish and puritan twisting of motives and conduct of the pop cowboy myth at its worst, there does lurk a set of ideals of honesty and courage and staunchness and other basic virtues.

But art concerns itself with the ideal as well—if only, sometimes, with its absence—and while the possibilities for esthetic argument are endless, I doubt many of us believe that the value, as art, of a piece of bronze bucking-bronco sculpture is lessened by the fact that it may convey an ideal of cowboy guts and skill, perhaps more guts and skill than most real cowboys had. It may or may not be lousy art; much Western stuff fails through the same sentimental distortion and misfired talent that devil artists everywhere. But if it is lousy, the fact that an element of the ideal is present is not the reason. Art can thus become myth, or myth become art, so that many times it's not possible to say which is which. . . .

Another curious point is that myth can influence the direction of human life, as can art, and may even influence its live subject matter if the timing is right. The popular cowboy myth was not shaped for cowboys, but for (and in a sense by) a non-Western public, worldwide in extent as time passed, which seized on it with a passion that could only have come from deep need. But it reached real cowboys as well, the later ranch-working kind, and they seized on it too—some of them, indeed, having left home to get to be cowboys on account of its potent pull. It is well known that much of the favorite reading matter around chuckwagons and bunkhouses was pulp Western fiction, and when cowboy movies started being shown in towns across the cattle country their audiences included plenty of men who might guffaw and slap their legs over technical bloopers involving animals or the details of work and language—might in fact grouse bitterly about them later—but who soaked up the messages just about as appreciatively as any Philadelphian. Passing by the question of possibly reinforced egotism, what this appears to mean is that the myth, operating with a sort of reverse English on it, entered and reentered them and flavored their perception of what they were. Maybe it made some of them a bit pop-mythic themselves, if anybody can be. Ideals not being intended to serve as laws, but as reference points.

It may well be simpleminded of me, but I admit I have a hard time seeing this as always bad, whether or not the myth involved is pure and true. No doubt it can sometimes lead to posing and self-worship and trying to be one's own grandfather and the like, as it did in the maudlin, alcoholic Panhandle protagonist, not a favorite of Texans, of Jane Kramer's acidly anti-mythic *The Last Cowboy*. But myself, I find it quite pleasant to consider that that poor drunk Tom Mix figure of my youth, yorking publicly into a gutter on North Main Street in Fort Worth, may have had the cinematic Tom's sterling presence working inside him as an antidote to degradation. Just as some kid bouncing a pickup across a pasture today in, say, Borden County, Texas, hauling feed cubes to steers and checking heifers for calving trouble, mooning about a girl with whom he nearly made it last night, can have a hunk of both Charlie Russell and John Wayne in his soul and is undoubtedly better off for it—nobler, by God, if you like.

Then, for that matter, there's history—including such things as memoirs, and honest photographs snapped in time to put old ways on record—which seldom overlaps with myth except to report it, but can be art if it's good enough or, if it's not, can serve as art's (and thus myth's) prime subject matter. Let us not, however, ride our pinto ponies any farther down that analytical trail.

There is no doubt that the myth in both its forms got its hooks into my own psyche when I was young, and that some traces of its influence still remain there despite the countervailing effects of experience and of a lifelong effort as a writer, maybe vain, to arrive at facts and truths unsentimentally. I am in no sense a cowboy and never got close to becoming one. What little illusion I ever attained in that respect came sporadically during adolescence on what the big-ranch cowboys would have called shirttail outfits, small operations where farming might loom as large as cattle in the scheme of things. It consisted of being allowed sometimes to ride out and help drive animals in for working or shipping, getting to wrestle a few calves now and then, and being tricked aboard an occasional un-

friendly horse with results that usually satisfied the hopes of whoever it was that had tricked me.

Notwithstanding this unheroic cowboy past of mine, these
days I find myself living in cattle country by choice and for about
two decades now I've run a small, not highly profitable herd of Angus and crossbred beef cows under stock-farm conditions, doing
the work that needs to be done with them and liking practically all
of it outside of a few obstetrical crises. This atavism in me, if that's
what it is, is not a simple thing and it comes from no single source,
but I'm aware that it has at least some slight connection with those
fragments of the myth still lodged in me like shards of an old grenade, even if an observer of our methods might have a hard time
seeing this. We deal with our calves in a chute with a headgate, and
are so far removed from the ki-yi-yippee side of things that we usually toll beasts to the corral with rattling buckets of feed, unless
they're sullen from recent handling and have to have their minds
changed by my daughter on her mare. The only real cowboy aptitude for which I can discern a lingering juvenile yen in myself is
the ability to throw a rope with a fair certainty of catching a creature
in motion, but I hardly ever seem to feel compelled to try it
any more.

Something down inside me, though, would still have liked to
be one. A cowboy is not the only thing that some part of me would
have liked to be, but it's one of them. Not at this point Tom Mix,
not the Virginian or the Lone Ranger or any other of their virtuous
ilk. Not even good, solid, lately departed John Wayne, himself
damned nearly a work of art. Just a competent friend of Teddy Blue
Abbott's, say, or one of those lean and weathered types riding rough
wild country in a Russell painting, in that simpler time when freedom could be a literal and physical thing for proud, tough, dexterous, reliable men on horseback. Or so at least that something inside
me, and inside a lot of other people, does profoundly wish to
believe.

So we shall not look upon their like again, or look again at any
rate upon the like of those weathered fellows who lived the cowboy
life whole. Shall we then add our verse to the somewhat dissonant

chorus which over the years, with asperity or irony or praise, has been saying farewell? Goodbye, American Cowboy: is that our message too?

To a fat extent it has to be, I guess. The old ones are as finally gone as the wild red men that went away before them, and in the kind of world we have on hand, even in the West where all that land you can't farm is still mainly used by cows, what remains of that way of being seems ever less relevant to wherever it is that we're headed. Its skills and lore have been abraded by economics and chutes and pickup trucks, and maybe more importantly, the romantic pull it once had for young recruits, its glamor so to speak, is being sucked away elsewhere, partly by the old myth itself and some offspring it has spawned.

There is glamor enough, for instance, in big-time rodeo, where some of the old skills, plus others that have no range use, are brilliantly employed in ritual form for the pleasure of a growing and avid public. But rodeo is increasingly show business and its successful "cowboy" participants are increasingly professionals—athletes, performers, whatever you want to call them—whose connection with the management of beef cattle on grassland, when it exists at all, runs second to the pull of the arena's acclaim and its cash and the tightly cowgirl-clad groupies at beerhall and motel-room parties after the show. More and more the sort of youngsters who once might have wanted to be the real thing are yearning toward that world instead, taking jobs sometimes on ranches for a living and for experience while they wait to break into the money and the glory. A man I knew who ranched in New Mexico had to furlough two of his three hands, one a Navaho, whenever the season for certain rodeos rolled around. He would have lost them otherwise. Neither ever won anything to brag about, but they had to hang onto the illusion that they might. With a slightly paranoid note in his voice, he claimed they also knocked weight off his calves by running and roping them for practice when he wasn't around.

There is glamor too, with far less connection to the old cowboy way of being, in some other things—in, for instance, wearing two or three thousand bucks' worth of custom-made Western clothes (or, alternatively, forty bucks' worth of very scruffy ones) while you sing into a microphone and pluck on your guitar, or in just wearing that kind of clothes out for a night on the town in

Dallas or Houston or, according to report, New York. And this glamor like the rodeo kind has been inherited in part, however deviously, from that tough, adept, monastic, ever more dimly envisioned old brotherhood of the cow camps, leaving precious little of the stuff for any yahoo throwback who just wants to live out where it's lonesome and take care of cows for a meager wage—as, incredibly, some still do.

Because that's the hitch in saying with assurance goodbye, American Cowboy, goodbye. About the time you've put your farewell speech together in your head and have started waving a bandanna toward that lone, lean, mounted figure crossing a hogback ridge into the sunset, another cowboy, maybe not a cultural member of the vanished brotherhood but tough and able and legitimate nonetheless, may very well ease up inquisitively beside you and say, "What the hell are you doin'?"

You have to define him and recognize him for yourself, I guess, and he may be in a pickup or on a tractor when you first see him, though it's not where he looks best. He's not hard to find in Texas if you look in the right places, though for me he popped up most recently in Wyoming last fall, where I'd gone to cast a few flies for trout before cold weather set in. The ranch I was visiting lies among the foothills and the worn-down sculptured peaks of an ancient range east of the Rockies, and these days only steers are run on it, being bought as big calves in the spring, grazed all summer on the mineral-strong mountain grass, and sold when autumn comes at a profit, if any, which derives from the three hundred pounds or more each animal can gain in that time. Because of market ups and downs this kind of ranching has a strong element of gambling in it, but it gets around the heavy winter feeding and care required with cow-calf operations in northern country. Absentee-owned, the ranch is run by a foreman and his wife with help from two or three seasonal hands in the months when the steers are there, and during the time of my visit they were bringing animals down from the higher country and assembling them for shipping.

A couple of nearby ranchers came to pitch in as well, bringing along hired hands or wives and horses, and the size and makeup of the small working crew varied from day to day according to what different ones of them found had to be done at home. Such neighboring-up for main jobs, by people who know they'll all be thus helped in their turns, is a time-hallowed institution in cow country, especially where family-sized operations are common. Working ten- and twelve-hour days during which they covered a given tract of country and gathered up its steers, they knew the land's shape and knew one another, and the way they functioned together was pretty to see as they were coming in at evening or, occasionally, when I could watch them during the day in some valley whose creek I was fishing. Mainly it wasn't elaborate cowboy work, just herding, but in that intricately up-and-down terrain, with beasts that were spooky and stubborn from living five fat months on their own, it was fancier—more picturesque, anyhow— than what you usually see in rolling Texas in these degenerate times, with a good bit of hard, fast riding and cutting and heading off, and more rarely a little rope work with some part-Brahman outlaw that had to be choked down or busted to convince him that the herd's winding route of march was the appropriate one for him too.

They were efficient rather than showy in the way they did things, and a couple of the women were about as good as most of the men—not a new or remarkable thing either, where families do their own work. In general the old-timers, the foreman and the neighbors and their wives, were steadier and more knowledgeable than the younger paid hands, a couple of whom had a sort of dapper, mythic, rodeo look about them, at least to my outlander's eye. There was an exception, though, an unprepossessing specimen at first glance. He was in his twenties, scrawny and slightly stooped when afoot, with small darting close-set green eyes, a pointed nose, and a flow of frizzy red-blonde hair hanging down between his shoulders and sticking out over his ears. All his outer gear looked second- or third-hand, being worn and battered and soiled from use—scuffed boots with spurs, greasy scarred chaps, a stained and ripped down vest, and one of the more disastrous hats I've ever seen worn, filthy, its brim drooping down at an angle all around, with a home-made band of rattlesnake skin in which he'd stuck a tall frayed eagle feather. But the clothes next to his body were clean, and the wife of the man he worked for said with a smile that he washed that long hair every day. They called him, aptly, Wild Man, and I never heard his real name.

He watched me when I was around and dodged any talk, and I thought this was because I was an aging, alien non-cowboy till I noticed he was shy and short with all the others as well. He was also more skillful than any of them at the work that had to be done. Mounted, all his scrawniness went away and he was so tightly fluid and balanced that the old cliché about being part of the horse was wrong; instead the horse, whatever horse he was on, turned into a swift, strong, quick-turning part of him. He could think like a cow only faster, they said, and rope like a Mexican, and one evening when they came over the shoulder of a mountain with the three hundred or so steers they had gathered up that day, the Wild Man was not with them, showing up a little later from a different direction with fifteen beasts he was driving on his own. "They tore off up the worst canyon we got," the ranch's foreman said. "I knowed the funny-lookin' little son of a bitch was the only one I had could bring them things out by himself, and I needed everybody else to help with the main bunch."

He'd worked for one of the neighbor ranchers for three summer seasons so far, and within a couple of weeks now he would throw his bedroll and suitcase and saddle in the back of an old yellow pickup and take off for Arizona where on some ranch, they didn't know which, there was a winter job waiting. The rancher, a quiet man of sixty-five or so, said he was the best help they'd ever had, as deft and willing at building fences or constructing sheds and feeders as he was with horses and cows.

I asked if he did any rodeoing, because it was something most of those people seemed to talk about.

He shook his head. "I haven't got the least idea," he said. "You've seen for yourself what a talky scutter he is. I don't much think he likes all that stuff, though. What he likes is work, and getting things done right." He paused and spat tobacco juice and said, "Me, what I hope is old Wild Man just shows up next spring."

"Lord, I do too," said his wife with feeling.

And so for my own reasons, mythic or not, do I.

"Cowboys" was published as the introduction to *Cowboy Life on the Texas Plains: The Photographs of Ray Rector* (College Station: Texas A&M University Press, 1982).

Composed in Horley types with Augustea Shaded initial.

A LOSER

IT WAS THE KIND OF FARM auction that mainly countrymen and a few implement dealers attend, for it was in an out-of-the-way part of the upper West Cross Timbers and the classified ad announcing it in the Fort Worth paper had mentioned no churns, crocks, wagonwheels, or other aging curiosities of the sort that lure crowds of city people to such affairs. There was to be a disposal of everything on hand, including the farm itself— "125 a. sandy land, 45 in cultivation, rest improved grass and timber, 2 tanks, barn, new brick home 3 b.r. 2 baths, all furnishings." Though it lay about two hours north of my own place and I'm not much addicted to those sellout auctions—melancholy events nearly always, aromatic with defeat and often with death—I drove up that Saturday in late winter because among the items listed for sale was an Allis-Chalmers grain combine of the antiquated type that is pulled and powered by a tractor.

In my rough area these relatively small harvesting machines, none of them less than about twenty years old, are still in demand if they've been kept in working order. Most of our field land is in little tracts strewn about between the hills, and even when you can find a custom combine operator willing to bring his shiny self-propelled behemoth to your place for the sake of reaping just twelve or twenty or thirty acres of oats or wheat, he will most likely balk when he gets a good look at the narrow rocky lanes and steep stream crossings through which it must be jimmied to arrive at its work. As a result we often let our cattle keep on grazing winter grain fields past mid-March, when they ought to be taken off if harvest is intended, or we cut and bale the stuff green for hay. But sometimes when you'd like a bin full of grain to carry your horses and goats through winter and maybe to fatten a steer or so for slaughter, you wish you had a bit more of the sort of control that possession of your own varied if battered machinery gives.

A front had pushed heavy rains through the region the day before and the morning was bleak, with gray solid mist scudding not far overhead and the northwest wind jabbing the pickup toward the shoulder as I drove. It grew bleaker after I left our limestone hills, with their liveoaks and cedars that stay green all year, and came into country where only a few brown leaves still fluttered on winter-bare post oaks and briers and hardwood scrub. Sandy fields lay reddish and wet and sullen under the norther's blast, and in some rolling pastures, once tilled but now given over to grass and brush, gullies had chewed through the sand and eaten deep into the russet clay underneath. Outlying patches of such soil and vegetation occur even in my own county, and for that matter since childhood I've known and visited this main Cross Timbers belt, a great finger-shape of sand and once-stately oak woods poking down into Texas from the Red River. But it has always had a queerly alien feel for me, in part undoubtedly because I grew up surrounded by limestone and black prairie dirt and the plants they favor and, with the parochialism dear to the human heart, I simply like them.

Others for their part prefer the sand, and locals of this stamp seemed to make up a majority of the hundred and fifty or so people who were standing around in clumps when I parked alongside a narrow dirt road, slithered up a clay hill past a low suburban-style house, and entered the farmyard where, arranged in a wide ellipse, stood the relics and trophies of someone's ruptured love affair with the soil. Bushel baskets and nail kegs filled with random hand tools and pipe fittings and bolts and log chains and mason jars and whatnot. A section harrow, three tandem disks, plows of various sorts, a row planter, a cultivator, a grain drill, a hay swather, two balers of which one was riddled with rust and good only for parts cannibalization, a corral holding twenty or more good crossbred beef cows with their calves, a tin barn half full of baled Coastal Bermuda and, as the ad had promised, other items too numerous to mention, though I can't help mentioning one: a large and gleaming tuba. Much of the farm machinery had a scarred third-hand look quite familiar to me, for it was the kind of stuff that we marginal small-timers tend to end up with. But this fellow had invested in a much greater variety of it than I had ever ventured to, and here and there sat something fairly expensive with the sheen of relative newness on it—a good medium-sized tractor, a heavy offset-disk plow, a fancy wheeled dirt scoop with hydraulic controls. . . .

The blocky orange shape of the A.-C. combine loomed at the far end of the ellipse, and as I walked toward it wind-hunched locals in caps and heavy jackets and muddy boots viewed me with taciturn distaste, another outlander plunked down among them to run the bidding up and make them shell out more for whatever it was they had their eyes and hearts set on. Two of them were studying the combine and stopped talking when I came near, but started again in lower tones after I began jiggling levers and checking belts and chains and opening flaps to peer at intricacies inside the big box. Its paint job wasn't bad, so it had been kept under cover for at least some of its long life, and those metal working parts that came in contact with moving grain and straw and chaff were shiny-bright in testimony, I thought, of fairly recent use, a hawk-eyed Holmesian observation confirmed by one of the other interested parties.

"They cut twenty-four acres with it last summer," he said to his friend. "I know because I seen it. It didn't blow hardly no oats out on the ground."

"What about the canvases?" I asked, for those wide ribbed belts that elevate materials from the cutter bar to the machine's complicated interior matter greatly, and are expensive to replace if worn out or rotten from neglect.

He snapped his stubble jaw shut and glared but had to answer, minimally. "In the barn," he said.

I found them on a shelf there and they looked all right too. The combine was worth trying to buy, though while examining it I had begun to have misgivings about towing its eleven-and-a-half-foot width over the fifteen miles of narrow muddy humpbacked roads, with waterfilled ditches, that I had traversed since leaving pavement, and then maneuvering it through the Saturday traffic of three fair-sized county seats that stood between this place and home. However, these thoughts were cut short by the crackle and burp of a bullhorn near the house and a jovial brassy voice announcing the auction's start. Together with most of the others I moved toward the scarlet pickup from whose bed the bullhorn blared, but a few dogged figures remained beside implements or other objects they had chosen, establishing what they hoped was priority and waiting for the sale to come to them.

The auctioneer was a pro as nearly all are these days, Stetsoned and paunched and lump-jawed with sweet Red Fox tobacco. He knew a few of the people present—Western-clad and cliquish, probably dealers—and jollied them by name between spells of ribba-dibba chanting and exhortation to higher bids as an assistant held up the containers of smaller stuff to view and they were sold off batch by batch. Loading the cold moving air with urgent sound, his amplified voice fanned greed and fuzzed rational thought among less inured listeners, as it was intended to do, but the crowd wasn't a prosperous one and at this early stage the bidding stayed low. I felt a twinge of avarice as a basket of good wrenches and pliers and screwdrivers and such, worth probably eighty or ninety dollars at retail, went for $4.75, but forced myself into the reflection that I already owned at least one specimen of every tool there—as, probably, did the grim skinny oldster who bought them and bore them away in triumph. . . . The pickup inched forward along the line of ranked items as they were sold, and when it reached the farming implements the visiting dealers moved in for the kill and things began to get hotter, to the disgruntlement of us amateurs. Thwarted, a young farmer delivered a hard sodden kick to the beam of the handsome yellow offset-disk over which I had earlier seen him practically salivating, but for whose sake he had been unwilling or unable to top the seven hundred and fifty dollars it brought, about half of its market value even second-hand. "Them son of a bitches sure make things hard," he said.

I was looking at a hatless thin-clad man who sat on the edge of the pickup's bed beside the auctioneer. He was in his forties, pale and slight and balding and with the pinched waxy look of sickness on him, maybe even of cancer, and as I watched his dark worrier's eyes switch anxiously from bidder to bidder and saw the down-tug of his lips when something sold far too low, I knew very well who he was. He was the erstwhile lord of this expanse of wet sand and red mud, the buyer and mender and operator of a good bit too much machinery for forty-five arable acres, the painstaking nurturer and coddler of those fat penned cows, the player perhaps of a tuba, the builder of a hip-roofed brick-veneer castle, 3 b.r. 2 baths, from which to defend his woman and his young against the spears of impending chaos. Except that chaos, as is its evil custom, had somehow stolen in on him unawares and confounded all his plans. He was, in short, the Loser.

"I got a scoop," the auctioneer cried. "I got a big red dirt scoop. I got a great big pretty red dirt scoop that'll dig you a ditch and build you a terrace and haul one whole cubic yard of gravel or sand up out of your creek bed, and all you got to do is touch a little lever and she dumps it right where you want it. Eight-ply tires and the whole thing just about new from the looks of it. What you say, men?"

"Thirty-five," ventured one of his auditors in a tentative voice. I saw the Loser twitch and tense, and surmised that to him, for whatever reason, the scoop had special meaning, as occasional implements do.

"That ain't no bid, it's an insult," said the auctioneer.

"Cylinder's busted," the bidder answered with a defensive air, and I remembered noting that the arm of a hydraulic piston on the scoop was bent and useless, though repair or replacement probably wouldn't cost much.

"Urba durba dibba rubba hurty-fie," said the auctioneer in abandonment of the subject. "Hurty-fie hurty-fie hurty-fie, who say fitty? Fitty, fitty, fitty, fitty, durba dubba ibba dibby who say forty-fie? Forty-fie, forty-fie, come on, folks. . . ."

"Forty!" somebody yelled.

The Loser rose trembling to his full five foot seven or so beside the large auctioneer, and his unamplified voice was reedy but the feeling behind it carried it out over the crowd. "God-amighty, boys," he said. "I paid out three seventy-five for that thing not six months ago and the fellow I got it from he hadn't never used it but twice. Another fellow come by one day when I was digging a tank with it and he wanted to give me five hundred. That there's a *good* machine. I just can't see . . ."

And sat down, staring at his toes. As if in imitation, many in the crowd looked earthward toward their own muddy footwear, and an almost visible feeling enveloped us like thick gas, and was not blown away by the steady wind. Faced with erosion of the mood he had been building, the auctioneer spat brown juice and stared briefly, cynically, toward the gray horizon before returning to the fray. "Man's right," he said. "Listen to him, boys. It's a good scoop. You got to remember what the Bible says, Thou shalt not steal."

Urba dibby, etc., and in the end the scoop fetched ninety bucks, which may have been a trifle more than it would have brought without the little man's outburst. Nobody, it seemed, really wanted a scoop, and the dealers for their own private reasons were not interested. The Loser shortly thereafter got down from the pickup and went to what was at that point still his house, followed by numerous furtive eyes.

"Poor booger," somebody said.

In large part our lingering fog of feeling was made up of shame, of the guilt most of us had brought along with us to the sale, knowing that if we found any bargains there it would be because of someone else's tough luck. Some of us hadn't been aware that we carried this load until we heard the Loser speak, but it was waiting there within us nonetheless, needing only a pinprick to flow out.

There was another thing, though, less altruistic and thus maybe stronger. But for the grace of God, there through the red mud trudged we, stoop-shouldered toward a brick-veneer house soon not to be our own. At three o'clock in the morning, once or twice or often, many of us had known ourselves to be potentially that small pale man as we sweated against the menaces of debt not to be covered by non-farm earnings or a job in town, of drouth, of a failing cattle or grain or peanut market, of having over-extended ourselves on treasured land or machinery or a house, of perhaps a wife's paralyzed disillusionment with the rigors of country life, and above all of the onslaught of sickness with its flat prohibition of the steady work and attention that a one-man operation has to have, or else go under. The Loser had made us view the fragility of all we had been working toward, had opened our ears to the hollow low-pitched mirth of the land against mere human effort.

No, I didn't get the little A.-C. combine. If all of us there had been amateur buyers I would have had it for a hundred and seventy-five dollars, for that was where the other countrymen stopped bidding. But a dealer type in lizard boots and a spotless down jacket and a large black hat stayed with me, as I had suspected he would, for the old machine with a bit of furbishing would be worth seven hundred or so on his lot. Enjoying the growth of his cold resentment, I carried him up to four hundred and quit, partly because of my doubts about bulling that orange hulk through ninety difficult miles and perhaps getting caught by darkness, but mainly I believe because thinking about the Loser and all he stood for had made me start wondering hard if I really, honestly, badly needed the damned thing.

Nor did I stay to watch the bidding for the cattle and the house and land. What I wanted, and what I did, was to flee back home to black dirt and limestone country, where I could have a drink beside a fire of liveoak logs and consider the Loser's alien, sandy-land troubles with equanimity from afar.

First published as "The Loser" in *Texas Monthly* (August 1978), "A Loser" appears in *From a Limestone Ledge: Some Essays and Other Ruminations about Country Life in Texas* (New York: Knopf, 1980; Austin: Texas Monthly Press, 1985; Houston: Gulf Publishing Company, 1991). Reprinted by permission of Alfred A. Knopf, Inc.

Composed in Times New Roman types with Fry's Ornamental initial.

CONCLUSION OF *HARD SCRABBLE*

IN PHILOSOPHICAL TERMS of "being" and "becoming" there is not much question that life at Hard Scrabble, with so much always still to do and the problem of whether it will ever all get done, has leaned strongly toward the latter, kinetic state. Unstatically, the house sprouts new rooms, barns and sheds grow out of nothingness, fields change from briery tangles to expanses of worked soil furred with tame greenery, and grassed stretches of new pasture lie where only a year or so ago old cedar used to brood on past human error.

Yet now that there is a house which though small can shelter us through the year, and some growing sense that the place is moving toward function, life here has a tinge of "being" too. The seasons roll by toward wherever it is that they go: tawny wind-fanged winters give way to long lush springs, and summers with (perhaps) small sheeplike clouds riding above the southwest shove of searing Chihuahuan air finally yield to moist and melancholy and exultant falls with northers and high skeins of big birds trumpeting overhead. New generations of cattle and goats appear in their time, and frolic in fresh life-joy and are admired and sometimes named, and the recurrent work with them and with the soil takes on a known and welcome pattern. Children find out for themselves, rummaging afoot or horseback, the cedar's secret places and what kinds of birds build what kinds of nests and how dark hills nose out into green and winding valleys when viewed from the high Booker, and by finding out these things they take on ownership too. Seeding and harvest, heat and cold, rain and drouth, birth and death, lushness and dormancy, earth and air and fire and water are with us closely all around, year by rhythmic year.

That this is an archaic and sideline sort of existence in a pulsating technological time is obvious. That it bespeaks no hot noble desire in the Head Varmint for immersion in twentieth-century humanity's rub and stink and clamor, the Varmint readily admits. This is not, however, sour Weltschmerz. I have moved about a good bit in the world, if in an uncontemporary sort of way. And while finding much that seemed sorrowful and wrong and reaching stout disaccord with some main forces of the age, I have been barred always from glumness by the rather ridiculous fact that I've liked so many people I've known and have always been so bloody glad to be alive. The only truly philosophical question, as Camus noted, being suicide. . . .

But it strikes me as more than a possibility that archaism, in times one disagrees with, may touch closer to lasting truth than do the times themselves—that, for instance, the timbre and meaning of various goat-bleats may be at least as much worth learning as the music and mores of the newest wave of youths to arrive at awareness of the eternal steaming turmoil of the human crotch. Therefore, having at least the illusion of choice, one chooses for the moment at any rate isolation and an older way of life.

Not that isolation itself is more than relative now, or that we have sought it fully. Like most other people these days, we have in us much that is urban, and contemporaneity comes at us through sometimes complex kinships and friendships in cities fifty or eighty or two hundred or two thousand miles away, through magazines and newspapers and electronic boxes in the helter-skelter house, through influences on children in school, through the fact that both Madame and I have work we do and like that relates to the world outside, through highlines and fuel companies that feed energy to the machines and gadgets on which we depend in lieu of the hired help and draft animals another age might have required for the less than truly simple life we lead, through raiding dogs and sonic booms and cruising helicopters and the faint groan of big trailer trucks fighting a grade on U.S. 67 two or three miles away, on quiet nights with a slight drift of southerly air. . . . Most of the time at Hard Scrabble you can feel yourself remote from the world and its moil if you want to, and one city friend of ours says that on getting out of his car here he always experiences "culture shock." But isolation and simplicity are not what they used to be.

Other prospective intrusions loom. A nuclear power plant is scheduled for construction on Squaw Creek a few miles east, with whatever titillating possibilities for malfunction and dire leakage there may be inherent in the state of that art. Its output is intended to satisfy new demands to arise in the 1980s in a "metroplex" of losangelization on erstwhile excellent farmland between Fort Worth and Dallas, sixty miles from us, which speculators and other boomers are prophesying will grow up in the environs of a new regional airport. . . . And the indefatigable Army Engineers, rumor says, keep nosing quietly up and down the Paluxy valley with some sort of big dam in mind. I am told that outcrops of the porous Trinity Sand upstream would prevent a reservoir from holding water, and hope this may be so, for otherwise we might end up either submerged or part of one of the shrill suburban playgrounds that are promoted around such lakes.

Isolation, indeed. Bells still toll for one and all—and, God knows, for the land.

Relative isolation, then.

There is always the question of whether or not you are doing your children a favor shielding them even this much from the world as it is— whether you may just be setting them up for trauma when they barge out into its jostle, as barge out they will. I tend to think otherwise. Anyone who has been shown clearly that natural and rural basics contain a good measure of irrationality and violence and injustice and pain and lust and greed has at least a start toward comprehending adult social and professional life when the time comes to face it. And even if it does turn out that the world as it is gives them some knocks, as the world as it is surely will, who would want to cheat them of someone to blame for trauma later, when it hurts? At any rate, life at Hard Scrabble is providing them with some time to build up strength, some responsibility for living things, some awareness of biological and natural truth—and, perhaps wrongly, I suspect that these are among the more meaningful things you can furnish a child in any era.

If this were a different sort of book, the reader would have been getting warm glimpses along the way of the Happy Homestead Family, of John and Jane and Helen and Sally and dog Blue and cat Kitty and goat Door Bell and ponies Ladybird and Penny and the other personified members of the place's population, laboring and playing and producing in honest rustic joy and fulfillment. Well, we do so labor and play and produce, more or less, and we do find rustic joy and fulfillment, but somehow in the process we do not manage greatly to resemble the families in back-to-the-land magazines and books or to exhibit constant hearty unison in regard to our common goals, if indeed they are common. For just as the world is often with us, so is individuality, and the voice of genial Lord Hard Scrabble is sometimes heard to swell quite loud in speaking of such matters as whose turn it may be to feed the horses, or who left what gate open endangering the heifers' virtue, or what set of small hands and feet shall go forthwith in search of kindling wood, or how he intends callously to carry the beloved pet Nubians off to auction at Meridian if someone doesn't get hot and clean their shed. . . .

But it isn't that sort of book. . . .

If it fitted into still another category, that of Triumphant Returns to the Land, now would likely be the time for a few wind-up pages of ringing affirmation and a proud recital of the universal principles symbolized by one's years of labor and rumination amid the Tonkish hills. But when you come down to it, the main idea in truth seems to have been not so much triumph as comprehension, though I suppose there is a certain minor degree of triumph in what little has been accomplished here and in the fact that it all still seems worthwhile. And if some universal principles are truly very much involved—how could they not be, with the land?—I am sure I have pointed a bony finger toward them a bit too often already.

You have the power to make a choice, or at least from long habit you think you do. And when the time comes to choose land you choose, against all good sense, a patch of rocky rough cedar hills with a few tired little fields and pretty water flowing past them over ledge limestone. In the short, disastrous, backwater history of its use by men of your race, its swift decline from primal richness, you come to see that there is a summary of the relationship between men and land on all parts of this planet, in the ages succeeding a golden time of harmony between men and the natural order that may or may not have ever been, anywhere. Because there is in you a need to know certain things—though why the need is there you do not at first discern—you undertake this bit of land's uneconomic restoration to what you hope is gentler human use, with no certainty at all that those who come after you will be gentle with it too or that in long time what you do here will matter a mote for good or bad, these being needful illusions as is land ownership itself, existing only in your head.

Yet out of the work and the illusions come in time some scraps of understanding—tardy and incomplete perhaps, but there were other things to do before, and maybe for that matter it was only now time to learn about scrub brush and rhizobia and goat-bleats and all those other things. And through the understanding comes abruptly and at long last a glimpse of old reality, indestructible, hiding among the creatures wild and tame and the stones and the plants, and in the teeming dirt. Without having known fully till now that it was what you sought, you see it there as clearly as does any battered ancient pensioner who leans on a hoe and picks his nose beyond the fringes of suburbia, contemplating the rituals of bantam hens that are not even all the same color, uncontemporary, at one with vanished medieval peasants in his fundamental thrusts and rhythms, at one with Sumerian farmers working in fields beside the Tigris and hearing from far off the clash and clang of mad kings murdering one another.

You see it and it sees you. Old reality survives, blinking at you there, lizard-eyed. Survives and will prevail.

That is perhaps enough to know. Yes.

Hard Scrabble: Observations on a Patch of Land was published in 1974 (New York: Knopf) and reissued in 1985 (Austin: Texas Monthly Press) and 1993 (Houston: Gulf Publishing Company). Reprinted by permission of Alfred A. Knopf, Inc.

Composed in Sabon types with Thorne Shaded initial.

Texas Past

THE LAST RUNNING

*T*HEY CALLED HIM PAJARITO, in literal trader-Spanish interpretation of his surname, or more often Tom Tejano, since he had been there in those early fighting days before the Texans had flooded up onto the plains in such numbers that it became no longer practical to hate them with specificity.

After the first interview, when he had climbed down from the bed where an aching liver held him and had gone out onto the porch to salute them, only to curse in outrage and clump back into the house when he heard what they wanted, the nine of them sat like grackles about the broad gray-painted steps and talked, in Comanche, about Tom Texan the Little Bird and the antique times before wire fences had partitioned the prairies. At least, old Juan the cook said that was what they were talking about.

Mostly it was the old men who talked, three of them, one so decrepit that he had had to make the trip from Oklahoma in a lop-sided carryall drawn by a piebald mare, with an odd long bundle sticking out the back, the rest riding alongside on ponies. Of the other six, two were middle-aged and four were young.

Their clothes ran a disastrous gamut from buckskin to faded calico and blue serge, but under dirty Stetsons they wore their hair long and braided, plains style. Waiting, sucking Durham cigarettes and speaking Comanche, they sat about the steps and under the cottonwoods in the yard and ignored those of us who drifted near to watch them, except the one or two whom they considered to have a right to their attention. Twice a day for two days they built fires and broiled unsymmetrical chunks of the fat calf which, from his bed, furiously, Tom Bird had ordered killed for them. At night — it was early autumn — they rolled up in blankets about the old carry-all and slept on the ground.

"They show any signs of leaving?" Tom Bird asked me when I went into his room toward evening of the second day.

I said, "No, sir. They told Juan they thought you could spare one easily enough, since all of them and the land too used to be theirs."

"They didn't used to be nobody's!" he shouted.

"They've eaten half that animal since they got here," I said. "I never saw anybody that could eat meat like that, and nothing but meat."

"No, nor ever saw anything else worth seeing," he said, his somber gray eyes brooding. He was one of the real ones, and none of them are left now. That was in the twenties; he was my great-uncle, and at sixteen he had run away from his father's farm in Mississippi to work his way to the brawling acquisitive Texas frontier. At the age of eighty-five he possessed — more or less by accident, since cattle rather than land had always meant wealth to him — a medium-large ranch in the canyon country where the Cap Rock falls away to rolling prairies, south of the Texas Panhandle. He had buried two wives and had had no children and lived there surrounded by people who worked for him. When I had showed up there, three years before the Comanches' visit, he had merely grunted at me on the porch, staring sharply at my frail physique, and had gone right on arguing with his manager about rock salt in the pastures. But a month later, maybe when he decided I was going to pick up weight and live, we had abruptly become friends. He was given to quick gruff judgments and to painful retractions.

He said in his room that afternoon, "God damn it, I'll see them in hell before they get one, deeper than you can drop an anvil."

"You want me to tell them that?"

"Hell, yes," he said. "No. Listen, have you talked any with that old one? Starlight, they call him."

I said that neither Starlight nor the others had even glanced at any of us.

Tom Bird said, "You tell him you're kin to me. He knows a lot, that one."

"What do you want me to say about the buffalo?"

"Nothing," he said and narrowed his eyes as a jab of pain shot through him from that rebellious organ which was speaking loudly now of long-gone years of drinking at plains mudholes and Kansas saloons. He grunted. "Not a damn thing," he said. "I already told them."

Starlight paid no attention at all when I first spoke to him. I had picked up a poor grade of Spanish from old Juan in three years but was timid about using it, and to my English he showed a weathered and not even disdainful profile.

I stated my kinship to Tom Bird and said that Tom Bird had told me to speak to him.

Starlight stared at the fourteen pampered bison grazing in their double-fenced pasture near the house, where my great-uncle could watch them from his chair in the evenings. He had bred them from seed stock given him in the nineties by Charles Goodnight, and the only time one of them had ever been killed and eaten was when the governor of the state and a historical society had driven out to give the old man some sort of citation. When the Comanches under Starlight had arrived, they had walked down to the pasture fence and had looked at the buffalo for perhaps two hours, hardly speaking, studying the cows and the one calf and the emasculated males and the two bulls — old Shakespeare, who had killed a horse once and had put innumerable men up mesquite trees and over fences, and his lecherous though rarely productive son, John Milton.

Then they had said, matter-of-factly, that they wanted one of the animals.

Starlight's old-man smell was mixed with something wild, perhaps wood smoke. His braids were a soiled white. One of the young men glanced at me after I had spoken and said something to him in Comanche. Turning then, the old Indian looked at me down his swollen nose. His face was hexagonal and broad, but sunken where teeth were gone. He spoke.

The young man said in English with an exact accent, "He wants to know what's wrong with old Tom Bird, not to talk to friends."

All of them were watching me, the young ones with more affability than the others. I said Tom Bird was sick in the liver, and patted my own.

Starlight said in Spanish, "Is he dying?"

I answered in Spanish that I didn't think so but that it was painful.

He snorted much like Tom Bird himself and turned to look again at the buffalo in the pasture. The conversation appeared to have ended, but not knowing how to leave I sat there on the top step beside the old Comanche, the rest of them ranged below us and eyeing me with what I felt to be humor. I took out cigarettes and offered them to the young man, who accepted the package and passed it along, and when it got back to me it was nearly empty. I got the impression that this gave them amusement, too, though no one had smiled. We all sat blowing smoke into the crisp evening air.

Then, it seemed, some ritual biding time had passed. Old Starlight began to talk again. He gazed at the buffalo in the pasture under the fading light and spoke steadily in bad Spanish with occasional phrases of worse English. The young Indian who had translated for me in the beginning lit a small stick fire below the steps. From time to time one of the other old men would obtrude a question or a correction, and they would drop into the angry Comanche gutturals, and the young man, whose name was John Oak Tree, would tell me what they were saying.

The story went on for an hour or so; when Starlight stopped talking they trooped down to the carryall and got their blankets and rolled up in them on the ground. In the morning I let my work in the ranch office wait and sat down again with the Comanches on the steps, and Starlight talked again. The talk was for me, since I was Tom Bird's kinsman. Starlight did not tell the story as I tell it here. Parts I had to fill in later in conversation with Tom Bird, or even from books. But this was the story.

WITHOUT KNOWING his exact age, he knew that he was younger than Tom Bird, about the age of dead Quanah Parker, under whom he had more than once fought. He had come to warrior's age during the big fight the white men had had among themselves over the black men. Born a Penateka or Honey Eater while the subtribal divisions still had meaning, he remembered the surly exodus from the Brazos reservation to Oklahoma in 1859, the expulsion by law of the Comanches from all of Texas.

But white laws had not meant much for another ten years or so. It was a time of blood and confusion, a good time to be a Comanche and fight the most lost of all causes. The whites at the Oklahoma agencies were Northern and not only tolerated but sometimes egged on and armed the parties striking down across the Red, with the full moon, at the line of settlements established by the abominated and tenacious Texans. In those days, Starlight said, Comanches held Texans to be another breed of white men, and even after they were told that peace had smiled again among whites, they did not consider this to apply to that race which had swarmed over the best of their grass and timber.

In the beginning, the raids had ritual formality and purpose; an individual party would go south either to make war, or to steal horses, or to drive off cattle for trading to the New Mexican comancheros at plains rendezvous, or maybe just reminiscently to run deer and buffalo over the old grounds. But the distinctions dimmed. In conservative old age Starlight believed that the Comanches' ultimate destruction was rooted in the loss of the old disciplines. That and smallpox and syphilis and whiskey. And Mackenzie's soldiers. All those things ran in an apocalyptic pack, like wolves in winter.

They had gone horse raiding down into the Brazos country, a dozen of them, all young and all good riders and fighters. They captured thirty horses here and there in the perfect stealth that pride demanded, without clashes, and were headed back north up the Keechi Valley near Palo Pinto when a Texan with a yellow beard caught them in his corral at dawn and killed two of them with a shotgun. They shot the Texan with arrows; Starlight himself peeled off the yellow scalp. Then, with a casualness bred of long cruelty on both sides, they killed his wife and two children in the log house. She did not scream as white women were said to do, but until a hatchet cleaved her skull kept shouting, "Git out! Git, git, git."

And collecting five more horses there, they continued the trek toward the Territory, driving at night and resting at known secret spots during the days.

The leader was a son of old Iron Shirt, Pohebits Quasho, bullet-dead on the Canadian despite his Spanish coat of mail handed down from the old haughty days. Iron Shirt's son said that it was bad to have killed the woman and the children, but Starlight, who with others laughed at him, believed even afterward that it would have been the same if they had let the woman live.

What was certain was that the Texans followed, a big party with men among them who could cut trail as cleanly as Indians. They followed quietly, riding hard and resting little, and on the third evening, when the Comanches were gathering their herd and readying themselves to leave a broad enclosed creek valley where they had spent the day, their sentry on a hill yelled and was dead, and the lean horsemen with the wide hats were pouring down the hillside shouting the long shout that belonged to them.

When it happened, Starlight was riding near the upper end of the valley with the leader. The only weapons with them were their knives and Starlight's lance, with whose butt he had been poking the rumps of the restive stolen horses as they hazed them toward camp below. As they watched, the twenty or more Texans overrode the camp, and in the shooting and confusion the two Comanches heard the end of their five companions who had been there afoot.

"I knew this," the leader said.

"You knew it," Starlight answered him bitterly. "You should have been the sentry, Know-much."

Of the other two horse gatherers, who had been working the lower valley, they could see nothing, but a group of the Texans rode away from the camp in that direction, yelling and firing. Then others broke toward Starlight and the leader a half mile above.

"We can run around them to the plain below," the son of Iron Shirt said. "Up this creek is bad."

Starlight did not know the country up the creek, but he knew what he felt, and feeling for a Comanche was conviction. He turned his pony upstream and spurred it.

"Ragh!" he called to the leader in farewell. "You're dirty luck!" And he was right, for he never saw the son of Iron Shirt again. Or the other two horse gatherers either.

But the son of Iron Shirt had been right, too, because ten minutes later Starlight was forcing his pony among big fallen boulders in a root tangle of small steep canyons, each of which carried a trickle to the stream below. There was no way even to lead a horse up their walls; he had the feeling that any one of them would bring him to a blind place.

Behind him shod hoofs rang; he whipped the pony on, but a big Texan on a bay horse swept fast around a turn in the canyon, jumping the boulders, and with a long lucky shot from a pistol broke Starlight's pony's leg. The Comanche fell with the pony but lit cat-bouncing and turned, and as the Texan came down waited crouched with the lance. The Texan had one of the pistols that shot six times, rare then in that country. Bearing down, he fired three times, missing each shot, and then when it was the moment Starlight feinted forward and watched the Texan lurch aside from the long bright blade, and while he was off balance, Starlight drove it into the Texan's belly until it came out the back. The blade snapped as the big man's weight came onto it, falling.

Starlight sought the pistol for a moment but not finding it ran to the canyon wall and began climbing. He was halfway up the fifty feet of its crumbling face when the other Texan rode around the turn and stopped, and from his unquiet horse, too hastily, fired a rifle shot that blew Starlight's left eye full of powdered sandstone.

He was among swallows' nests. Their molded mud crunched under his hands; the birds flew in long loops, chittering about his head. Climbing, he felt the Texan's absorbed reloading behind and below him as the horse moved closer, and when he knew with certainty that it was time, looked around to see the long caplock rifle rising again. . . . Watched still climbing, and guessing at the instant, wrenched himself hard to the right, seizing the roots of a cedar that grew almost at the top of the cliff.

The bullet smashed through his upper left arm, and he hung only by his right, but with the long wiry strength of trick horsemanship he swung himself up and onto the overhanging turf of the cliff's top. A round rock the size of a buffalo's head lay there. Almost without pausing he tugged it loose from the earth and rolled it back over the cliff. It came close. The Texan grabbed the saddle as his horse reared, and dropped his rifle. They looked at each other. Clutching a blood-greasy, hanging arm, the Comanche stared down at a big nose and a pair of angry gray eyes, and the young Texan stared back.

Wheeling, Starlight set off trotting across the hills. That night before hiding himself he climbed a low tree and quavered for hours like a screech owl, but no one answered. A month later, an infected skeleton, he walked into the Penateka encampment at Fort Sill, the only one of twelve to return.

That had been his first meeting with Tom Bird.

WHEN TELLING of the fights, Starlight stood up and gestured in proud physical representation of what he and others had done. He did not give it as a story with a point; it was the recountal of his acquaintance with a man. In the bug-flecked light of a bulb above the house's screen door the old Indian should have looked absurd — hipshot, ugly, in a greasy black hat and a greasy dark suit with a gold chain across its vest, the dirty braids flying as he creaked through the motions of long-unmeaningful violence.

But I did not feel like smiling. I looked at the younger Indians expecting perhaps to find amusement among them, or boredom, or cynicism. It was not there. They were listening, most of them probably not even understanding the Spanish but knowing the stories, to an ancient man who belonged to a time when their race had been literally terrible.

In the morning Starlight told of the second time. It had been after the end of the white men's war; he was a war chief with bull horns on his head. Thirty well-armed warriors rode behind him when he stopped a trail herd in the Territory for tribute. Although the cowmen were only eight, their leader, a man with a black mustache, said that four whoa-haws were too many. He would give maybe two.

"Four," Starlight said. "Texan."

It was an arraignment, and the white man heard it as such. Looking at the thirty Comanches, he said that he and his people were not Texans but Kansas men returning home with bought cattle.

"Four whoa-haws," Starlight said.

The white man made a sullen sign with his hand and spoke to his men, who went to cut out the steers. Starlight watched jealously to make certain they were not culls, and when three of his young men had them and were driving them away, he rode up face to face with the white leader, unfooled even though the mustache was new.

"Tejano," he said. "Stink sonabitch." And reached over and twisted Tom Bird's big nose, hard, enjoying the rage barely held in the gray eyes. He patted his scarred left biceps and saw that the white man knew him, too, and reached over to twist the nose again, Tom Bird too prudent to stop him and too proud to duck his head aside.

"Tobacco, Texan," Starlight said.

Close to snarling, Tom Bird took out a plug. After sampling and examining it and picking a bit of lint from its surface, Starlight tucked it into his waistband. Then he turned his horse and, followed by his thirty warriors, rode away.

In those days revenge had still existed.

He had been, too, with Quanah Parker when the half-white chief had made a separate peace with Tom Bird — Tom Tejano the Pajarito now, looming big on the high plains — as with a government, on the old Bird range up along the Canadian. There had been nearly two hundred with Quanah on a hunt in prohibited territory, and they found few buffalo and many cattle. After the peace with Tom Bird they had not eaten any more wing-branded beef, except later when the Oklahoma agency bought Bird steers to distribute among them.

They had clasped hands there in Quanah's presence, knowing each other well, and in the cowman's tolerant grin and the pressure of his hard fingers Starlight had read more clearly the rout of his people than he had read it anywhere else before.

"Yah, Big-nose," he said, returning the grip and the smile. Tom Bird rode along with them hunting for ten days and led them to a wide valley twenty miles long that the hide hunters had not yet found, and they showed him there how their fathers had run the buffalo in the long good years before the white men. November it had been, with frosted mornings and yellow bright days; their women had followed them to dress the skins and dry the meat. It was the last of the rich hunting years.

After that whenever Tom Bird passed through Oklahoma he would seek out the Indian who had once pulled his nose and would sometimes bring presents.

But Starlight had killed nine white men while the fighting had lasted.

DRESSED, TOM BIRD CAME OUT onto the porch at eleven
o'clock, and I knew from the smooth curve of his cheek that the
liver had quit hurting. He was affable and shook all their hands
again.

"We'll have a big dinner at noon," he told Starlight in the same
flowing pidgin Spanish the old Comanche himself used. "Juan's
making it especially for my Comanche friends, to send them on
their trip full and happy."

Still unfooled, Starlight exhumed the main topic.

"No!" Tom Bird said.

"You have little courtesy," Starlight said. "You had more once."

Tom Bird said, "There were more of you then. Armed."

Starlight's eyes squinted in mirth which his mouth did not let
itself reflect. Absently Tom Bird dug out his Days O' Work and bit
a chew, then waved the plug apologetically and offered it to the
Comanche. Starlight took it and with three remaining front teeth
haggled off a chunk, and pretended to put it into his vest pocket.

They both started laughing, phlegmy, hard-earned, old men's
laughter, and for the first time — never having seen Tom Bird out-
argued before — I knew that it was going to work out.

Tom Bird said, "Son of a coyote, you . . . I've got four fat
castrados, and you can have your pick. They're good meat, and I'll
eat some of it with you."

Starlight waggled his head mulishly. "Those, no," he said.
"The big bull."

Tom Bird stared, started to speak, closed his mouth, threw
the returned plug of tobacco down on the porch, and clumped back
into the house. The Indians all sat down again. One of the other
older men reached over and picked up the plug, had a chew, and
stuck it into his denim jacket. Immobility settled.

"Liberty," Starlight said out of nowhere, in Spanish. "They
speak much of liberty. Not one of you has ever seen liberty, or
smelled it. Liberty was grass, and wind, and a horse, and meat to
hunt, and no wire."

From beyond the dark screen door Tom Bird said, "The little
bull."

Starlight without looking around shook his head. Tom Bird
opened the door so hard that it battered back against the house
wall, loosening flakes of paint. He stopped above the old Indian

and stood there on bowed legs, looking down. "You rusty old bastard!" he shouted in English. "I ain't got but the two, and the big one's the only good one. And he wouldn't eat worth a damn."

Starlight turned his head and eyed him.

"All right," Tom Bird said, slumping. "All right."

"Thank you, Pajarito," Starlight said.

"Jimmy," the old man said to me in a washed-out voice, "go tell the boys to shoot Shakespeare and hang him up down by the washhouse."

"No," John Oak Tree said.

"What the hell you mean, no?" Tom Bird said, turning to him with enraged pleasure. "That's the one he wants. What you think he's been hollering about for two whole days?"

"Not dead," John Oak Tree said. "My grandfather wants him alive."

"Now ain't that sweet?" the old man said. "Ain't that just beautiful? And I can go around paying for busted fences from here to Oklahoma and maybe to the God damn Arctic Circle, all so a crazy old murdering Comanche can have him a pet bull buffalo."

Starlight spoke in Spanish, having understood most of the English. "Tom Tejano, listen," he said.

"What?"

"Listen," Starlight said. "We're going to kill him, Tom Tejano. We."

"My butt!" said Tom Bird, and sat down.

IN THE AFTERNOON, after the fried chicken and the rice and mashed beans and the tamales and the blistering chili, after the courteous belching and the smoking on the porch, everyone on the ranch who could leave his work was standing in the yard under the cottonwoods as the nine Comanches brought their horses up from the lot, where they had been eating oats for two days, and tied them outside the picket fence, saddled.

After hitching Starlight's mare to the carryall, without paying any attention to their audience they began to strip down, methodically rolling their shed clothes into bundles with hats on top and putting them on the back of the carryall. Starlight reeled painfully among them, pointing a dried-up forefinger and giving orders.

When they had finished, all of them but he wore only trousers and shoes or moccasins, with here and there scraps of the old bone and claw and hide and feather paraphernalia. John Oak Tree had slipped off the high-heeled boots he wore and replaced them with tennis sneakers.

A hundred yards away, gargling a bellow from time to time, old Shakespeare stood jammed into a chute where the hands had choused him. Between bellows, his small hating eye peered toward us from beneath a grayed board; there was not much doubt about how *he* felt.

The Indians took the long, blanketed bundle from the carryall and unrolled it.

"For God's sake!" a cowboy said beside me, a man named Abe Reynolds who had worked a good bit with the little buffalo herd. "For God's sake, this is nineteen damn twenty-three?"

I chuckled. Old Tom Bird turned his gray eyes on us and glared, and we shut up. The bundle held short bows, and quivers of arrows, and long, feather-hung, newly reshafted buffalo lances daubed with red and black. Some took bows and others lances, and among the bowmen were the two old men younger than Starlight, who under dry skins still had ridged segmented muscles.

"Those?" I said in protest, forgetting Tom Bird. "Those two couldn't . . ."

"Because they never killed one," he said without looking around. "Because old as they are, they ain't old enough to have hunted the animal that for two whole centuries was the main thing their people ate, and wore, and made tents and ropes and saddles and every other damn thing they had out of. You close your mouth, boy, and watch."

Starlight made John Oak Tree put on a ribboned medal of some kind. Then they sat the restless ponies in a shifting line, motley still but somehow, now, with the feel of that old terribleness coming off of them like a smell, and Starlight walked down the line of them and found them good and turned to raise his hand at Tom Bird.

Tom Bird yelled.

The man at the chute pulled the bars and jumped for the fence, and eight mounted Indians lashed their ponies into a hard run toward the lumpy blackness that had emerged and was stand-ing there swaying its head, bawling-furious.

Starlight screeched. But they were out of his control now and swept in too eagerly, not giving Shakespeare time to decide to run. When the Indian on the fastest pony, one of the middle-aged men, came down on him shooting what looked like a steady jet of ar-rows from beside the pony's neck, the bull squared at him. The Indian reined aside, but not enough. The big head came up under the pony's belly, and for a moment horse and rider paused reared against the horns and went pin-wheeling backward into the middle of the on-rushing others.

"Them idiots!" Abe Reynolds said. "Them plumb idiots!"

One swarming pile then, one mass with sharp projecting heads and limbs and weapons, all of them yelling and pounding and hacking and stabbing, and when old Shakespeare shot out from under the pile, shrugging them helter-skelter aside, he made a run for the house. Behind him they came yipping, leaving a gut-ripped dead horse on the ground beside the chute and another running riderless toward the northeast. One of the downed hunters sat on the ground against the chute as though indifferently. The other — one of the two oldsters — was hopping about on his left leg with an arrow through the calf of his right.

But I was scrambling for the high porch with the spectators, those who weren't grabbing for limbs, though Tom Bird stood his ground cursing as Shakespeare smashed through the white picket fence like dry sunflower stalks and whirled to make another stand under the cottonwoods. Some of the Indians jumped the fence and others poured through the hole he had made, all howling until it seemed there could be no breath left in them. For a moment, planted, Shakespeare stood with arrows bristling brightly from his hump and his loins and took someone's lance in his shoulder. Then he gave up that stand, too, and whisked out another eight feet of fence as he leveled into a long run down the dirt road past the corrals.

They rode him close, poking and shooting.

And finally, when it was all far enough down the road to have the perspective of a picture, John Oak Tree swung out leftward and running parallel to the others pulled ahead and abruptly slanted in with the long bubbling shriek, loud and cutting above all the other noise, that you can call rebel yell or cowboy holler or whatever you want, but which deadly exultant men on horseback have likely shrieked since the Assyrians and long, long before. Shakespeare ran desperately free from the sharp-pointed furor behind him, and John Oak Tree took his dun pony in a line converging sharply with the bull's course, and was there, and jammed the lance's blade certainly just behind the ribs and pointing forward, and the bull skidded to his knees, coughed, and rolled onto his side.

"You call that fair?" Abe Reynolds said sourly.

Nobody had. It was not fair. Fair did not seem to have much to do with what it was.

Starlight's carryall was headed for the clump of horsemen down the road, but the rest of us were held to the yard by the erect stability of Tom Bird's back as he stood in one of the gaps in his picket fence. Beside the chute, Starlight picked up the two thrown Indians and the saddle from the dead horse, the old hunter dis-arrowed and bleeding now, and drove on to where the rest sat on their ponies around Shakespeare's carcass.

Getting down, he spoke to John Oak Tree. The young Indian dismounted and handed his lance to Starlight, who hopped around for a time with one foot in the stirrup and got up onto the dun pony and brought it back toward the house at a run, the lance held high. Against his greasy vest the big gold watch chain bounced, and his coattails flew, but his old legs were locked snugly around the pony's barrel. He ran it straight at Tom Bird where he stood in the fence gap, and pulled it cruelly onto its hocks three yards away, and held out the lance butt first.

"I carried it when I pulled your nose," he said. "The iron, anyhow."

Tom Bird took it.

"We were there, Tom Tejano," Starlight said.

"Yes," my great-uncle said. "Yes, we were there."

The old Comanche turned the pony and ran it back to the little group of his people and gave it to John Oak Tree, who helped him get back into the carryall. Someone had caught the loose pony. For a few moments all of them sat, frozen, looking down at the arrow-quilled black bulk that had been Shakespeare.

Then, leaving it there, they rode off down the road toward

Oklahoma, past the fences of barbed steel that would flank them all the way.

A cowhand, surveying the deadly debris along the route of their run, said dryly, "A neat bunch of scutters, be damn if they ain't."

I was standing beside old Tom Bird, and he was crying. He felt my eyes and turned, the bloody lance upright in his hand, paying no heed to the tears running down the sides of his big nose and into his mustache.

"Damn you, boy," he said. "Damn you for not ever getting to know anything worth knowing. Damn me, too. We had a world, once."

First published in *Atlantic Monthly* (June 1959), "The Last Running" appeared in *The Best American Short Stories 1960* (Boston: Houghton Mifflin, 1960). This version was published as a book in 1974 (Austin: Encino Press) and in 1990 (New York: Lyons & Burford).

Composed in Cochin types with Gavotte initial.

THE DREAMER

IT WAS A BIG DOG, a black-and-tan hound with maybe some mastiff in it, and no one knew where it had come from except that it had clearly come a long way. A fleshless, graceful, scarred, hide-hung skeleton, it trotted sorefooted down the dirt valley road by the river, paying no mind to any man though at John Ferris's tavern some would have been glad to stop it and own it. It went on into the hills to August Doppelwein's place and then to the third hill beyond August's where August's daughter Sophie and her quiet redheaded husband and their children lived in a rock house. There it went to the flagstone-floored gallery where the quiet redheaded man, Joe McNeill, was sitting in a hide-bottomed chair, and it licked his hands and lay down. The morning afterward it died, and Joe McNeill wept.

"He cried, Papa," Sophie told her father in the soft Bavarian German they used between themselves, though her mother had been English-speaking. "He cried over it. He never cried before. You know him. It was a wild beast, and it bit little Otto's leg when he tried to play with it, and Joe cried over its dying."

Old August in his side-whiskers sighed and spat. He was old-country and did not understand his son-in-law. It did not help to know that the people born in this new country did not understand him either. August knew that he liked Joe McNeill. Sophie had been happy with him and they had given August three fat loud grandchildren, his first ones. His other two daughters had married and moved away, but Joe and Sophie were there beside him with three children, and August liked that.

"Husbands are strange cattle," he told her, not believing it really, never having been especially strange as a husband himself. "The dog had some meaning for him. Let it be."

>   <

He had come among them violently, but it was a violent time and place, South Texas in the Fifties. His violence was directed, with provocation, at a man he did not know, a loner like himself who had no relatives or close friends on whom the duty of revenge might devolve.

John Ferris had a still and kept a drinking-place beside his gristmill on the river, at a rockbottomed rapids between high limestone hills from which wild Plains Indians threaded down by moonlight from time to time, to steal and kill and sometimes to be killed themselves. Settlement was strung up and down the river valley from the mill, the people mixed Teutons and Anglo-Saxons, with a scattering of the darker people whom the Revolution against Mexico twenty years before had practically disenfranchised. There were few slaves, and no free blacks. Some of the community's people farmed and some ranched, and most did a little of both.

The redheaded man arrived afoot and alone and without a hat one morning, dressed in filthy fringed buckskins and moccasins, and stopped at Ferris's tavern to stand through the dinner hour, quietly and slowly and steadily drinking white liquor at one end of the long plank that served for a bar. He was still there later when ranchers began to drift in and formed a conversational clot. Armored against brush in boots and chaps and jackets of coarse cowhide, they spoke of cattle, of horses, of Indians, and a little—not much, for among them were both Germans and Anglos—of the recent Staats-Saengerfest in San Antonio where many Texas Germans had written down their names in favor of Abolition. They let the stony-eyed redheaded man alone and he seemed to pay no attention to their talk.

To John Ferris behind his plank bar one of the Anglos said, "We'd ought to pay you to set a barrel of red-eye outside on a table, moonlight nights."

"I wouldn't charge but half price," Ferris told him.

"Drunk Injuns make good killing," said a big black-haired man named Peter Wilkinson.

The first one looked at him. "You'd know," he said. "You was sure as hell there, wasn't you?"

"I took care of what was mine," Wilkinson said flatly. "How many horses you say you lost?"

On the night of the last raid a half-dozen Comanches had hatcheted through the door of the tavern and had gotten drunk, and in the morning aroused whites had found them squabbling and sick in brush a half-mile from the valley road, and had shot them down before riding on futilely to trail their vanished comrades with the stolen livestock and the scalps of two women. But Peter Wilkinson had not been along. He had stayed at his own ranch as always, his horses penned, his Mexican vaqueros posted about with rifles. If everybody would take care of himself right, he often said, there would be a hell of a sight fewer rich Indians up in the buffalo country. His vaqueros stuck by him not so much it seemed from loyalty as from pride in his womanless hard-working brutality, and he had prospered.

Stung a little, however, by what the other man had said, Wilkinson looked down the bar where the redheaded man stood drinking, lapped in his own unlistening calm.

"Hey, Red!" Wilkinson said.

The man did not notice.

"Injun!"

The man turned.

"The way that hair's cut, looks like it was braids not long ago," Wilkinson said.

"Could've been."

"Braid-headed Injuns is son of a bitches. You been squawin' with 'em?"

The man said quietly, not in any of the various accents of that place, "Strikes me you're wantin' a scrap."

"I scrap mean," Wilkinson said, slitting his eyes. It was true enough; a couple of years before he had killed a quarrelsome horse buyer.

"All right," the redheaded man said, and moved. Wilkinson grabbed at a long Walker Colt that he carried holstered against his left hipbone. But the other man from somewhere behind his neck pulled a great bone-handled knife and in a smooth single motion brought it up and over his head and down and threw it, and it stuck straight and deep into Peter Wilkinson's belly below his breastbone. He stood for a moment and fired one chamber of the revolver into the dirt floor, and dropped it, and fell, and died.

Fluidly and almost without pause, the stranger stooped and yanked his red knife free and backed toward a corner where a rifle stood. But nobody among the Texans moved. They had the push and the fortitude to care for themselves in a hard time and place, but Peter Wilkinson through long effort had made his own troubles his own.

There was a thing, though. One of them named Ted Lackey said it: "You sabe Comanch? You run with those red devils?"

"No," he answered.

They studied him, but he had spoken flatly and they believed him. Old August Doppelwein spat in his usual punctuation of discussion. "Aw right, boy," he said. "Nobody's look for more trouble. Vas right, you."

Two of Wilkinson's vaqueros came in and unemotionally took the body away, and the loner drank himself numb before suppertime, when August threw him into the back end of a wagon with his knife and rifle and took him to the house up Grindstone Creek where he lived with his three motherless daughters. Three months later the redheaded man married Sophie Doppelwein, the middle daughter, still without having told more about himself than that his name was Joe McNeill. He had been a good hand for old August, deft with horses, new to cattle but quick to learn. August got masons from San Antonio to build them a plain rock house three hills over from his own, and gave them land and a little herd of snuffy longhorns to start out with, and the fat loud grandchildren began arriving one a year.

Somebody said that having rid them of Peter Wilkinson, Joe McNeill had stayed on as a replacement, but it was a joke. Like Wilkinson he wanted no help, but he gave help when it was needed, and at the spring and fall cow hunts he labored steadily and well and quietly, all bone and fiber, proof against thorns and horns and hooves and dust. And his rectitude in the matter of which calves belonged to which cows and what brand was to be burned into them, even if their owner lived forty miles away in other country, made some of the valley's less punctilious residents uncomfortable.

By then the frontier had moved its outposts far enough north and west of this region that Indian raids came less often. It was a long time now since the white treachery at the Council House in San Antonio and the fierce retribution that it had evoked from the wild people. It would be another few years before white weakness during the Civil War would bring red men with frequency that deep into the state again. But they came sometimes.

Once a big party did, fifty or sixty of them. They rode out of the valley's region with a herd of stolen horses and five scalps, all taken in the night and unrevenged. A party of the valley people, Joe McNeill among them, struck out after the raiders under the command of a fat slave-owner named Friedrich von Helmstedt. But they moved fumblingly and McNeill left them to ride ahead. Two days later he met them, riding a mouse-colored mare that he had swapped at night from the Comanches' own stolen herd. He told them to hurry; the Indians were close ahead.

"How far?" von Helmstedt asked.

"Eighteen mile, twenty," McNeill answered. "We can get up with 'em tomorrow."

"Too far," Friedrich said. "Are tired, our horses."

"So are theirn, Mister Fred, God damn it. They've done started movin' slow because they think they're safe. Come on!"

In command now whether Friedrich von Helmstedt liked it or not, Joe McNeill lashed the party into quick movement and kept them going all night, and the following afternoon hid them in an elm motte, in a valley up which the Comanches came ambling easily with their herd, unwary. In an ambuscade and a charge the settlers killed twenty or more and scattered the rest, chasing them until they began to regroup, more numerous still than the whites. Both parties stopped, three hundred yards of rolling grassland between them. The whites had most of the stolen herd behind them now, theirs again, and the fight was over. But, for face, a burly war chief on a paint horse rode out between the groups and cantered up and down, shaking a lance and shouting unintelligible brag talk.

"Because he knows he's lost," Ted Lackey said grinning. "Damn old fool."

"Hold this," Joe McNeill told him, handing over his rifle. Pulling out the big bear knife with which he had killed Peter Wilkinson, he put the mouse-colored mare into a dead run toward the war chief. They met like knights. McNeill shoved the point of the Indian's lance up and over his own shoulder and bored in slashing, and so quickly that nobody later could claim to have seen how it was done, the paint horse was loping riderless away and Joe McNeill was dragging the dead chief by his braids and taking the scalp even as other Comanches came at him, and then had it and hard-raced back toward his own people, laughing back over his shoulder and shouting Indian words. Mad glee was in his face for a moment when he pulled up among the Texans again, before the mask of always settled on his mouth and eyes.

"I don't care," a man said at one of the campfires that night where they stopped, the recovered herd secure in a little canyon. "You say brave. I say flat looney-tic. I don't care."

"They sure as hell ain't gonna follow us after that business," Ted Lackey said. "You know how many coups a knife fight like that counts with Indians? You think McNeill didn't know that?"

"I think crazy," the other said, and just beyond the firelight fat Friedrich von Helmstedt rumbled surly corroboration.

"It's God's truth that he's queer," Ted Lackey said. "I told him I thought it was real fine, what he did, and he never even split a grin. Just looked at me."

But he had earned a respect, and in time people smiled at his quietness on those days when he would come to John Ferris's to drink himself into stupor—less and less frequently now, once every month or so or even sometimes letting a half-year go by without leaving his family and the farming and the cow work in the hills.

> <

Then the big black-and-tan hound came, and licked his hand, and bit his little son, and died, and Joe McNeill wept. That afternoon he got drunk again at the tavern and fought three loud strangers in a group, and went down only after they had clubbed him with a loaded quirt. Old August came to haul him home.

The next day he sat empty-eyed and silent on the gallery of his house, not speaking to Sophie or the awed children or to August when he came over. Just staring across the hills. Not even eating or answering her when she asked him to come to the table. Late that afternoon he let out a long wild yell that brought her running out. He was stropping the big knife against his canvas trousers.

"What, honey?" Sophie said. "What?"

He looked up with a touch of shame in his face, and the vacancy had left his eyes. "I was just daydreamin' a little, I reckon," he said.

Hot with relief, she tousled his red crisp hair, and he reached up to take her firm wrist in the circle of his thumb and forefinger and to shake it slowly, with affection. There was warmth in him despite his strangeness, and they had had a good marriage.

"Whoo-ee!" she said. "Where's that smell comin' from?"

"What smell?"

"Like on the air," she said, sniffing. "Like somebody was boilin' an old coon that had been dead too long."

"I can't smell it," McNeill said whose nose was usually like a predator's.

"Strong," his wife said, and went into the house to sing Bavarian songs at her loom in celebration of the fact that her man was back with her again. Wherever it was he'd been gone to.

Joe McNeill sat in the hide-bottomed chair, musing not back into his dream but about it. He had been dreaming of a hound. Not of the hound that had come and found him and died, but of a hound that had never been. Bigger than a mountain lion by far. Mean as a grizzly. Made to hunt big rough things with, like bears and bulls and lions and even men. A hound to clear out a piece of country with. The damnedest hound the world would ever have seen.

> <

He was a mountain man, though not as purely one as he would have been if he had been born a few years earlier. The mountains' big lonesomeness and the good reasons for being there had begun to crumble by the time he reached them. He had learned a little trapping young when, at sixteen, the rootless by-blow of an Irishman and a French Canuck servant girl, he had drifted up the Missouri from St. Louis. He had fallen in with one of the old ones who had taught him trapping, and drinking, and sign, and to keep his mouth shut, and other things that he had put to use later as a meat hunter for exploring and Army parties in the middle Rockies.

Then he had quit that and had hunted only for himself. Not for meat, which was easy to come by in the lonesome places that he sought and found, but for the hunting itself. For the fight, for the kill. With a straggling pack of dogs he had drifted for years, north and high up in the summer, south and low in the winter, hunting down big killer animals simply because it was in him to do that, alone. Lions and once jaguars far in the south, but for preference grizzlies, sometimes leaping astraddle them where the dogs held them bayed and killing them with his knife. He owned nothing but weapons and animals, and in cold times slept nestled among his hounds, and if he was a little crazy, as the Utes thought respectfully among whom he settled for a while, later, it was a craziness not uncommon in that age. A craziness of the wild solitary places that still existed.

He had left the Utes after six months. A big sow grizzly had killed most of his dogs in one fight, and white miners had shown up in the region, and in a raid on the Ute village with the men away, Pawnees had raped and killed the wife he had taken on. Reading the signs, he had abruptly abandoned the big lonesomeness and the fierce hunting, and leaving his two surviving hounds with his Indian brother-in-law he had struck out south and east, vaguely seeking white people who did not know what a mountain man was. In the valley he had found them.

> <

He thought of the old black-and-tan hound coming all that way to die.

"It ought to've died in the mountains," he said aloud on the gallery. "It didn't have no business down here."

Did he himself? Dreaming daydreams of a hound like nothing the world had ever seen raging down the valley ahead of him, Joe McNeill, killing out men and cattle and horses, everything, leaving only a lonesomeness?

A daughter in gingham, three, cotton-blonde like Sophie, stood at his knee and watched his face. He had not seen her come. He picked her up beneath the arms and threw her into the air and caught her as she fell and both of them whooped with pleasure.

"Bad old dog bite Otto," she said.

McNeill nodded. "Bad. But he's gone now, Cissy. He won't come back no more."

The other one did, though, the big one, the dream one. He couldn't keep it away. Life went on in the rhythm of cow work and plowing and planting and harvesting. Far to the east there now rattled threats of war between South and North, but they did not yet echo loud in the valley. McNeill no longer went to the tavern at all. Now, on those rare days when the emptiness and the restlessness and the nausea of being surrounded by people rose in him like a bitter fluid, when the shove inside him was the same shove that at sixteen had taken him up the Missouri toward the big savage lonesomeness that was petering out—now on those days he would sit in the hide-bottomed chair and daydream. Sophie and the children came to recognize those days and to let him alone while the spell was on him. He would sit there on the gallery silent and apart from everything around him. No feel of Joe McNeill was there, only an absence, and the smell. The smell always. Sophie came to know the smell and even to have a sense of what it meant. She believed that it did not belong to Joe but to that mood. It was deadliness. It was what a Comanche's rotted corpse would smell like, though she had never smelled one. Wild, obscene.

Redheaded Joe McNeill and the great hound that had never existed, the damnedest hound, would hunt their way down farming valleys, ripping to pieces people and livestock that they did not hate, that they were only meant to hunt. Sometimes they would hunt a swath through the whole of Texas and up into the Territory, sniffing out and baying down and killing all tameness, leaving broken-doored silent houses and bloody pens and lonesomeness behind.

Afterward, as he had once been after the big drunks, he would be quiet, hard-working, hard-riding Joe McNeill again, a family man who had come to be the person his neighbors sent for to lead all chases of Indians, whom the Rangers themselves consulted when they worked through the region. He would not own a dog, nor even go along when Ted Lackey, who liked him, invited him on hunts to chase down the occasional cougars or red wolves that showed up in the hills and killed calves. For one thing, he had known grizzlies, but that was not it. Once when somebody gave his oldest boy a pup, a floppy soft little part-hound, he waited till the children had been put to bed and tied a rock to its neck and dropped it regretfully into the blue cypress-shaded pool on the creek, where the big catfish were.

To Sophie in flat explanation he said, "No dogs. I don't want no dogs around. You don't know nothin' about me and dogs."

>   <

War began in the East and loomed suddenly big in the valley. The people split into factions. Its Anglos, though few of them owned slaves, were mainly Southerners or Southern-connected, and there was talk of raising a company. Ted Lackey rode up to talk with Joe McNeill.

"They'd elect you captain," he said. "Hell, there's not a one that wouldn't be proud to ride behind you."

"I thank you," Joe McNeill said, and shook his head.

Ted Lackey looked at him. "Old August, is it? I know there's some of the Dutchmen that don't care shoot for Secession. Not that I blame 'em."

"No. It just ain't none of my fight."

"All right," Lackey said, and then frankly, "You're a hell of a queer one, you are."

"I am," McNeill said.

Reining his horse to turn away, Lackey said, "You watch out for that fat old Friedrich. He's all of a sudden more Rebel than anybody, and he don't like you much."

Three weeks later the company left to join a ragtag cowboy cavalry regiment in San Antonio, taking with it two thirds of the valley's younger men. Those remaining, young and old, clumped into family groups that watched one another untrustingly. John Ferris died and the tavern closed, war tensions among its patrons having ruined business months before. Some of the Germans, reared to a political humanism that had brought them or their fathers across an ocean to escape feudal ways, went to Kerr County and joined a group that marched out toward Mexico where they planned to organize for the Union, but home guards caught up with them on the Nueces and slaughtered most of them. Absurdly, gentle old August Doppelwein was among those killed. Sophie named her next child after him.

Others, both Anglos and Germans, joined the valley's own small Confederate home guard under Friedrich von Helmstedt, and rode out at night to burn corncribs and barns and to shout violence at the darkened houses of men who had failed to register for conscription. It was not a good time. Taking advantage, the Comanches came down with the full moons to steal horses and kill cattle and people, and most men became as Peter Wilkinson had been, taking care of themselves and their own as best they could. After a year or so maimed soldiers began to come back, Ted Lackey among them, with a rawhide cup-stirrup on his saddle to accommodate a new peg leg.

Joe McNeill cared for his own, not missing companionship he had never sought. With two Mexican hands he built a barrier of stakes and thorny brush a hundred yards out from his house, clearing the trees from the space inside it. Within a few months he lost most of his horses and cattle to Indians, but he and Sophie and the children stayed safe. Once the home guard, disguised under sheets, came with torches and sat on their horses along the barricade and shouted filth, but then a voice spoke from the cedars behind them, outside the enclosure.

"Mister Fred," it said calmly, "there is three shotguns settin' here, right acrost my lap. Six barrels, and buckshot in 'em. How many bedsheets you reckon I could put holes in, with all that lead?"

In the ensuing jostle Friedrich von Helmstedt got his best horse's leg broken in a deep gully, and there was no more of that for a time. Quite soon the Comanches grew so violent, not even bothering to go all the way back to the plains between raids, that trouble among the valley's whites seemed to simmer down, not enough energy and hatred being left over for it. A few strong houses became nuclei of protection where people forted up during the worst times. Joe McNeill's house was one such place—mainly neutral and Union-leaning Germans came there, and two or three un-Confederate Anglo families—and von Helmstedt's place was another, as was Ted Lackey's father's at the head of the valley. People no longer thought about pursuing the Indians, but simply fought them off from the gathering-forts and let them do what they wanted elsewhere. The rattling war in the East went on, but the valley cared much less about it than it had before. It held a good many refugees from the crumpled frontier fringe farther north and west, and it was hungry and afraid.

There were lulls. Sometimes the wild people, bribed and soothed at plains conferences with Confederate officers, would let the frontier alone for two and three months at a time, and the valley's people would relax enough to start hating one another again. Von

Helmstedt's home guard, posing sometimes as Indians, rode again at night, burning now less than they looted. August Doppelwein's place was put up for auction as enemy property, and von Helmstedt bought it cheaply. Joe McNeill, forgetting now to daydream, watched the valley and the hills and kept on taking care of himself and his own.

In Sixty-four a notable lull came after Kit Carson's Federals out of New Mexico angered the Comanches and Kiowas by striking them at the Adobe Walls, far up on the High Plains, and the red raiders became almost Confederate for a while. During that hiatus Joe McNeill began gathering up scattered cattle in the brushy hills, not to consolidate property but to have meat. Alone or with his vaqueros he was much away, not knowing how long the quiet period would last or how lean the period would be that came after it. Scrupulous, he kept tally of all brands, intending to pay back beef for beef after the bad times were past, if they ever were.

In the gray hour before dawn on one of the nights when Joe was gone, Sophie McNeill heard sounds at the corrals. Wrapping herself, she slipped out without waking her children, picking up a shotgun by the door. It was dim outside, but not so dim that she could not recognize Friedrich von Helmstedt among the men who were driving seven steers and a horse toward the open gate-gap of the brush barricade.

"What are you doing?" she demanded in German.

"Your swine of a husband stole them," he said. "They are marked with others' brands."

"Not all. Nor the horse. And it doesn't matter anyhow. There was an agreement, for now."

"Agreements with traitors do not hold," he said, wheeling his horse aside.

She saw that he and the others wore moccasins, to leave confusing tracks. She raised the shotgun, held till now inconspicuously by her side. "You will replace the beasts in the pen," she said.

The horse of one of the other men stumbled and shied and she swung the gun toward him. When she did, Friedrich von Helmstedt shot her. Her solid firm womanhood melted away and she fell lumpishly. Von Helmstedt dismounted and walked to the body.

"You damned old fool," one of the home guardsmen said, an Anglo named Wofford. "That's Joe McNeill's woman you kilt."

The German stared at him pouch-eyed. "Comanches have killed her," he said. "Know you that?"

"Yes," Wofford said. "Hell, yes, a big fat Comanche done it. But I got better sense than to like it."

Von Helmstedt took out his knife.

> <

So that what Joe McNeill came riding home to that afternoon, with his two vaqueros and a trio of rope-linked mossy-horned steers, was five hysterical children unsoothed by a flock of scared neighbor women, and a gallery bristling with the guns of his friends gathered against Indians, and the scalped, sheet-covered corpse of his wife on a table in the stone house's little parlor.

When he had listened to what people had to say, he went to the corrals and studied the footprints in the dust and the signs of unshod ponies' hooves, and a single red feather. Then he came back to the house.

"Git on home," he said to the men on the gallery who had been watching him. "There ain't no Injuns."

"You sure?" one asked. "They stole stock at Theiss's, too, and left sign."

"I'm sure," he said. "I know white folks' feet, moccasins or no. Git home."

They believed him, but one of the women said that somebody would have to sit up with Sophie's body till the preacher came; it was only right. . . .

"I'll set," he said.

"You want us to take the kids till the burying?"

"Yes," he said. "Yes. Yes. Now git on home, God damn it!"

They left. Joe McNeill went into the house and pulled down the sheet and looked at his dead wife for a time. Then he returned to the gallery and sat down in the hide-bottomed chair. The vaqueros came and asked what to do with the three steers, but he did not answer or look at them. Uneasy, they went to the corral where they untied the steers and gave them water, then they slouched murmuring toward their shack at the rear of the compound.

Something inside Joe McNeill was saying that he was alone and that was good. There was a big lonesomeness and it felt good. He sat there on the flagged gallery in the hide-bottomed chair.

>   <

Ted Lackey heard the huge hound voice in the night. It was faint, for a wind was blowing the sound away from him and rustling the brush around his father's house. But it was enormous. He had kept a pack of hounds since childhood and had hunted with many other men's dogs, but he had never heard a baying like that. He eased from bed and strapped on his peg leg and steadying himself against the wall to prevent the peg's clump from waking his people, went out onto the long moonlit gallery strewn with saddles and hides. The baying was a good way down the valley, somewhere toward von Helmstedt's, and he could hear it only fitfully between bursts of wind. From his room it had sounded like a trailing note, steady and knowing, but now, from what he could hear, it had something treed. Then the wind picked up and he could hear nothing more.

A hell of a dog, he thought, returning to his bed. A dog like I never heard. Whose?

In the morning he and his young brother had business at von Helmstedt's. Though he did not like the man, their ranges over-lapped and there was a question of an outlaw bull that was tolling cows away, even out of enclosures. They rode down the dirt road by the clear stream, then forded it and headed up the valleyside toward a cluster of stone buildings among liveoaks where Friedrich and his people lived. There were no noises as they approached it, and when they entered the yard they saw why. Nothing there was alive. In the pens horses and cattle lay torn and bloody under a fog of blowflies. Under the oaks dead dogs and chickens and geese were scattered. Across the house's threshold, its oaken door ajar and awry, chopped open, lay a thick solid body that by its shape they knew was Friedrich von Helmstedt's. But only by its shape, for it had no head.

Ted Lackey's brother drew in his breath and cursed. "I never heard of 'em takin' any whole head before. Scalps, yes. But not a whole head."

They knew beforehand through premonition and the buzzing of flies what they would find inside, and they found it, seven bodies of old and young persons, male and female, ripped by an unimaginable violence and tossed like dolls into corners, and with an evil smell around them that was not theirs. When the two came outside again Ted Lackey sucked at the clean wind.

"No," he said in answer to his brother's question. "No, leave 'em lay for now. We'll come back later, with people. I want to look around the valley some."

His brother said, "Ted, I ain't yellow and you know it, but I ain't a damn fool either. They can just as easy still be around."

"There isn't any 'they.' No human somebody ripped up that old Dutchman that way."

"The hell they didn't. It was a human somebody that chopped down that door."

"Maybe," Ted Lackey said. "Come on."

A half-mile below they met three men, big-eyed. "God A'mighty, you ought to see Wofford's!" one shouted when they came within hearing. "You ought to see what they done!"

"We already saw somethin'," Lackey said.

"Von Helmstedt's?"

When he nodded the man looked with scared eyes at the hills on the north side of the valley, then at those on the south. "God, it was lonesome at Wofford's," he said. "It was the lonesomest thing I ever seen."

"We'll find more," Ted Lackey said, and they did. Along the road and in little fenced fields all kinds of stock lay torn and dead, but it was at the houses—where death had struck in a zigzag pattern, skipping some and taking others—that the lonesomeness and the silence ruled and the terrible smell lingered in sheltered spots. Here and there other valley men joined them and the party grew, and as it increased in size and saw more, it made less talk.

"Must have been two hundred of 'em," someone said in grief-struck fear after one of the houses with its shattered door and all the rest. "Three hundred. They've gone flat crazy. I'm headin' back to Mississippi tomorrow, Yankees or no Yankees. There ain't any Yankees like this."

"No, nor any Injuns either," said Lackey, but nobody was listening. They were pointed up Grindstone Creek now, toward Joe McNeill's rock house.

"Reckon they got him too," a man said. "Tough and mean as he was. They got his wife, night before last."

"Bluebellied bastard," Ted Lackey's younger brother said.

"You're wrong, Billy," said Lackey. "It just wasn't his fight, that one."

They rode to the thorny barricade and through its open gap. Beside the house the two McNeill vaqueros lay torn in the way they had come to know and the corral was lumpy with red things, but on the gallery redheaded Joe McNeill was sitting quietly in a hide-bottomed chair, with the glare of madness in his eyes and his hand around the helve of a blood-marked axe. In his lap was the fat-cheeked head of Friedrich von Helmstedt, its eyes half open.

Approaching close, they ran into a wall of the fearsome smell, and one of them retched and vomited suddenly, down past his horse's neck. The redheaded man looked up at Ted Lackey, who leaned from his saddle across the gallery's rail, studying those eyes.

"It was a dog," said Joe McNeill. "It was the God-damnedest dog anybody ever seen."

John Graves wrote "The Dreamer" in 1959 or 1960. It was published in *Readers & Writers* (May–June 1966).

Composed in Janson types with Trafton Script initial.

Side Roads

CHAPTER 10 OF *GOODBYE TO A RIVER*

T HERE WAS AN ISLAND, long and slim, built up of the variegated Brazos chert gravel which, when wet and shining, looks like the jewels in a storybook treasure chest. Its top was padded with white sand and bordered by big willows and small cottonwoods. Toward the blunt upper end, where spring's drouth-breaking floods had worked to most effect, lay a bare-swept sandy plain, and the few trees along the shoreline there were bent downstream at steep angles. Against stubs and stumps down the length of the island the same force had laid up tangled jams of driftwood from ash and cedar elm and oak and other trees, good fuel. Here and there where silt had accumulated, Bermuda grass or weeds bristled in patches.

Because I liked the look of it, I stopped there in the middle of a quiet bright afternoon and made a solid camp on flat gravel under willows, eight feet above the water but only a few nearly vertical steps from the canoe. I was tired and my gear needed tending, and it looked like the kind of place I'd been waiting for to spend a couple of nights and to loaf through a little of what the abstractly alliterative military schedules used to call "matériel maintenance." Islands are special anyhow, as children know with a leaping instinct, and when they lie in public domain you can have a fine sense of temporary ownership about them that's hard to get on shores, inside or outside of fences.

By the time I'd finished setting up camp and hauling my chattels from the canoe—all of them, since they all needed cleaning or fixing— it was nearly evening. The stronger of the channels flanking the island ran on the side where I was camped; I walked up the narrow beach and put out a catfish line just below where the water dropped out of a rapids, tying a rock to the line's end and throwing it straight out so that when the line came taut the rock dropped gurgling and anchored the line in a long bow across the head of the deep run, back to a willow stub beside me. Trotlines from shore to shore get you more fish and bigger ones, but they're also more labor. After I'd finished with the line I worked along the beach, spin-casting bootlessly for bass. Four Canada geese came diagonally over the river, low, calling, and in a moment I heard a clamor at the head of the island, shielded from me by the island's duned fringe and by willows. I climbed up through them to look. At least 200 more honkers took off screaming from the sandbar at the upper end of the bare plain. The passenger ran barking after them. Calling him back, I squatted beside a drift pile, and in the rose half-light of dusk watched through the field glass as they came wheeling in again, timid but liking the place as I had liked it, and settled by tens and twenties at the bar and in the shallows above it where the two channels split.

Nine skeptics, maybe the ones that had seen me at first and raised the alarm, circled complaining for a time before they flew on elsewhere. Black against water that held the west's reflected red, the others stalked about till their alertness had softened, then began to drink and cavort, lunging at one another, leaping into the air with their wings spread and circling two by two in a kind of dance.

Old John Magnificence was with me:

> *What call'st thou solitude, is not the Earth*
> *With various living creatures, and the Aire*
> *Replenisht, and all these at thy command*
> *To come and play before thee? . . .*

He was. I used to be suspicious of the kind of writing where characters are smitten by correct quotations at appropriate moments. I still am, but not as much. Things do pop out clearly in your head, alone, when the upper layers of your mind are unmisted by much talk with other men. Odd bits and scraps and thoughts and phrases from all your life and all your reading keep boiling up to view like grains of rice in a pot on the fire. Sometimes they even make sense.

I thought of the shotgun at my camp a hundred yards below, but it would have been useless if I'd had it; they were a long way from any cover. And for that matter there was about them something of the feel that the bald eagle had had for me in the mountain country. I'd been a hunter most of my life, except for two or three years after the war. Young, I'd made two-hour crawls on my belly through standing swamp water for the mere hope of a shot at a goose, nearly always frustrated. Just now, though, it seemed to matter little that these were safe out of range. Watching the red-and-black shadow show of their awkward powerful play was enough, and listening to their occasional arrogant horn shouts. I squatted there watching until nearly dark, then backed down quietly to the beach and went to camp.

Supper was a young squirrel who had nevertheless achieved an elder's stringiness, roasted in foil on the embers, and a potato baked in the same way. I'd been going lazy on the cooking lately, mostly because I had little appetite, and that little most generally for things I'd have disliked in town—bouillon, or coffee thickly sweet with honey, or the stewed mixed fruit that made my breakfasts. From such sparse eating and from exercise I'd lost weight—maybe twelve or fifteen pounds since Possum Kingdom, to judge from the slack in my waistband. I ate the potato and chewed a little on the squirrel and gave the rest of it to the pup.

Hearing the geese honk still from time to time, I knew it would have been easy enough, on that moonless night, to ease up the defiladed beach near them and sneak across the sand on my stomach for a sniping shot. All it would take was patience. But I was years past being tempted by that kind of dirtiness. The contradictory set of rules that one works out for killing, if he keeps on killing past a certain age, usually makes an unreasonable distinction between ways that are honorable and ways that aren't, and for me night potshots weren't. . . . And for that matter I didn't think I needed anything as big as a goose.

Someone else's rules were less strict, or maybe his need was greater; when I'd put a couple of heavy chunks of elm on the fire and sat watching them, sniffing the faintly urinal sharpness of their burning, two rapid shots sounded far off down the river and a minute later geese were calling confusedly in the sky. Stacked alongside my own abstention it angered me a little, but on the other hand it was none of my right business.

From brief yards away, in a cottonwood, a barred owl cut loose with flourishes: *Who, who, whoo, whoo, whah, whah, hah, HAH, HAH, WHO ALL!*

Then, an afterthought, he said, *YOU ALL!*

Certain it meant specifically him, the passenger barked back once almost under his breath, growled a little with an angry ridge of short hair dark along his spine, and sought my lap.

*

Elm stinks, wherefore literal farmers give it a grosser name, but it makes fine lasting coals. That morning I was up before dawn to blow away the ashes from the orange-velvet embers underneath, and to build more fire on them with twigs and leaves and brittle sticks of dead cottonwood. I huddled over it in the cold, still, graying darkness and watched coffee water seethe at the edges of a little charred pot licked by flame, and heard the horned owl stop that deceptively gentle five-noted comment he casts upon the night. The geese at the island's head began to talk among themselves, then to call as they rose to go to pastures and peanut fields, and night-flushed bobwhites started whistling *where-you? where-you?* to one another somewhere above the steep dirt riverbank. Drinking coffee with honey in it and canned milk, smoking a pipe that had the sweetness pipes only have in cold quiet air, I felt good if a little scratchy-eyed, having gone to sleep the night before struck with the romance of stars and firelight, with the flaps open and only the blanket over me, to wake at two-thirty chilled through.

On top of the food box alligator-skin corrugations of frost had formed, and with the first touch of the sun the willows began to whisper as frozen leaves loosed their hold and fell side-slipping down through the others that were still green. Titmice called, and flickers and a redbird, and for a moment, on a twig four feet from my face, a chittering kinglet jumped around alternately hiding and flashing the scarlet of its crown. I sat and listened and watched while the world woke up, and drank three cups of the syrupy coffee, better I thought than any I'd ever tasted, and smoked two pipes.

You run the risk of thinking yourself an ascetic when you enjoy with that intensity the austere facts of fire and coffee and tobacco and the sound and feel of country places. You aren't, though. In a way you're more of a sensualist than a fat man washing down sauerbraten and dumplings with heavy beer while a German band plays and a plump blonde kneads his thigh. You have shucked off the gross delights, and those you have left are few, sharp, and strong. But they're sensory. Even

Thoreau was guilty of this, if I remember right a passage or so on his cornbread, though mainly he was a real ascetic.

Real ones shouldn't care. They ought to be able to live without caring on pâté and peaches and roast suckling pig or alternatively on cheese and garlic in a windmill or on the scraps that housewives have thrown into begging bowls. Groceries and shelter should matter only as fuel and frame for life, and life only as energy for thought or beyond-communion or (Old Man Charlie Goodnight has to fit somewhere, and a fraught executive or two I've known, and maybe Davis Birdsong hurling his bulldozer against the tough cedar brush in a torn shirt and denim pants, coughing yellow flu sputum while the December rain pelts him, not caring) for action.

But I hadn't set up as an ascetic, anyhow. I sat for a long time savoring the privilege of being there, and didn't overlay the taste of the coffee with any other food. A big red-brown butterfly sat spread on the cottonwood log my axe was struck in, warming itself in the sun. I watched until it flew stiffly away, then got up and followed, for no good reason except that the time seemed to have come to stir and I wanted a closer look at the island than I'd gotten the evening before.

It was shaped like an attenuated teardrop or the cross section of an airplane's wing, maybe three quarters of a mile long and 200 yards or so wide at its upper, thicker end. Its foundation everywhere appeared to be a heavy deposit of the multicolored gravel, and its flat top except for a few high dunes of the padding sand was eight or ten feet above the present level of the river. All around, it dropped off steeply, in spots directly to the water, in others to beaches, and toward the pointed tail the willows and weeds stood rank. I rooted about there and found nothing but coon tracks and a few birds still sleepy and cold on their roosts, but emerging among cockleburs above a beach by the other channel I scared four ducks off of a quiet eddy. I'd left the gun in the tent; shots from here and there under the wide sky's bowl reminded me that busier hunters than I were finding game.

Let them. I considered that maybe in the evening I would crouch under a bush at the island's upper end and put out sheets of notepaper on the off chance that more geese would come, and the off-off chance that if they did they'd feel brotherly toward notepaper. You can interest them sometimes in newspapers.

And maybe I wouldn't.

The river's shores on either side from the island were dirt and steep, twenty feet high, surmounted by pecans and oaks with the bare sky of fields or pastures beyond. They seemed separate from the island. It was big enough, with a strong enough channel on either side, to seem to have a kind of being of its own distinct from that of the banks—a sand and willow and cottonwood and driftwood biome—though in dry times doubtless there would be only one channel and no island, but just a great bar spreading out below the right bank.

Jays, killdeers, wrens, cardinals, woodpeckers . . . With minute and amateurish interest, I found atop a scoop in the base of a big, drifted, scorched tree trunk five little piles of fox dung, a big owl's puke ball full of hair and rat skulls, and three fresher piles of what had to be coon droppings, brown and small, shaped like a dog's or a human's.

Why, asked intrigued ignorance, did wild things so often choose to stool on rocks, stumps, and other elevations?

Commonsense replied, Maybe for the view.

On the flat beach at the head of the island the night's geese had laid down a texture of crisscrossed toe-prints. Elsewhere, in dry sand, I found little pointed diggings an inch in diameter and four to five inches deep, much like those an armadillo makes in grassland but with no tracks beside them. A bird? A land-foraging crawfish? Another puzzle for my ignorance, underlined now by the clear note of an unknown sad-whistling bird in a willow a few steps from me. He wouldn't show himself, and when I eased closer said irascibly, *Heap, heap!* and fluttered out the other side.

The trouble was, I *was* ignorant. Even in that country where I belonged, my ken of natural things didn't include a little bird that went *heap-heap* and, with melancholy:

$$\underline{\qquad}$$
$$— \; — \; —, \quad — \; — \; —, \quad — \; — \; —,$$
$$\underline{\qquad}$$

and a few moronic holes in the sand. Or a million other matters worth the kenning.

I grew up in a city not far from that river—more or less a city, anyhow, a kind of spreading imposition on the prairies—that was waked from a dozing cow-town background by a standard boom after the First World War and is still, civic-souled friends tell me, bowling right along. It was a good enough place, not too big then, and a mile or so away from where I lived, along a few side streets and across a boulevard and a golf course, lay woods and pastures and a blessed river valley where the stagnant Trinity writhed beneath big oaks. In retrospect it seems that my friends and I spent more time there than we did on pavements, though maybe it's merely that remembrance of that part is sharper. There were rabbits and squirrels to hunt, and doves and quail and foxes and skunks. A few deer ran the woods, and one year, during a drouth to the west, coyotes that we wanted to believe were wolves. Now it is mostly subdivisions, and even then it lay fallow because it was someone's real-estate investment. The fact that caretakers were likely to converge on us blaspheming at the sound of a shot or a shout, scattering us to brush, only made the hunting and the fishing a bit saltier. I knew one fellow who kept a permanent camp there in a sumac thicket, with a log squat-down hut and a fireplace and all kinds of food and utensils hidden in tin-lined holes in the ground, and none of the caretakers ever found it. Probably they worried less than we thought, for there weren't very many of us.

I had the Brazos, too, and South Texas, where relatives lived, and my adults for the most part were good people who took me along on country expeditions when they could. In terms of the outdoors, I and the others like me weren't badly cheated as such cheatings go nowadays, but we were cheated nevertheless. We learned quite a lot, but not enough. Instead of learning to move into country, as I think underneath we wanted, we learned mostly how to move onto it in the old crass Anglo-Saxon way, in search of edible or sometimes just mortal quarry. We did a lot of killing, as kids will, and without ever being told that it was our flat duty, if duty exists, to know all there was to know about the creatures we killed.

Hunting and fishing are the old old entry points into nature for men, and not bad ones either, but as standardly practiced these days, for the climactic ejaculation of city tensions, they don't go very deep. They aren't thoughtful, but hold themselves too straitly to their purpose. Even for my quail-hunting uncles in South Texas, good men, good friends to me, most smaller birds of hedge and grass were "chee-chees," vermin, confusers of dogs' noses. And if, with kids' instinctive thrustingness, we picked up a store of knowledge about small things that lived under logs and how the oriole builds its nest, there was no one to consolidate it for us. Our knowledge, if considerable, remained random.

This age, of course, is unlikely to start breeding people who have the organic kinship to nature that the Comanches had, or even someone like Mr. Charlie Goodnight. For them every bush, every bird's cheep, every cloud bank had not only utilitarian but mystical meaning. Awareness of all that was an extension of their sensory systems, an antenna as rawly receptive as a snail's. Even if their natural world still existed, which it doesn't, you'd have to snub the whole world of present men to get into it that way.

Nor does it help to be born in the country. As often as not these days, countrymen know as little as we others do about those things. They come principally out of the old hard-headed tradition that moved onto the country instead of into it. For every Charlie Goodnight there were several dozen Ezra Shermans, a disproportion that has bred itself down through the generations. Your standard country lore about animals—about the nasal love life of the possum, or the fabled hoop snake—is picturesque rather than accurate, anthropocentric rather than understanding.

But Charlie Goodnight and the Ezra Shermans and their children and grandchildren all combined have burned out and chopped out and plowed out and grazed out and killed out a good part of that natural world they knew, or didn't know, and we occupy ourselves mainly, it sometimes seems, in finishing the job. The rosy preindustrial time is past when the humanism of a man like Thoreau (*was* it humanism?) could still theorize in terms of natural harmony. Humanism has to speak in the terms of extant human beings. The terms of today's human beings are air conditioners and suburbs and water impoundments overlaying whole countrysides, and the hell with nature except maybe in a cross-sectional park here and there. In our time quietness and sun and leaves and bird song and all the multitudinous lore of the natural world have to come second or third, because whether we wanted to be born there or not, we were all born into the prickly machine-humming place that man has hung for himself above that natural world.

Where, tell me, is the terror and wonder of an elephant, now that they can be studied placid in every zoo, and any office-dwelling sport with a recent lucky break on the market can buy himself one to shoot through telescopic sights with a cartridge whose ballistics hold a good fileful of recorded science's findings? With a box gushing refrigerated air (or warmed, seasonally depending) into a sealed house and another box flashing loud bright images into jaded heads, who gives a rat's damn for things that go bump in the night? With possible death by blast or radiation staring at us like a buzzard, why should we sweat ourselves over where the Eskimo curlew went?

The marvel is that a few people do still sweat themselves, that the tracks of short varmints on a beach still have an audience. A few among that audience still know something, too. If they didn't, one wouldn't have to feel so cheated, not knowing as much. . . . Really knowing, I mean—from childhood up and continuously, with all of it a flavor in you. Not just being able to make a little seem a lot; there is enough of that around. I can give you as much book data about the home life of the yellow-breasted chat as the next man can. Nor do I mean vague mystic feelings of unity with Comanche and Neanderthal as one wanders the depleted land, gun at the ready, a part of the long flow of man's hunting compulsion. I mean *knowing*.

So that what one does in time, arriving a bit late at an awareness of the swindling he got—from no one, from the times—is to make up the shortage as best he may, to try to tie it all together for himself by reading and adult poking. But adult poking is never worth a quarter as much as kid poking, not in those real terms. There is never the time for that whole interest later, or ever quite the pure and subcutaneous receptiveness, either.

I mean, too—obviously—if you care. I know that the whicker of a plover in the September sky doesn't touch all other men in their bowels as it touches me, and that men whom it doesn't touch at all can be good men. But it touches me. And I care about knowing what it is, and—if I can—why.

Disgruntled from caring, I went to run my throwline. Coons' fresh tracks along the beach overlaid my own of the evening before; one had played with the end of the line and had rolled the jar of blood bait around on the sand trying to get inside it. The passenger followed some of the tracks into a drift tangle but lost interest, not knowing what he was trailing, robbed by long generations of show-breeding of the push that would have made him care. In my fingers the line tugged with more than the pulse of the current, but when I started softly hand-over-handing it in, it gave a couple of stiff jerks and went slacker, and I knew that something on it in a final frenzy had finished the job of twisting loose. They roll and roll and roll, and despite swivels at last work the staging into a tight snarl against whose solidity they can tear themselves free. Whatever it had been, channel or yellow or blue, it had left a chunk of its lip on the second hook, and two hooks beyond that was a one-pounder which I removed, respectful toward the sharp septic fin spines.

In the old days we had taken the better ones before they rolled loose by running the lines every hour or so during the night, a sleepless process and in summer a mosquito-chewed one. Once in Hood County, Hale and I and black Bill Briggs had gotten a twenty-five-pounder, and after an argument with Bill, who wanted to try to eat it, we sold it to a bridge-side café for a dime a pound. Another time on the Guadalupe to the south—but this is supposed to be about the Brazos. . . .

Tethering the little catfish to the chain stringer by the canoe, I got a rod and went down to the sharp tail of the island to cast a plug into green deep eddies I'd seen there while exploring. Without wind, the sun was almost hot now. From a willow a jay resented me with a two-note muted rasp like a boy blowing in and out on a harmonica with stuck reeds, and in an almost bare tree on the high riverbank a flock of bobolinks fed and bubbled and called, resting on their way south.

Cast and retrieve, shallow and deep, across current and down and up, and no sign of bass. The sun's laziness got into me and I wandered up the lesser channel, casting only occasionally into holes without the expectation of fish. Then, on a long flow-dimpled bar, something came down over my consciousness like black pain, and I dropped the rod and squatted, shaking my head to drive the blackness back. It receded a little. I waddled without rising to the bar's edge and scooped cold water over my head. After four or five big throbs it went away, and I sat down half in the water and thought about it. It didn't take much study. My stomach was giving a lecture about it, loud. What it amounted to was that I was about half starved.

I picked up the rod, went back to camp, stirred the fire, and put on a pot of water into which I dumped enough dried lima beans for four men, salt, an onion, and a big chunk of bacon. Considering, I went down to the stringer and skinned and gutted the little catfish and carried him up and threw him in the pot, too. While it boiled, I bathed in the river, frigid in contrast to the air, sloshed out the canoe and sponged it down, and washed underclothes and socks. In shorts, feeling fine now but so hungry it hurt, I sat by the fire and sharpened knives and the axe for the additional hour the beans needed to cook soft in the middle. Hooking out the skeleton of the disintegrated catfish, I used the biggest spoon I had and ate the whole mess from the pot almost without stopping, and mopped up its juices with cold biscuit bread.

Then I wiped my chin and lay back against the cottonwood log with my elbows hanging over it behind and my toes digging into the sand, and considered that asceticism, most certainly, was for those who were built for it. I hadn't seen God in the black headache on the sandbar and I didn't want to try to any more, that way. Starving myself hadn't had much to do with spirituality, anyhow, but only with the absence of company.

Philosophically equilibrated, I rolled down into the sand and went to sleep for two or three hours, waking into a perfect blue-and-yellow afternoon loud with the full-throat chant of the redbird.

Wood . . . I went roaming with the honed axe among the piles of drift, searching out solid timber. Bleached and unbarked as much of it is, you have a hard time seeing what it may be, but a two-lick notch with the axe usually bares its grain enough to name it. Cottonwood and willow slice soft and white under the first blow, and unless you're hard up you move on to try your luck on another piece, for they are not serious fuel:

> The fire devoureth both the ends of it, and the
> midst of it is burnt. Is it meet for any work?

But the river is prodigal of its trees, and better stuff is usually near.

If food is to sit in the fire's smoke as it cooks, any of the elms will give it a bad taste, though they last and give good heat. Cedar's oil eats up its wood in no time, and stinks food too, but the tinge of it on the air after supper is worth smelling if you want to cut a stick or so of it just for that. Rock-hard bodark—Osage orange if you want, bois d'arc if you're etymological—sears a savory crust on meat and burns a long time, if you don't mind losing a flake out of your axe's edge when you hit it wrong.* For that matter, not much of it grows close enough to the river to become drift. Nor does much mesquite—a pasture tree and the only thing a conscientious Mexican cook will barbecue kid over. Ash is all right but, as dry drift anyhow, burns fast. The white oaks are prime, the red oaks less so, and one of the finest of aromatic fuels is a

---

*I learned more about bodark as a fuel years after writing this passage, when living in an old farmhouse with a stack of weathered bodark posts out back. It can "sear a savory crust on meat" sometimes, but other pieces burn with a smell like that of the old coal-fired locomotives, and occasionally a knot will erupt in thousands of flying sparks for minutes on end, a display that can lead to frantic stamping on smoldering spots in carpets and other nearby combustibles.

twisted, wave-grained branch of liveoak, common in the limestone country farther down the river.

Maybe, though, the nutwoods are best and sweetest, kind to food and long in their burning. In the third tangle I nicked a huge branch of walnut, purple-brown an inch inside its sapwood's whitened skin. It rots slowly; this piece was sound enough for furniture making—straight-grained enough too, for that matter. I chopped it into long pieces. The swing and the chocking bite of the axe were pleasant; the pup chased chips as they flew; and I kept cutting until I had twice as many billets as I would need. Then I stacked them for later hauling and went to camp to use up the afternoon puttering with broken tent loops and ripped tarps and sprung hinges on boxes, throwing sticks for the passenger, looking in a book for the differences among small streaked finches, airing my bed, sweeping with a willow branch the sandy gravel all through a camp that I would leave the next day.

I lack much zeal for camping, these years. I can still read old Kephart* with pleasure: nearly half a century later hardly anyone else has come near him for information and good sense. But there is detachment in my pleasure now. I no longer see myself choosing a shingle tree and felling it and splitting out the shakes for my own roof, though if I did want to he would tell me how. Nor have I passion for canoeing, as such; both it and the camping are just ways to get somewhere I want to be, and to stay there for a time. I can't describe the cross-bow rudder stroke or stay serene in crashing rapids. I carry unconcentrated food in uncompact boxes. I forget to grease my boots and suffer from clammy feet. I slight hygiene, and will finger a boiled minnow from the coffee with equanimity, and sleep with my dog. My tent in comparison to the aluminum-framed, tight-snapping ones available is a ragged parallelogrammatic disaster.

Nevertheless, when camping for a time is the way of one's life, one tries to improve his style. One resolves on changes for future trips—a tiny and exactly fitted cook box, a contour-cut tarp over the canoe hooking to catches beneath the gunwales, no peaches in the mixed dried fruit. . . . One experiments and invents, and ends up, for instance, with a perfect aluminum-foil reflector for baking that agreeable, lumpy, biscuit-mixed bread that the Mexicans call "pan ranchero" and the

---

*Horace Kephart, *Camping and Woodcraft* (New York: Macmillan, 1917).

northwoods writers "bannock" and other people undoubtedly other names.

One way or the other, it all generally turns out to be work. Late that afternoon, carrying abrasive armloads of the walnut from where I'd chopped it to camp, I got as though from the air the answer to a question that used to come into my mind in libraries, reading about the frontiersmen and the Indians. I used to wonder why, knowing that Indians were around, the old ones would let themselves be surprised so often and so easily. Nearly all the ancient massacres resulted from such surprise.

The answer, simple on the island, was that the old ones were laboring their tails off at the manifold tasks of the primitive life, hewing and hauling and planting and plowing and breaking and fixing. They didn't have time to stay wary. Piped water and steam heat and tractors might have let them be alert, just as I had been among the stacked tomes of the Southwest Collection.

It was a good day, work and all. At evening I sat astraddle the bow of the canoe on the beach, putting new line on the spinning reel, when three big honkers came flying up the river slowly, low searchers like the first ones of the evening before. The gun was at hand. Even though they veered, separating, as I reached for it, they still passed close, and it needed only a three-foot lead on the front one's head to bring him splashing solidly, relaxed, dead, into the channel. I trotted downstream abreast of him as he drifted and finally teased him ashore with a long crooked piece of cottonwood.

Till then I'd had the visceral bite of the old excitement in me, the gladness of clean shooting, the fulfillment of quarry sought and taken. But when I got him ashore and hefted the warm, handsome eight or nine pounds of him, and ran my fingers against the grain up through the hot thick down of his neck, the just-as-old balancing regret came into it. A goose is a lot of bird to kill. Maybe size shouldn't matter, but it seems to. With something that big and that trimly perfect and, somehow, that meaningful, you wonder about the right of the thing.

For a while after the war I did no shooting at all, and thought I probably wouldn't do any more. I even chiseled out a little niche for that idea, half Hindu and tangled with the kind of reverence for life that Schweitzer preaches. But then one day in fall beside a stock tank in a mesquite pasture a friend wanted me to try the heft of a little engraved

L. C. Smith, and when I'd finished trying it I had dropped ten doves with sixteen shots and the niche didn't exist any longer.

Reverence for life in that sense seems to me to be like asceticism or celibacy: you need to be built for it. I no longer kill anything inedible that doesn't threaten me or mine, and I never cared anything about big-game hunting. Possibly I'll give up shooting again and for good one of these years, but I believe the killing itself can be reverent. To see and kill and pluck and gut and cook and eat a wild creature, all with some knowledge and the pleasure that knowledge gives, implies a closeness to the creature that is to me more honorable than the candle-lit consumption of rare prime steaks from a steer bludgeoned to death in a packing-house chute while tranquilizers course his veins. And if there is a difference in nobility between a Canada goose and a fat white-faced ox (there is), how does one work out the quantities?

Although I threw the skin and head and guts into the river to keep them away from the pup, an eddy drifted them into shore and he found them and ate a good bit before I caught him at it. The two big slabs of breast hissed beautifully in foil on the fire after dark. When they were done I hung them up for a time uncovered in the sweet walnut smoke and then ate nearly all of one of them. The other would make sandwiches at noon for two or three days, tucked inside chunks of biscuit bread. Despite his harsh appetizers, the passenger gobbled the drumsticks and organs I had half-roasted for him, and when I unrolled the sleeping bag inside the tent he fought to be first into it.

Later, in half-sleep, I heard a rattle of dirty metal dishes beside the fire. I shot the flashlight's beam out there and a sage, masked face stared at me, indignant. Foreseeing sport, I hauled the pup up for a look. He blinked, warm and full, and dug in his toes against ejection into the cold air, and when I let him go he burrowed all the way down beside my feet, not a practical dog and not ashamed of it, either. The coon went away.

Later still, the goosefeathers began their emetic work and I woke to the rhythmic *wump, wump, wump* that in dogs precedes a heave. Though the account of it may lack wide interest, later it seemed to me that there had been heroic coordination in the way I came out of sleep and grabbed him, holding his jaws shut with one hand while I fought to find the bag's zipper with the other, then fought to find and loose the zipper of the tent too, and hurled him out into the night by his nose. He stayed there for a while, and when I was sure he had finished I let him back in, low-eared and shivering, but I preferred his unhappiness to what might have been.

It came to me then who it was in a book that had slept with a dog for his health. Leopold Bloom's father. The dog's name had been . . . Athos! Old Man Bloom had slept with Athos to cure his aches and pains.

One can get pretty literary on islands.

Goodbye to a River: A Narrative was published in 1960 (New York: Knopf) and issued in paperback in 1971 (New York: Sierra Club/Ballantine). Three paperback editions have followed (Lincoln: University of Nebraska Press, 1977; Austin: Texas Monthly Press, 1985; and Houston: Gulf Publishing Company, 1993). In 1989, The Book Club of Texas published a limited edition. Reprinted by permission of Alfred A. Knopf, Inc.

Composed in Garamond types with Codex initial.

FISHING THE RUN

I'd made the mistake, the evening before, of mentioning to my younger daughter that I'd heard the crappie and sand bass were running in the Brazos. Therefore that Saturday morning, a clear and soft and lovely one of the sort our Texas Februaries sometimes offer in promise of coming spring, filled with the tentative piping of wrens and redbirds, I managed to get in only about an hour and a half's work in my office at the rear of the barn before she showed up there, a certain mulish set to her jaw and eyelids indicating she had a goal in mind and expected some opposition.

I said I needed to stay a while longer at the typewriter and afterward had to go patch a piece of net-wire boundary fence in the southeast pasture, shredded by a neighbor's horned bull while wrangling through it with my own Angus herd sire. She reminded me that the winter before we had missed the best crappie day in local memory because I'd had something else to do, one somewhat greedy fellow whom we knew having brought home eighty-three in a tow sack. She was fifteen and it struck me sometimes, though not to the point of neurosis, that maybe she deserved to have been born to a younger, less preoccupied father. In answer to what she said I raised some other negative points but without any great conviction, for I was arguing less against her than against a very strong part of myself that wanted badly to go fishing too.

The trouble was that those two or three weeks of late winter when the crappie and the sandies move up the Brazos out of the Whitney reservoir, in preparation for spawning, can provide some of the most pleasant angling of the year in our region on the fringes of dry West Texas, where creeks and rivers flow trickingly if at all during the warmer parts of a normal year. Even when low, of course, the good ones have holes and pools with fair numbers of black bass and bream and catfish, and I've been fishing them all my life with enjoyment. But it's not the same flavor of enjoyment that a hard-flowing stream can give, and those of us who have acquired—usually elsewhere—a penchant for live waters indulge it, if we've got the time and money, on trips to the mountain states, and look forward with special feeling to those times when our local waters choose to tumble and roll and our fish change their ways in accordance.

The Brazos in this section, my own personal river of rivers if only because I've known it and used it for so long, is a sleepy cat-fishing stream most of the time, a place to go at night with friends and sit beneath great oaks and pecans, talking and drinking beer or coffee and watching a fire burn low while barred owls and hoot owls brag across the bottomlands, getting up occasionally to go out with a flashlight and check the baited throwlines and trotlines that have been set. Its winter run of sand bass and crappie is dependable only when there's been plenty of rain and the upstream impoundments at Granbury and Possum Kingdom are releasing a good flow of water to make riffles and rapids run full and strong, an avenue up which the fish swim in their hundreds of thousands. To catch them in drouthy winters you have to drive down to Whitney's headwaters above the Kimball Bend, where the Chisholm Trail used to cross the river and the ruins of stone factory buildings recall old Jacob De Cordova's misplaced dream of water-powered empire, back in the 1860s. But that is lake fishing, best done from a boat and short on the concentrated excitement that a strong current full of avid live things can give.

Generally you fish the river run blind, choosing a likely spot where fast water spews into a slow pool, casting across the flow and letting it sweep your lure or fly in a long arc downstream to slack water near shore, working it in with what you hope are enticing twitches and jerks and pauses, then casting again. It is the venerable pattern still most often used with Atlantic salmon and the West Coast's steelheads, though our local quarry is far less impressive than those patrician species, since a pound-and-a-half crappie is a good one and the sandies—more properly known as white bass—only occasionally exceed a couple of pounds or so. There are plenty of them when a good run is on, though, and unless you overmatch them with heavy stiff tackle they can put up a reasonable fight in the strong water. For that matter there's always an outside chance of hooking a big striped bass, a marine cousin of the sandy introduced to the salty Brazos reservoirs in recent years and reaching fifteen or eighteen pounds or more. To have a horse like that on a light rig is quite an emotional experience, at least if you're of the tribe that derives emotion from angling, but the end result is not ordinarily triumphant. The annoyed striper hauls tail swiftly and irresistibly downriver while you hang onto your doubled, bucking rod and listen to the squall of your little reel yielding line, and when all the line has run out it breaks, at the fish's end if you're lucky, at the reel if you're not.

★   ★   ★

I've never been very happy fishing in crowds, and after word of a run of fish has seeped around our county the accessible areas along the river can be pretty heavily populated, especially on weekends in good weather and even more especially at the exact riverbank locations most worth trying. So that morning when without much resistance I had let Younger Daughter argue me down, I got the canoe out, hosed off its accumulation of old mud-dauber nests and barn dust, and lashed it atop the cattle frame on the pickup. If needed, it would let us cross over to an opposite, unpeopled shore or drop downriver to some other good place with no one at all in sight.

After that had been done and after we had rooted about the house and outbuildings in search of the nooks where bits of requisite tackle had hidden themselves during a winter's disuse, the morning was gone and so was the promise of spring. A plains norther had blown in, in northers' sudden fashion, and the pretty day had turned raw. By the time we'd wolfed down lunch and driven out to the Brazos, heavy clouds were scudding southeastward overhead and there was a thin misty spit of rain. This unpleasantness did have at least one bright side, though. When we'd paid our dollar entrance fee to a farmer and had parked on high firm ground above the river, we looked down at a gravel beach beside some rapids and the head of a deep long pool, a prime spot, and saw only one stocky figure there, casting toward the carved gray limestone cliffs that formed the other bank. There would be no point in using the canoe unless more people showed up, and that seemed unlikely with the grimness of the sky and the cold probing wind, which was shoving upriver in such gusts that, with a twinge of the usual shame, I decided to use a spinning rig.

Like many others who've known stream trout at some time in their lives, I derive about twice as much irrational satisfaction from taking fish on fly tackle as I do from alternative methods. I even keep a few streamers intended for the crappie and white bass run, some of them bead-headed and most a bit gaudy in aspect. One that has served well on occasion, to the point of disgruntling nearby plug and minnow hurlers, is a personal pattern called the Old English Sheep Dog which has a tinsel chenille body, a sparse crimson throat hackle, and a wing formed of long white neck hairs from the amiable friend for whom the concoction is named, who placidly snores and snuffles close by my chair on fly-tying evenings in winter and brooks without demur an occasional snip of the scissors in his coat. Hooks in sizes four and six seem usually to be about right, and I suppose a sinking or sink-tip line would be best for presentation if you keep a full array of such items with you, which I usually don't. . . .

But such is the corruption engendered by dwelling in an area full of worm-stick wielders and trotline types, where fly-fishing is still widely viewed as effete and there are no salmonids to give it full meaning, that increasingly these days I find myself switching to other tackle when conditions seem to say to. And I knew now that trying to roll a six-weight tapered line across that angry air would lead to one sorry tangle after another.

We put our gear together and walked down to the beach, where the lone fisherman looked around and greeted us affably enough, though without slowing or speeding his careful retrieve of a lure. A full-fleshed, big-headed, rather short man with a rosy Pickwickian face, in his middle or late sixties perhaps, he was clearly enough no local. Instead of the stained and rumpled workaday attire that most of us hereabouts favor for such outings he had on good chest waders, a tan fishing vest whose multiple pouch pockets bulged discreetly here and there, and a neat little tweed porkpie hat that ought to have seemed ridiculous above that large pink face but managed somehow to look just right, jaunty and self-sufficient and good-humored. He was using a dainty graphite rod and a diminutive free-spool casting reel, the sort of equipment you get because you know what you want and are willing to pay for it, and when he cast again, sending a tiny white-feathered spinner bait nearly to the cliff across the way with only a flirt of the rod, I saw that he used them well.

Raising my voice against the rapids' hiss and chatter I asked him if the fish were hitting.

"Not bad," he answered, still fishing. "It was slow this morning when the weather was nice, but this front coming through got things to popping a little. Barometric change, I guess."

Not the barometer but the wind had me wishing I'd mustered the sense to change to heavier clothing when the soft morning had disappeared. It muffled the pool's water darkly, working against the surface current. Younger Daughter, I recalled, had cagily put on a down jacket, and when I looked around for her she was already thirty yards down the beach and casting with absorption, for she was and is disinclined toward talk when water needs to be worked. My Pickwickian friend being evidently of the same persuasion, I intended to pester him no further, though I did wonder whether he'd been catching a preponderance of crappie or of sand bass and searched about with my eyes for a live bag or stringer, but saw none. When I glanced up again he had paused in his casting and was watching me with a wry half-guilty expression much like one I myself employ when country neighbors have caught me in some alien aberration such as fly-fishing or speaking with appreciation about the howls of coyotes.

"I hardly ever keep any," he said. "I just like fishing for them."

I said I usually put the sandies back too, but not crappie, whose delicate white flesh my clan prizes above that of all other local species for the table and, if there are many, for tucking away in freezer packets against a time of shortage. He observed that he'd caught no crappie at all. "Ah," I said, a bilked gourmet. Then, liking the man and feeling I ought to, I asked if our fishing there would bother him.

"No, hell, no," said Mr. Pickwick. "There's lots of room, and anyhow I'm moving on up the river. Don't like to fish in one spot too long. I'm an itchy sort."

That being more or less what I might have said too had I been enjoying myself there alone when other people barged in, I felt a prick of conscience as I watched him work his way alongside the main rapids, standing in water up to his rubber-clad calves near the shore, casting and retrieving a few times from each spot before sloshing a bit farther upstream. It was rough loud water of a type in which I have seldom had much luck on that river. But then I saw him shoot his spinner-bug out across the wind and drop it with precision into a small slick just below a boulder, where a good thrashing sand bass promptly grabbed it, and watched him let the current and the rod's lithe spring wear the fish down before he brought it to slack shallow shore water, reaching down to twist the hook deftly from its jaw so that it could drift away. That was damned sure not blind fishing. He knew what he was doing, and I quit worrying about our intrusion on the beach.

By that time Younger Daughter, unruffled by such niceties, had caught and released a small sandy or two herself at the head of the pool, and as I walked down to join her she beached another and held it up with a smile to shame my indolence before dropping it back in the water. I'd been fishing for more than three times as many years as she had been on earth, but she often caught more than I because she stayed with the job, whereas I have a long-standing tendency to stare at birds in willow trees, or study currents and rocks, or chew platitudes with other anglers randomly encountered.

"You better get cracking," she said. "That puts me three up."

I looked at the sky, which was uglier than it had been. "What *you'd* better do," I told her, "is find the right bait and bag a few crappie for supper pretty fast. This weather is getting ready to go to pieces."

"Any weather's good when you're catching fish," she said, quoting a dictum I'd once voiced to her while clad in something more warmly waterproof than my present cotton flannel shirt and poplin golfer's jacket. Nevertheless she was right, so I tied on a light marabou horsehead jig with a spinner—a white one, in part because that was the hue jaunty old Mr. Pickwick had been using with such skill, but mainly because most of the time with sand bass, in Henry Fordish parlance, any color's fine as long as it's white. Except that some days they like a preponderance of yellow, and once I saw a fellow winch them in numerously with a salt-water rod and reel and a huge plug that from a distance looked to be lingerie pink. . . .

I started casting far enough up the beach from Younger Daughter that our lines would not get crossed. The northwest wind shoved hard and cold and the thin rain seemed to be flicking more steadily against my numbing cheeks and hands. But then the horsehead jig found its way into some sort of magical pocket along the line where the rapids' forceful long tongue rubbed against eddy water drifting up from the pool. Stout sand bass were holding there, eager and aggressive, and without exactly forgetting the weather I was able for a long while to ignore it. I caught three fish in three casts, lost the feel of the pocket's whereabouts for a time before locating it again and catching two more, then moved on to look for another such place and found it, and afterward found some others still. I gave the fish back to the river, or gave it back to them: shapely, forktailed, bright-silver creatures with thin dark parallel striping along their sides, gaping rhythmically from the struggle's exhaustion as they eased away backward from my hand in the slow shallows.

I didn't wish they were crappie, to be stowed in the mesh live bag and carried off home as food. If it wasn't a crappie day, it wasn't, and if satisfactory preparation of the sandies' rather coarse flesh involves some kitchen mystery from which our family's cooks have been excluded, the fact remains that they're quite a bit more pleasant to catch than crappie—stronger and quicker and more desperately resistant to being led shoreward on a threadlike line or a leader. In my own form of piscatorial snobbery, I've never much liked the sort of fishing often done for them on reservoirs, where motorboaters race converging on a surfaced feeding school to cast furiously toward its center for a few minutes until it disappears, then wait around for another roaring, roostertailed race when that school or another surfaces somewhere else. But my basic snobbery—or trouble, or whatever you want to call it—is not much liking reservoir fishing itself, except sometimes with a canoe in covish waters at dawn, when all good roostertailers and waterskiers and other motorized hypermanics are virtuously still abed, storing up energy for another day of loud wavemaking pleasure.

In truth, until a few years ago I more or less despised the sand bass as an alien introduced species fit only for such mechanized pursuit in such artificial waters. But in a live stream on light tackle they subvert that sort of purism, snapping up flies or jigs or live minnows with abandon and battling all the way. It isn't a scholarly sort of angling. Taking them has in it little or none of the taut careful fascination, the studious delicacy of lure and presentation, that go with stalking individual good trout, or even sometimes black bass and bream, but it's clean fine fishing for all that.

Checking my watch, I found with the common angler's surprise that nearly three hours had gone a-glimmering since our arrival at the beach, for it was after four. Younger Daughter and I had hardly spoken during that time, drifting closer together or farther apart while we followed our separate hunches as to where fish might be lying. At this point, though, I heard her yell where she stood a hundred yards or so downshore, and when I looked toward her through the rain—real rain now, if light, that gave her figure in its green jacket a pointillist haziness—I saw she was leaning backward with her rod's doubled-down tip aimed toward something far out in the deep pool, something that was pulling hard.

If she had a mature striper on her frail outfit there wasn't much prayer that she'd bring him in. But I wanted to be present for the tussle that would take place before she lost him, and I hurried toward her shouting disjointed, unnecessary advice. She was handling the fish well, giving him line when he demanded it and taking some back when he sulked in the depths, by pumping slowly upward with the rod and reeling in fast as she lowered it again. She lost all that gained line and more when he made an upriver dash, and he'd nearly reached the main rapids before we decided that he might not stop there and set off at a jogtrot to catch up, Younger Daughter reeling hard all the way to take in slack. But the run against the current tired him, and in a few minutes she brought him to the beach at about the point where we'd met Mr. Pickwick. It was a sand bass rather than a striper, but a very good one for the river. I had no scale along, but estimated the fish would go three and a half pounds easily, maybe nearly four.

"I'm going to keep him," she said. "We can boil him and freeze him in batches for Kitty, the way Mother did one time. Kitty liked it."

"All right," I said, knowing she meant she felt a need to show the rest of the family what she'd caught, but didn't want to waste it. The wind, I noticed, had abated somewhat but the cold rain made up for the lack. "Listen," I said. "I'm pretty wet and my teeth are starting to chatter. Aren't you about ready to quit?"

A hint of mulishness ridged up along her jawline. "You could go sit in the truck with the heater and play the radio," she said.

I gave vent to a low opinion of that particular idea.

"There's his hat," she said. "The man's."

Sure enough there it came, the tweed porkpie, shooting down the rapids upside down and half submerged like a leaky, small, crewless boat, and no longer looking very jaunty. It must have blown off our friend's head somewhere upstream. Riding the fast tongue of current to where the pool grew deep, it slowed, and I went down and cast at it with a treble-hooked floating plug till I snagged it and reeled it in.

"I guess we can drive up and down and find his car, if we don't see him." I said. "It's a pretty nice hat."

She said in strange reply, "Oh!"

The reason turned out to be that Mr. Pickwick was cruising downriver along the same swift route his hat had taken but quite a bit more soggily, since his heavy chest waders swamped full of water were pulling him toward the bottom as he came. He was in the lower, deepening part of the rapids above us, floating backward in the current—or rather not floating, for as I watched I saw him vanish beneath surging water for five or six long seconds, surfacing enormously again as his large pink bald head and his shoulders and rowing arms broke into sight and he took deep gasps of air, maintaining himself symmetrically fore-and-aft in the river's heavy shove. He stayed up only a few moments before being pulled under again, then reappeared and sucked in more great draughts of air. It had a rhythmic pattern, I could see. He was bending his legs as he sank and kicking hard upward when he touched bottom, and by staying aligned in the current he was keeping it from seizing and tumbling him. He was in control, for the moment at any rate, and I felt the same admiration for him that I'd felt earlier while watching him fish.

I felt also a flash of odd but quite potent reluctance to meddle in the least with his competent, private, downriver progress, or even for that matter to let him know we were witnesses to his plight. Except that, of course, very shortly he was going to be navigating in twelve or fifteen feet of slowing water at the head of the pool, with the waders still dragging him down, and it seemed improbable that any pattern he might work out at that extremely private point was going to do him much good.

Because of the queer reluctance I put an absurd question to the back of his pink pate when it next rose into view. I shouted above the hoarse voice of the water, "Are you all right?"

Still concentrating on his fore-and-aftness and sucking hard for air, he gave no sign of having heard before he once more sounded, but on his next upward heave he gulped in a breath and rolled his head aside to glare at me over his shoulder, out of one long blue bloodshot eye. Shaping the word with care, he yelled from the depths of his throat, "NO!"

And went promptly under again.

Trying to gauge water speed and depth and distances, I ran a few steps down the beach and charged in, waving Younger Daughter back when she made a move to follow. I'm not a powerful swimmer even when stripped down, and I knew I'd have to grab him with my boots planted on the bottom if I could. Nor will I deny feeling a touch of panic when I got to the edge of the gentle eddy water, up to my nipples and spookily lightfooted with my body's buoyancy, and was brushed by the edge of the rapids' violent tongue and sensed the gravel riverbed's sudden downward slant. No heroics were required, though—fortunately, for they'd likely have drowned us both, with the help of those deadweight waders. Mr. Pickwick made one of his mighty, hippo-like surfacings not eight feet upriver from me and only an arm's length outward in the bad tongue-water, and as he sailed logily past I snatched a hold on the collar of his many-pocketed vest and let the current swing him round till he too was in the slack eddy, much as one fishes a lure or a fly in such places. Then I towed him in.

Ashore, he sat crumpled on a big rock and stared wide-eyed

at his feet and drank up air in huge, sobbing, grateful gasps. All his pinkness had gone gray-blue, no jauntiness was in sight, and he even seemed less full-fleshed now, shrunken, his wet fringe of gray hair plastered vertically down beside gray ears. Younger Daughter hovered near him and made the subdued cooing sounds she uses with puppies and baby goats, but I stared at the stone cliff across the Brazos through the haze of thin rain, waiting with more than a tinge of embarrassment for his breathing to grow less labored. I had only a snap notion of what this man was like, but it told me he didn't deserve being watched while he was helpless. Maybe no one does.

He said at last, "I never had that happen before."

I said, "It's a pretty tough river when it's up."

"They all are," he answered shortly and breathed a little more, still staring down.

He said, "It was my knees. I was crossing at the head of this chute, coming back downriver. They just buckled in the current and whoosh, by God, there we went."

"We've got your hat," Younger Daughter told him as though she hoped that might set things right.

"Thank you, sweet lady," he said, and smiled as best he could.

"That was some beautiful tackle you lost," I said. "At least I guess it's lost."

"It's lost, all right," said Mr. Pickwick. "Goodbye to it. It doesn't amount to much when you think what I . . ."

But that was a direction I somehow didn't want the talk to take, nor did I think he wanted it to go there either. I was god-awfully cold in my soaked, clinging, skimpy clothes and knew he must be even colder, exhausted as he was. I said I wished I had a drink to offer him. He said he appreciated the thought but he could and would offer me one if we could get to his car a quarter-mile down the shore, and I sent Younger Daughter trotting off with his keys to drive it back to where we were. The whiskey was nice sour-mash stuff, though corrosive Skid Row swill would have tasted fine just then. We peeled him out of the deadly waders and got him into some insulated coveralls that were in his car, and after a little he began to pinken up again, but still with the crumpled shrunken look.

He and I talked for a bit, sipping the good whiskey straight from plastic cups. He was a retired grain dealer from Kentucky, and what he did mainly now was fish. He and his wife had a travel trailer in which they usually wintered on the Texas coast near Padre Island, where he worked the redfish and speckled trout of the bays with popping gear or sometimes a fly rod when the wind and water were right. Then in February they would start a slow zigzag journey north to bring them home for spring. He'd even fished steelhead in British Columbia—the prettiest of all, he said, the high green wooded mountains dropping steeply to fjords and the cold strong rivers flowing in from their narrow valleys. . . .

When we parted he came as close as he could to saying the thing that neither he nor I wanted him to have to say. He said, "I want . . . Damn, I never had that happen to me before." And stopped. Then he said, "Jesus, I'm glad you were there."

"You'd have been all right," I said. "You were doing fine."

But he shook his strangely shrunken pink head without smiling, and when I turned away he clapped my shoulder and briefly gripped it.

In the pickup as we drove toward home, Younger Daughter was very quiet for a while. I was thinking about the terrible swiftness with which old age could descend, for that was what we'd been watching even if I'd tried not to know it. I felt intensely the health and strength of my own solid body, warmed now by the whiskey and by a fine blast from the pickup's heater fan. If on the whole I hadn't treated it as carefully as I might have over the years, this body, and if in consequence it was a little battered and overweight and had had a few things wrong with it from time to time, it had nonetheless served me and served me well, and was still doing so. It housed whatever brains and abilities I could claim to have and carried out their dictates, and it functioned for the physical things I liked to do, fishing and hunting and country work and the rest. It had been and was a very satisfactory body.

But it was only ten or twelve years younger than the old grain dealer's, at most, and I had to wonder now what sort of sickness or accident or other disruption of function—what buckling of knee, what tremor of hand, what milkiness of vision, what fragility of bone, what thinness of artery wall—would be needed, when the time came, to push me over into knowledge that I myself was old. Having to admit it, that was the thing. . . .

Then, with the astonishment the young bring to a recognition that tired, solemn, ancient phrases have meaning, my daughter uttered what I hadn't wanted to hear the old man say. She said, "You saved his life!"

"Maybe so," I said. "We just happened to be on hand."

She was silent for a time longer, staring out the window at the rain that fell on passing fields and woods. Finally she said, "That's a good fish I caught."

"Damn right it is," I said.

"Fishing the Run" first appeared in *Texas Monthly* as "Going Under" (March 1981) and was later published in *The Ultimate Fishing Book* (Boston: Houghton Mifflin, 1981).

Composed in Trump Mediaeval types with Charlemagne initial.

THE WATER OF LIFE

Maybe there exists somewhere a satisfying historical account of ethyl alcohol in relation to mankind, but if so I haven't seen it, and I've read a few attempts. My interest in the subject, I'd better establish to begin with, does not stem from being what one of my daughters as a child, having read the word but not heard it, used to call a drun*kard*. Rather it derives from a longstanding friendship with the substance, appreciative for the most part but also reasonably wary in later years, so that my appreciation has managed to survive a good many decades during which I have watched quite a few harder-drinking contemporaries, true drun*kards* some of them although others were stout fellows, go down a one-way road to psychic wreck, cirrhosis, or dire abstinence.

What I've wondered for a long time now is whether humanity's affinity for the stuff isn't fundamentally inborn. Much of botanic nature is an alcohol factory at times, and many lesser creatures take pleasure in this fact, as anyone knows who has watched wasps and beetles and mockingbirds gloriously swacked on spoiled fruit fallen from trees, or waxwings merry after a feast of fermented pyracantha berries, or cows and pigs clumsily full of well-being from a bait of extra-stout silage. Thus it isn't hard to call up the image of some shambling bristly forebear of *H. sapiens*, who with the beginnings of thrift and foresight flickering in whatever he had for a brain, gorged himself at some point on a happy bonanza of fruit or wild grain or honey, stashed what he couldn't eat in a tree hollow, and came back a few days later to find that moisture and other forces had wrought a wonder. The cache was now a mush of rudimentary beer or wine that made him feel magnificent when he downed it, at least for a brief while, after which he may have felt worse than he ever had before.

Perhaps in losing its fears and worries for that short time, his thinking apparatus achieved a liberation and grew creative in the manner sometimes attributed to drunkenness by far later generations of hominids. Maybe he was inspired to crunch his fellows' skulls with a sharp rock, thus gaining possession of whatever they had accumulated in the way of fruit or grain or honey or females. And in turn this may have given him dominance and an edge in the Darwinian contest, which he passed down to his descendants, along with a taste for hooch. (I know there is a touch of discredited Lamarckism here, but let it stand.) At any rate it could have happened in more or less that way, being no more improbable than such genetic arrangements as the symbiosis between yucca moths and yucca plants.

Nor can there be much doubt that this same intermediate product of sugar on its way to becoming vinegar has been a factor, at times a potent one, in human history of the sort we read in books. We all know that there is usually a good bit of difference—not necessarily in flavor but in degree—between an individual's normal sober behavior and what he does when drunk, in which condition the irrational id comes closer to the surface of things and sometimes takes command. We know too that a certain proportion of people, when social restraints are lacking or shucked off and alcohol is available, will stay drunk pretty much of the time.

What seems certain is that during vast reaches of history in places where democracy was not even a concept and the brute power of rulers was subject to few restraints save the brute power of other rulers or would-be rulers—under such conditions full many a brutal sot must have made full many a decision as to the waging of war, the slaughter of underlings in perhaps large numbers when they displeased him, and the elevation to high rank of idiots or psychopaths who did things he liked at a certain fuddled moment. I find it very hard otherwise to account for much that we know has taken place during the past three or four thousand years, even if certain forms of probably nonalcoholic intoxication must have come into play also, as with the religiously inspired massacres conducted by Assyrians and Hebrews and such, and the berserker rage of Vikings—though we are aware, of course, that the latter were heroic drinkers whenever they got a good chance.

The Vikings' tendency toward binges has been passed down, apparently, to large numbers of their relatively mild descendants the Scandinavians, and is shared for that matter by most North European peoples, including us Americans' principal Old World cousins and forebears, the British and the Irish. Whence it follows that we ourselves should show the tendency too, as the Lord knows we do and have ever since we first came to this side of the big water. Bills of lading from vessels serving these colonies in the old days, as well as diaries and recipe books and letters and the like, make it clear that a notable fraction of our ancestors, at least outside the more Godly parts of New England, found joy in having not only plenty to drink but often more than plenty.

Nor did conditions along the frontier, as Americans heroic or otherwise edged westward, do anything to weaken this ethnic affection for alcoholic excess when excess could be had. Raw hard liquor seems to have been just about as essential a fuel for the transcontinental movement as were salt pork and a sense of Manifest Destiny. And if at this range of years it is not hard to view as quaint the sometimes homicidal antics of men who capped off months of tough work and deprivation with mighty sprees at a fur trappers' rendezvous or a Kansas railhead cattle town, it isn't very hard either, if you live in a place like Texas, to find somewhat less quaint evidence of the legacy such men left us. All you have to do is pay a visit on Saturday night to the honkytonk fringe of one of our spraddling cities, where sprees and homicides flourish.

*

There are other ways to drink besides heroically, of course, as traditionally exemplified in those nationalities who for the most part sip their wine with moderation and quiet enjoyment along the sunlit shores of the Mediterranean, or nearby. Though the main difference between their habits and ours is undoubtedly cultural—racial, I've heard some Latin chauvinists claim—the question of what each culture chooses to drink comes into it too. The whole matter of the distinct effects produced by various liquids is fascinating, at least to drinkers, but it is also very hazy. One authoritative treatise that I read lumped all nonalcoholic components together as "congeners" and implied, as I remember, that they served only to give flavor and mystique to whatever it was you were drinking, without exerting any real influence on the nature of your reactions. The alcohol itself was all that counted.

I know from experience that this is nonsense in the case of such druggishly treacherous fluids as absinthe and mescal. Nor do I think it has much validity in terms of the cherished, hard-won lore of bibbers—that beer promotes good fellowship and music, for instance, champagne high merriment and romance, honest table wine a sense of well-being, skid row Sweet Lucy stumbling soddenness, excessive hard liquor combativeness and uproar, and so on infinitely.

There does appear to be scant variation in what is done to you by standard distilled spirits of the sort commonly used in this country—bourbon, Scotch, gin, vodka, rum—except for the size of the hangovers they or their mixers can evoke. But what is one to say about brandy, for instance, which, as all know who have on occasion let themselves love it too well, will wake you at three or four in the morning with your heart imitating a jackhammer and all the fears and pessimisms and inadequacies you've ever known dancing a hornpipe on your taut consciousness?

No difference, indeed.

To a degree, of course, drinkers' lore tends to come true even when its underpinnings are shaky. If you believe stoutly that sloe gin will help you whip a country cabaret full of pipeline workers, then sloe gin will probably make that sort of drunk out of you if not always that sort of fighter, just as Veuve Clicquot or Taittinger or Mumm's, coursing the arterioles of the faithful, will generate the illusion of gaiety and wit and seductive patrician charm, along with a special headache later.

Abstainers' notions about alcohol are a bit shakier, being less pragmatic. My firmly Baptist maternal grandmother believed, for instance, without having tried either one, that beer was stronger and more pernicious than whiskey. This was because she had listened to a lot of radio-station fundamentalist preachers in the 1930s, after the repeal of Prohibition, who sought to influence West Texas local-option elections—in which the sale of beer and wine was usually the only proposal—by specific assaults on beer as a sinful substance. They didn't say much about wine, being I suppose somewhat perplexed by it, since it was mentioned in Scripture and often with approval, as in harsh Saint Paul's much-quoted advice to use a little of it for the stomach's sake.

In her last days, in fact, that same grandmother used to receive from my father each evening a goodly tot of straight bonded bourbon laced with grenadine syrup, which he tactfully described as wine and she gladly accepted as such. She was bedridden and in some pain and it helped, just as I expect old Paul's approval helped her to enjoy it.

*

With a majority of Texans now living in cities and thus more or less liberated from the small-town scrutiny of people who know them and have known them all their lives, the old moral strictures on drinking have been changing rather fast, but in the countryside they're still around. I live in a place where still, if you're sitting out with a friend on his lawn in the evening and a car drives up, you ease your beer can down by the leg of the chair till you can see who it is, even though carry-out beer and wine have been legal in the county for a good many years. The furtiveness of this action does not bother me at all, for it is a genuine folkway, a part of the ethos of those wide reaches of our state where the harder-shelled forms of Protestantism still prevail. Any Texan of my age and background has been familiar with it all his life.

Despite some vigorously hard-shelled antecedents on my mother's side, I grew up in my father's people's church, the one that Virginia evangelicals still sneeringly call Whiskeypalian. I tend to be rather thankful for this fact though undoubtedly not for all the right reasons. Besides the superlative, ringing, peak English of the Authorized Version and the Book of Common Prayer (which, God help us, they have now quit using), this venerable institution offered its Texas communicants certain further rich gifts as well. Other people, I know, got much the same things from other fairly soft-shelled sects, or even on their own, but the benefits came to me with an Episcopalian flavor so that's where my gratitude flows.

Among them were a spotty, dubious, but enduring belief in free will, and a blessed if only partial release from the Calvinistic conviction of sinfulness that rolled all around us like a fog in those days, when even most Texas cities were basically still small towns, both for better and for worse. Sin to us Episcopalians was bad stuff and not to be taken lightly, but it was expiable too and hence didn't represent your irreversible progress toward the everlasting fires. Nor, except insofar as you might have inhaled a little secondhand Calvinism from the surrounding fog, did you have to go around looking for sin in all dark corners, wondering if every pleasure was a booby trap handcrafted by the forces of evil.

In terms of that pleasure called drinking, this meant that when you reached an age deemed proper, you were relatively free to go ahead and experiment without feeling the hot foul breath of Auld Reekie on your neck. And also without, I guess, the keen pleasure in forbidden sweets that puritan tipplers must have felt, though most of us had experienced some of that pleasure earlier, before we had reached the age deemed proper.

Like all young drinkers of whatever religious hue, I and others like me often overdid the thing for a while, but in this we were not encouraged by our elders. My father and the men he most often chose as friends had a general belief in what they called "holding your liquor," which was the dead opposite of spree drinking. They either drank all they felt like drinking and never showed it more than barely, mellowly, or they limited their intake to what they knew they could handle.

This reasonable standard of consumption may have created a good many more alcoholics than bust-loose spree drinking ever has, for spree drinking by its nature is usually sporadic and occasional. In some people, holding one's liquor fosters rather steady consumption, since they aren't being unruly and nobody objects. So that when age or other factors lessen their tolerance, as age or other factors inevitably will, the hooch sneaks up behind them and either turns them into staid and proper zombies, or makes them old-fashioned drun*kards* with all the trimmings, or eats at their livers and other components.

Sometimes it has more bizarre effects, as in the case of one gentleman of my father's generation who was famed for his wit and magnetism and his ability to knock back slug after slug of good Scotch without ever slurring a word. But one moonlit midnight this paragon went out on his lawn and started firing a revolver up into a Lombardy poplar that he claimed was full of obnoxious Bulgarians, and might have fired it also at the police who came to stop him except that by then he was out of ammunition. Convinced later by loved ones that whiskey had been the cause, he accepted clinical care and managed to get out from under the curse of drink. But sad to relate, along with his glow and those Bulgarians all of his charm and humor vanished, and he became a quite dull fellow.

*

That liquor is often handled wrongly I know as well as anyone. I am not amused by drunken slobs, and have watched for many years, sometimes from a lot closer than I wanted to be, the whole sorry spectacle of alcohol's misuse—the rotting of talent and self-respect, the decay of families and friendships, the collapse of health, the lifeblood spilled out on highways, and all of the miserable rest.

Yet I seem to be unable to rid myself of a quaint notion, maybe based on that spotty belief I still have in free will, that these are things that people do with alcohol rather than things that alcohol does to people. The stuff has been among us for untold ages and we all know its destructive potential, or damned well ought to know it. So that often when a conversation, or a book, or a TV show grows solemn about the Alcohol Problem, I find myself thinking of the beloved and bibulous cowboy artist Charles M. Russell, who in his pleasant, reminiscent book *Trails Plowed Under* began one tale with the words, "Whiskey has been blamed for lots it didn't do."

So have beer and wine and gin and brandy and vodka and rum, and so, I doubt not in the least, have ouzo and pulque and koumiss and aquavit and slivovitz and palm beer and sake and such, in societies where one or another of those delights is the fermented solace of choice. They didn't do it, whatever it was. People did.

And all the while more temperate people have been using those same liquids to relax when they need to relax, to ease disappointments and fears and angers and their bodies' aches and fatigues, to warm themselves when cold and cool themselves when hot, to render their tongues more eloquent, to get to know their fellows and on occasion to love them. To sing and dance and sometimes to think great thoughts even if in the aftermath, strangely, the greatness tends to wash away. And to live, most of them, to a ripeness of years while causing very scant trouble—far less, I would surmise, than is caused by most of the puritans, Calvinistic or not, who rant against the Water of Life. . . .

*

My own current ripeness of years has been blessed by the fact that so far nobody whether medical or otherwise has told me that I have to stop imbibing my few belts of the hard stuff each evening. I have never been a very heroic drinker save during some periods of careless youth, and like most people of my vintage who have escaped being sucked down that particular drain, I seem to have felt out a long while back what alcohol can do for or against me. I can't and don't use drink as a crutch for work, for instance, or even in connection with certain active forms of pleasure like fishing, which for me it blurs and dulls. I lay off entirely for a spell periodically, to prove to myself I still can and to help in losing weight, and I know that if a doctor I respect tells me at some point that I have to lay off for good, I will be able to do so. But I admit I do pray with muted Whiskeypalian piety that this will not come to pass.

I used to have an older friend who during a time of debt and other big personal troubles came to lean on whiskey quite heavily, without ever letting it get out of hand as far as anyone else could tell. Clearly it helped him to deal with the troubles, but when they were finally behind him he took a good look at himself and decided the stuff had clamped down too hard, and so one day he swore off—which, he being the man that he was, meant stopping for life.

Eight or ten years later he was put in the hospital to undergo surgery that nobody seemed to believe he'd survive—though, as it turned out, he did—and I went around to see him a day or so before the thing was scheduled. A reserved man by nature, he was a listener rather than a talker, but the sedatives they had given him, and perhaps his situation, had him in a thoughtful and not unhappy and almost loquacious mood. We spoke of matters I don't think we'd ever discussed in the past, basic matters for the most part—the ways of men with women and of women with men, the pitfalls of being born Southern and Texan, friendship, ambition, even immortality—in an easy and inquiring way, and he was far broader in his thinking than I had known. I remember feeling angry with myself for not having seen this long before.

Then he said, "I want to tell you something about John Barleycorn."

I was leading a bachelor life at the time, not a very gaudy one, and imagined someone had given him to believe I was drinking too much, which wasn't true. And remembering that long, unremitting abstinence of his, I supposed he was going to give me a lecture on the subject, as is some abstainers' unfortunate habit. I hadn't thought him to be of that ilk, but with things looking the way they did for him at that point, he had a right to moralize if he wished. Therefore I resigned myself and said, "What's that?"

"Old John Barleycorn," he said with a wide, crooked, reminiscent smile, "was the best friend I ever had."

Texas Monthly published this essay as "Drinking" (March 1982).

Composed in Caslon 540 types.

KINDRED SPIRITS

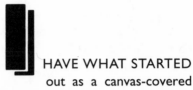

HAVE WHAT STARTED out as a canvas-covered wooden canoe, though with the years it has taken on some aluminum in the form of splinting along three or four fractured ribs, and this past spring I replaced its rotting cloth rind with resin-impregnated fiberglass. It is thus no longer the purely organic piece of handicraft that emerged from a workshop in Maine some decades back. Nor do I use it more than occasionally these days, to run a day's stretch of pretty river or just to get where fish may be. Nevertheless I retain much fondness for it as a relic of a younger, looser, less settled time of life.

While readying its hull for the fiberglass I had to go over it inch by inch as it sat on sawhorses in the barn—removing the mahogany outwales and stripping off the old canvas, locating unevennesses in the surface of the thin cedar planking, sanding and filling and sanding again so that protuberances and pits would not mar the new shell or lessen its adhesion, and finally taking out the seats and thwarts and readying the interior for fresh varnish. The process took up a good bit of my spare time for weeks, and during it I got to know a couple of Indians fairly well. At least I thought of them as Indians, for the canoe company which takes its name from the Old Town of the Penobscots used to employ many of that tribe's members as workers, and for all I know still does.

There was the Good Indian, as I came to call him, who had stood on the left side of the craft while it was being built ("port" and "starboard" will not serve, for the thing had lain sometimes rightside up on its trestle or table or whatever had held it, and sometimes upside down), selecting and trimming his planks with care and affixing them to the ribs so that their edges and butts fitted tightly and the tacks were driven precisely flush, drilling his screw and bolt holes true. And across from him on the right side had labored his confrere Slovenly Pete, a brooder and a swigger of strong waters during the long Maine winter nights, who with reddened eye and palsied hand had messed up everything he could without getting fired from his job. Their ghosts were with me, and I spoke to them as I went over their work and did my own. The Good Indian was a friend, a taciturn perfectionist in sympathy with my resolve to get things right. But somehow I took more interest in his shiftless mate, a sour and gabby type who responded to my gibes about hammer marks and ill-matched planks and protruding tackheads with irrelevant rhetoric on white men's viperish ways, or biting queries as to what business a Texan had fretting over a canoe in the first place. "Your God damn rivers," he said at one point, "ain't got no God damn water in them most of the God damn time."

I've been in this sort of touch with many artisans and laborers over the years, for I am both a putterer and a countryman, categories of humanity that frequently busy themselves in refurbishing and repairing things that other human beings have made or refurbished or repaired in times gone by, leaving personal imprints on them. An old Ford tractor, for example, whose hydraulic pump was replaced by a previous owner with a second one from another model, by dint of much ingenious grinding and shimming and drilling, can cause one to ponder and blaspheme for days over the question of why the costly new pump he has driven fifty miles to buy at a dealership can't be seated. And if, when starting casually to pull out a decayed forty-year-old fence cornerpost set four feet deep, in order to put a new one in its place, you discover that whoever installed it was such a fence nut that he filled the hole around it with angular crushed road gravel tamped down to grip like death, your emotions are mixed as you strive without success to budge his monument with a tractor drawbar or a jack rated at five thousand pounds' lift. On the one hand you have to admire the uncompromising correctness that made him go to such trouble; on the other, more strongly, you wish that in the matter of fence strength he had been a bit more of a slob, like yourself.

Sweatily romantic couples who have redone, maybe rebuilt, old houses with their own hands, ripping out ancient wallpaper and linoleum and pipes and wiring and such, searching out pockets of dry rot and settled foundation piers and chimney cracks, working everything down to bare wood and masonry or beyond, nearly always arrive at intimacy

with their predecessors in those abodes, their Good Indians and Slovenly Petes. Nearly always too they find the villains more interesting than
the nice guys. It is, of course, most pleasant to learn that underneath
some textoned plasterboard and eight or ten layers of bargain-basement
latex paint and wallpaper and white lead and alligatored varnish and the
like, you're the owner of a room paneled in wave-grained solid black
walnut beautifully fitted and joined, or that above the rusty stamped-tin
ceilings of a stone Hill Country cabin are beams of native post oak hewn
square with an adze by some ancestral Deutscher. But it's probably a bit
more fascinating to discover, as a friend of mine did, that the faint stink
which has seeped for years from a north kitchen wall and has lately
grown too stout to ignore derives from the grassroots inventive genius
of an anonymous former occupant who insulated that wall by filling its
stud spaces with cottonseed hulls, fermented now by a siding leak into
rich and miasmic silage.

One has to face also from time to time some effect or the other
of the powerful belief, among Prairie Gothic carpenters of a more innocent era, that a two-by-four would serve for just about any purpose.
I've seen whole upper floors sustained by joists of those dimensions, a
bit concave and springy underfoot but still functional, and in one antiquated farmhouse that my wife and I rented cheaply for several years
because we were willing to refinish it ourselves, I traced some mysterious cracks and sags to a small bracket built out of five or six short
lengths of two-by-four yellow pine nailed halfway up the wall of a closet
and sheathed in shiplap. It held up an entire brick woodstove flue that
must have weighed, according to my rough computation, about 4500
pounds avoirdupois. I had strange feelings about that chimney and the
ghost who'd put it there, and I hoped that whenever it fell it would
choose to collapse straight down toward where its foundation ought
to have been, rather than topple sideways through the attic and ceiling
onto the bed where gentle sleep enveloped us or the table where we
ate. But now, nine years after we moved out of that house and maybe
sixty or seventy after the chimney was erected, I note with interest
whenever I drive along that road that it is still poking up quite vertically
above the roofline, and in fact wintertime wisps of smoke tell me that a
current tenant enamored of alternative energy has hooked up a woodstove to it again.

Living now on this place we have owned for two decades where I
have built all the structures, sometimes with help but often not, the

ghost I most usually have to confront is myself. A chimney that leaks at its flashings, an outbuilding set up on blocks of wood through which termites have made a gleeful invasion, a sheet-iron barn roof that siphons rainwater at some seams when certain winds are blowing, a crawl-space inundated by storms through the place where waterpipes enter—all these joys and others are traceable not to the faulty theories or sloppiness of old-time carpenters and masons but to my own apprentice ignorance. An owner-builder lives with his botches, and working to correct them he waxes introspective, not necessarily with admiration.

I seldom work up the guts for that ultimate form of puttering which involves the patching or restoration of good antique furniture and other classic artifacts. Stout, relatively crude, country-made relics, whose charm is in their honesty and in the sheen of long hard use, I will tackle willingly enough, for the stout crude honest repairs that befit them are within my capacity and their native woods and other materials are usually easy to match. But it takes naïveté or a special sort of arrogance to tamper with the civilized products of vanished masters' vanished dexterity with hand tools. Their aged and chip-prone hardwoods, harvested perhaps in distant forests of the old British Empire where tigers burned bright and white men carried a metaphoric burden and dark men a literal one, are very hard to duplicate with inserts or patches made from woods available now. Furthermore the powered machines on which most present woodworkers depend won't reproduce the contours of their moldings and furbelows, and authenticity prohibits the use of epoxies and other miracle fillers and cements, mainstay substances in modern repair. Bungled work can lower their often considerable value, so like most other people I'm usually willing to leave restoration to professionals or to let the wounded things sit in their corners as is.

Spirits inhabit them too, of course, those of their gifted makers in the individual organic perfection of their shaping and joining and decoration, those of intermediate Slovenly Petes in crude repair jobs undertaken at some point in their history and showing up now as ill-seated reinforcement blocks and screwdriver nicks and other defects. And if one does let arrogance tempt him into essaying such a job himself, as I have on rare occasions, more often than not he ends up leaving a Slovenly Pete spoor also, or else giving up in the middle and either abandoning the object in question in a dismantled state or letting somebody else puzzle it back together. Sometimes with a flush of guilt I run across envelopes or cartons with labels on them in my own handwriting such as

"Trim from dressing room bureau" or "Pieces of rosewood snuffbox." This latter project hit a dead end some eleven years ago when I was unable to find any nickel silver of the right thickness for making a new delicate hinge to replace a broken one, and then it got forgotten in a round of very different puttering, the framing of a barn. I do still intend to seek out that metal and finish up the job, though, maybe in tremulous old age when my chances of being a Slovenly Pete will be even better than now.

In addition to being a putterer with things, I find with some surprise, having spent much of my younger life avoiding ownership when I could, that I have turned into a hoarder of them too. Marriage and parenthood are partly to blame, I guess, and country life even more. At any rate the owned objects that surround us now—some still serving a good purpose, some serving none at all, others awaiting a time of use or donation to somebody else—form massive clutters in workshop and office, and pile up in attics and on platforms under the barn roof and in any odd corner of our house and outbuildings that stays unoccupied for more than a week or so. I do sometimes muse out pleasurable fantasies of setting some large fires or holding a huge garage sale and then driving away with my mate to a spare life aboard a small ketch in coastal waters, but the fact is that I seem to be stuck with these belongings in a complex way. They *belong* where they are just about as much as I do, and if some morning I were to walk into the barn and note that an accustomed item was not there—say the battered Rube Goldberg seed cleaner that I picked up at a farm auction and use maybe once in three years, between which times it sits there stolidly collecting mud-dauber nests and goat-manure dust and blocking passage—I would feel my little world's foundations shudder slightly.

Undoubtedly the main trouble is that nearly all these impedimenta have spirits in them by now, either for me or my wife and daughters or simply for themselves. They were made by somebody, even if that somebody was only a stamping-machine jockey in some dark satanic mill of Pittsburgh or Chicopee Falls. Most bear marks of human use and misuse, and some, of the sort one starts accumulating as older relatives die off and one becomes an older relative oneself, have family stories and meanings attached to them. Heavy tables and sets of shelves put together by my late father, an inveterate putterer himself, tools and World War I stuff of his, a great-grandfather's gargoyled notary seal, large brass-latched Bibles with genealogical scribblings that omit most data about miscreants and black sheep, the cow's-horn cup that Great Uncle Billy Cavitt whittled out for his little sister, my grandmother, as he lay in a tent hospital getting used to the absence of a leg shot off at Pleasant Hill, the thirty-two that Grandpa bought for defense against a gambler in Cuero after a horsewhipping in which Grandpa had wielded the whip . . .

Others recapitulate past bits of my own existence and if, as has been claimed, the unexamined life is not worth living, I suppose they serve a useful end. Certainly if one has made a good many haphazard changes of direction in his lifetime it is at least instructive every now and then, after a certain point, to catch a glimpse of something that one was before. The Old Town canoe carries freight like that, along with its spectral red crew. An earring from an early love's rosy lobe can still rowel memory, as can things like a Boy Scout hatchet, still good, a set of black-ened silver lieutenant's bars, or a curious brass halyard snap given me long ago by a sailing friend in Mallorca and used now as a paperweight. A volume of James Branch Cabell, encountered lately in rummaging, made me pause and wonder over the very young me who admired and imitated his work, thank God without publishing the results, and a moth-tattered collection of trout flies that I tied up myself nearly thirty years ago, nymphs and wet flies and dries in all manner of patterns and sizes, brought back with freshness a compressed and separate parenthesis of time spent in a high valley of the Sangre de Cristo. I lived there alone for six months in a spruce-log shack rented from a rancher-Penitente, wrote earnest confused stories about the war, went down to Santa Fe for supplies and carousal when I felt like it or needed to, and with absorption fished the pools and riffles of a crystal alder-shaded creek either by myself or with an old and close and troublesome friend who would drive up from Albuquerque on weekends. Except that one Friday night he made a few bars before setting out and at two o'clock in the morning his car flipped over in the desert near a place called Galisteo and that was all of that, but I and the moth-gnawed Royal Coachmen and Bivisibles remain.

Freight enough . . . Despite everything, there does still dwell in me a remnant of that fellow who didn't want to own things, and for sanity on occasion I'm glad to know he's there. Sometimes he rears up and asserts himself and I muster the nerve to throw out a few cartons and sacks and pickup loads of unusable gear, or give them away, or burn them. But then the spirits start squeaking and gibbering in rage (ours do seem to make such noises, like Elizabethan spirits: not for them the quavering moan of midnight grade C movies) and I stay my hand before matters go too far. For it is well known among devotees of the occult that offended spirits are much less easy to live with than unoffended ones. And if one lives in a world dominated by things, how shall he know what spirits lurk where?

First published in *Texas Monthly* (November 1979), "Kindred Spirits" is included in *From a Limestone Ledge: Some Essays and Other Ruminations about Country Life in Texas* (New York: Knopf, 1980; Austin: Texas Monthly Press, 1985; Houston: Gulf Publishing Company, 1991). Reprinted by permission of Alfred A. Knopf, Inc.

Composed in Gill Sans types with Ephram Drop Shadow initial.

Some Friends

GEORGE WILLIAMS

*I*n the undulant course of an education, you run across a few first-rate teachers if you're lucky. From high school in Fort Worth I remember a couple of good bright ladies whose informed love of literature and languages managed to bore partway through my adolescent skull, and later, after World War II, I worked in graduate school under some big names like Lionel Trilling and Mark Van Doren and Joseph Wood Krutch, but their classes were large lecture affairs and the experience was somehow more scholarship than learning. The good teachers who mattered most to me came in between, at Rice in the late Thirties and early Forties, maybe because I was most ready for them then. At least three were special in the sense that if at this late date the understandings and feelings they transmitted, together with the other understandings and feelings that these led to, were excised from my being by some psychic knife, I'm certain I would be a different and diminished person. (Just as using that same knife on other realms of experience and other people, including some teachers, might enlarge one quite a bit. . . .)

Of these special mentors, one was the historian David Potter, a Georgia-born expert at—among other things—inducing late-adolescent provincial Confederates to level a critical gaze at their roots. He died later at Stanford, still young and having published only a fraction of the brilliant analytical work he had been born to do. Another was good gray Dr. McKillop, a scholar's scholar and also a man of such solid and dignified (and shy) integrity that he made you long to learn as much as you could of what he knew in the hope of attaining a scrap of that integrity for yourself. And the third was George Williams. The three were quite unlike, each carving designs on a different side of the partially shaped thing one was in those days, and I wouldn't want to have gone without what any of them had to give. Nor would I want to have to rank them one two three. I do know, however, that over the long haul of years whatever it was I got from George Williams seems to have meant the most to me.

And at this point the haul has indeed been long, with the other worlds and the numbers of other known people that have intervened, fuzzing exact recollection of things and persons from that somehow gentler time before the big war, and from after it too. What is left is mainly their sense, their feel. Even with George Williams, who mattered greatly to me and whom I have seen from time to time in later years, my memory of details is spotty and treacherous. I am not even certain how many courses I took from him—modern poetry and creative writing for sure, and maybe at least one other. But I remember how well he ran them, and the flavor of his teaching.

Its essence was . . . friendliness, I suppose. He was glad to be there himself and glad that you were there if you yourself seemed to be glad of it, as nearly all of us were who enrolled in those electives. He was still rather young then (it is unfailingly a jolt to look back at former stages of your life and to realize that only a few years' difference lay between you and some of the people you looked up to), but there was about his friendliness none of that excessive intimacy with which some young and uncertain pedagogues louse up good classes. He had control; he was the head conversationalist in the room and the conversation usually proceeded, often without our knowing it, more or less where he intended that it should.

But it *was* conversation, as it is supposed to be with things like writing and poetry when you care about them. Good conversation, too, intense and argumentative and at times excited. Even now when I run across certain pieces of language that I discovered through George Williams—Housman's "Terence, this is stupid stuff," for instance, that favorite with young self-dramatizing drinkers—there is somewhere in my mind an image of his mobile face, maybe wearing the quizzical pixie grin with which he often awaited your comment, maybe split wide open in high laughter, maybe somber or even scowling if that was where his mood or the subject went. He was "with it," whatever "it" happened to be at the moment—I can remember him actually stammering, the words stumbling over each other, when he was talking about a specimen of writing that was good and telling us why it was. And if you were with him, you were with it also.

Friendliness is one thing and friendship is another, but he offered that too to some of us in a quiet uninsistent way. He did not offer it lightly and if you had any sense you didn't accept it lightly either, for despite his wide firm knowledge there was a purity about George Williams, almost an innocence—about his beliefs, his values, his whole way of looking at the miserable, wonderful world—and pure friends are a responsibility, especially if you're not very pure yourself. You can hurt them. So can other people, and as a friend you feel obliged to keep it from happening. . . . I believe I hurt him once, and I wish I remembered more details rather than mainly the fact that I was wrong. Our talk in class that day was of the unlucky and downtrodden of the world (there were plenty of those around just then, at the tail end of the Great Depression), and I was just back from a summer of working in the wheatfields for a dollar and a half a day and beans and fatback, alongside large numbers of hard-edged floaters—dog-eat-dog philosophers from away back for the most part, definitely unlucky and downtrodden and not very nice about it. Therefore in response to something humanitarian that Mr. Williams said, I observed rebelliously that I didn't think the downtrodden needed all that much sympathy and even if they did I wasn't prepared to give it. Their troubles were their own and the hell with them. I was not to blame. Something like that . . . I remember the shock in his face, and the wariness that lay between us for a while even after I'd thought it over and apologized.

But mainly being around him was pleasure and stimulation, and instruction not only about poetry and writing but about other matters as well, for he knew a raft of things worth knowing. Birds and the natural world were one. Outdoors I was still mainly a hunter and fisherman at that time, not ready for the intricate knowledge he had and in fact rather resistant to it. But I recall walking with him a few times in that lovely tangled wilderness that used to stretch across the western part of the campus, where the Rice stadium and its parking lots now exhibit their cultural splendors, and seeing what he knew about hawks and sparrows and quail and bushes and herbs, and respecting it. Later on, it had something to do with my readiness to start learning that sort of thing for myself. The effects of teaching are often delayed.

One vignette without much relevance, except that it may have been the point at which I realized we were friends, because friends can enjoy your discomfitures . . . Houston in those days had a rather earnest if social ladies' literary club that offered an annual short-story prize of twenty dollars, a much tidier bit of cash back then than now. All of us in Mr. Williams's writing class entered something, and that year I won it with an autobiographical saga of young love, full of jealousy and despair and bungled sexuality, that stretched its mawkishness out to some five or six thousand words. Too late, I found that one of the conditions of winning was to read your masterpiece aloud to the assembled ladies. I sought out Mr. Williams in panic and ended by offering him the prize money if he would go to the Warwick Hotel and read the damned thing for me.

He was delighted, but for the wrong reasons, and broke into that big-mouthed cackling laugh of his. "You can't bribe me," he said (I don't pretend to be quoting exactly at this range of years). "You go down there and find out what writers have to put up with." And I did, and can still squirm remembering.

As a writer, I can find no way of defining the extent of my debt to George Williams, though I suspect it is quite large. There is a sort of digestive process by which writers take on influence from people and from books, distributing what they can use of it throughout their own dark psyches in cubbyholes and chinks. Thereafter they feed on it in ways hidden even from themselves, and when it comes back out into the light it comes out as their own. This happened to me a long long time ago with George Williams's specific teaching about things like fiction and imagery and whatnot, and also with much of the rest of what I learned from him. When I am aware of him at all in terms of writing, it is as a sort of reference point—of purity, of awareness of excellence and strong feeling about it, and nearly always of the gladness and delight that were so strong in him back then.

Just to have been provided with such a reference point early in life sets up a pretty fat debt all by itself. I have never since met anyone who was like him in the least, and am deeply grateful for the happenstance that brought me near him when it mattered.

This tribute to George Williams was published in the Rice University alumni magazine, *Sallyport* (November 15, 1976). Reprinted by permission.

Composed in Perpetua types with Floriated Initial.

JOSÉ MUT

$5/25/53$, Palma:

Nothing but hiding from women and from erstwhile fellow carousers, sailing, a slight cold, going to bed at night. Yesterday I took a really fine boat trip to La Fossa, alone going and with enough scary stuff to make it an adventure. Pleasant farting around there with Spaniards, with an eventful north wind on the return trip. It did me much good and I have more confidence in the boat and my ability to handle it.

1993 *note*: This was when my friendship with Pepe Mut, a Mallorquín by birth and blood, a superb boatman, and an officer in the Spanish military, was cemented. He and his younger brother Roberto, both of whom I knew slightly at the Club Náutico and liked, had invited me to go with them and another Spanish friend in their seven-meter cabin sloop Pegaso to La Fossa, a cove on the uninhabited, windswept southeastern shore of Palma Bay, where they swam and snorkeled and spearfished. The invitation evidently carried more weight than I realized (the Muts and their friends had very little to do with foreigners ordinarily, except in terms of pursuing tourist girls), and when I did not show up at the designated time, they shoved off without me.

Irritated—I hadn't been all *that* late—I took off in their path in my own smaller and much less seaworthy open boat and it was a

From a 1950s unpublished journal, edited with commentary in 1993. The piece on Alexander Brook, which follows this one, is from the same source.

truly hairy trip, with an onshore headwind that kept pushing me toward the rocks, and seas that half-filled the boat before I reached the cove. I had a scared yet exultant feeling of not giving a God damn as the jagged yellowish rock bottom (I can still see it, four decades later) slid by close underneath my keel on the inshore tacks. My voyage demonstrated to Pepe that I had cojones, a prime requisite to friendship with most Spaniards. What it mainly demonstrated to me was that I was a stubborn damned fool, but after that we were friends without question, to my great benefit. He was a lovely intelligent man with immense humor and a great stock of funny stories, a totally masculine and honorable person for whom friendship was nearly a religious thing. His acceptance of me also gave me access to a number of other good locals, for he was much respected.

Blue-eyed and strong-jawed, he came from a background that was basically peasant Balearic though somewhat elevated, for his father had been estate manager for one of the local titled families, and he and his brothers and sisters had all been educated well. He swam far out into Palma Bay and back each morning, and smoked two or three packs of Chesterfield cigarettes a day, cheaper there than in the U.S. because they came in illicitly and tax-free from Tangiers— smuggling being a major occupation of the islanders. Pepe was also a perfectionist about the use of the Spanish language and could not bear my mistakes, correcting them as I made them. We came from quite different cultural backgrounds and I suppose there were areas of philosophy and opinion that we couldn't traverse together, but that never seemed to matter. We were friends.

⤳

1993 note relating to June 1953, when I had moved to a secluded cottage to hide from fellow expatriates and to get some work done: Margarita, the pretty maidservant from the other house, came and cleaned up for me once a week, on her day off from the Cooks. She was a good friend by now and told me all her troubles. Ultimately one of these was fairly serious, since she had gotten herself involved with a black marketeer–smuggler type who promised to get her to France and took most of what little money she had, ostensibly for that purpose, but did nothing beyond trying to maneuver her into bed. Finally I spoke of this to Pepe Mut, and he pulled some local strings that I didn't want to know about, but at any rate Margarita

got her money back and I suspect the lustful and crooked estraper-
lista may have spent some time in a small dank cell.

⤚

*1993 note on an entry for 7/27/53, concerning a vacationing Span-
ish demimondaine with whom I had been briefly involved:* Pepe had
seen us sail away from the Club and later was caustic to me about
her, exercising his right as a Spaniard to criticize his own breed.
Laughing, I told him she claimed to be a marquesa. "Sí," he said
with that wry half-grin of his. "Una marquesa. La Marquesa de
Pollatiesa." The Marchioness of Stiffdick. Nevertheless she was fine,
and a delightful contrast to the neurotic women I had lately been
tangled with.

⤚

1/25/54, Madrid: Pepe telling of being a young foot-soldier
in the Nationalist ranks at Brunete and Guadalajara, and of the
great pride he and his fellows felt when the enemy Reds across
the way stopped Mussolini's crack Italian troops cold—"Es que
eran *españoles*! Tenían *cojones*!"

1993 note: That was where the Republican miners from the Asturias and Guipúzcoa had strapped dynamite around their waists
and jumped up on the Italian tanks and blown them up along with
themselves, and I am sure this tale was something that Pepe told me
in private, for his fellow officers and indeed most other Establish-
ment Spaniards of that time had very little flexibility in their view of
the Civil War and the Republican Reds. However, neither he nor I
was especially rigid about politics. Young and from a conservative
and Catholic background, he had enlisted for Franco, and he was still
quietly proud of having done so, but he had an ability to see things
whole, which was part of the reason I liked him as much as I did. He
viewed Falangists wryly, telling fine jokes about them, and could be
funny too about the titled Spanish aristocracy and their pretensions.

⤚

7/18/54, Mallorca: We spent the afternoon sweating and
loading the boat with Pepe Monserrat [a friend of the Muts who

was going along too]. Finally got away at 2035, but in the middle of the bay discovered we had left behind a big tin of olive oil and had to go back for it. Headed for Cabo Figuera, a good night with a light west wind in the beginning, then calming, then a light easterly, also calming. P. Monserrat went to sleep below [he was a decent little redheaded, freckled guy if not too bright, but his ways were a bit nerve-wracking and sleeping turned out to be his major talent]. At about 0325 at C. Figuera we caught a good north wind that carried us to the Islas de Malgrat, where we anchored at 0430 and figured to sleep late.

7/19: But at 0810 P. Monserrat, having slept long and well, was up and loudly jolly and making coffee for all, so that it was necessary to rise ill-rested and grumpy. They spearfished and got a couple of small specimens. 1100, hoisted sail and went to Cala Fornells, where our schedule was slightly messed up by the presence of Sr. Andía and his daughter [whom they were trying to marry to P. Mut] and a Frenchman with whom P. Mut had business. [A lot of wining and dining in that resort place, not wise because we were planning to catch a north or east night wind for Ibiza and to sail all night.] At around 2000, tired [and full of food and wine], we put to sea on bearing 243°, with a fresh east wind that turned stout as hell once we passed the capes. At around midnight it was necessary to take off the large jib and put on the little one (P. Monserrat sleeping nicely all the time), and the big one eventually blew overboard from atop the cabin, we having forgotten in the stormy uproar to stow it right.

Clear moonlight, huge seas, long nightmarish sleepy running before the big wind with the boom far out to starboard, rising up with the waves and sliding down their backs and half-afraid to look over your left shoulder at the next one, scudding through the last of the night-fishing fleet, scared shitless of a broach, watching for the Ibiza lighthouse on Tagomago and finally at around 0300 picking it up. [P. Mut and I were taking turns at the tiller and dozing in the little cabin below and when the steersman was nearly passing out from drowsiness he would slide forward holding the tiller and kick the other fellow awake to take over. P. Monserrat, however, slept fine the whole while.] Had real hallucinations built around that light toward which we steered, the one I remember best being a peasant family sitting around a table with a candle on it which was the lighthouse. The wind and the waves continued beastly strong but we passed Tagomago in gray dawn light at 0505 and a little later anchored in a cove where we slept until 1300.

1993: I think it's probably best to summarize most of this log, which, as can be seen above, is often detailed in terms of winds and seas and compass bearings and boat-handling and geographical detail and other such nautical matters. Over a period of about two weeks we circumnavigated the island of Ibiza, not hurrying, putting in at little coves at night and buying bread and wine from nearby peasants. Pepe Mut's mother had been born on the island and he spoke its dialect of Catalan, which helped a lot because the country folk knew little Spanish. Snorkeling, we speared fish and crustaceans and each day for the big noon meal made them into a seafood paella with rice and oil and saffron. "Un arroz," they called this dish simply, a rice, and it was usually very good, though there were occasional shortfalls, like the day when we got no fish and had to make our rice with limpets picked off of the rocks, extremely tough and not very palatable fare.

7/21/54, Ciudad Ibiza: Spent the whole day in town. Ran across Anthony Edkins [a wacky, demoralized, educated Britisher I had come to know and like in Madrid, who made a skimpy living as a guide on tour buses], drinking brandy at a café in midmorning with a friend of his who lives in a whorehouse here. The day passed nosing around the city, buying supplies, eating cheaply and well. In the evening I had to choose between nosing around some more with the two Pepes and a "funny people party" to which Edkins had invited me, and not feeling up to what E.'s funny people might be like, I chose the former. We went to a nightclub called El Corsario, not much of a place though good and noisy, and we didn't get back to the boat until 0330.

1993: There was another resort-city stop at San Antonio Abad on the west coast, where Pepe Mut and I vied for the attention of a slinky, vacationing, bikini-clad German brunette named Hannelore (I think that name needs an umlaut somewhere), but she didn't give a damn about either of us, just wanted to stay on good enough terms to be taken sailing, which she accomplished. Then there were more days of sailing from cove to lovely cove and spearfishing and swimming and eating our varied seafood paellas, along the steep, rugged, stupendous west side of the island, occasionally getting into tight spots with weather or currents or rocks but always getting out of them thanks to Pepe's quick and intuitive seamanship.

At one point we made a bread-and-wine expedition up a narrow valley to a very poor farm that should have been depressing but wasn't, and I fictionalized the episode twenty years later as a little chapter in my book *Hard Scrabble*.* We came back to Mallorca at Andraitx where the Germans had built a submarine base in WWII, and finally made it to the Club Náutico in Palma with a curiously empty but contented feeling of having "done it." It really was quite a voyage in a 23-foot wooden boat with no auxiliary power.

In a funny way, being mutually and irritably amused by P. Monserrat's constant sleeping in times of crisis or hard work, his ill-timed heartiness, and his eternal vocal worrying about constipation, etc., had drawn Pepe Mut and me closer together. The contretemps with the umlauted German girl had done that too, because we both knew how to laugh at things, at ourselves, and at each other. He was a hell of a man and a hell of a friend, and it tore me when he died of lung cancer (Chesterfield brand, I suppose) three or four years after I came back to the States. We had corresponded fairly often, but then there was a gap, and later a letter came from his brother Roberto telling what had happened.

---

*See *Hard Scrabble*, Chapter 13.

Composed in Minion types with Pepita initial line.

ALEXANDER BROOK

1993 note on an entry for Jan. 8, 1954,
which mentions the Brooks: There
is no notation in the journal of my first Madrid meeting with Alex
Brook and his wife Gina (hard "G"), but they became friends who
mattered a great deal to me. They were both painters, then in their
fifties, and when younger, Alex had made a considerable splash in the
American art world, winning a Carnegie Prize back in the 1930s.
Since then he had been pretty much eclipsed by the modern movement and had been doing mainly portraits, though very fine ones that
were much sought after. Lame from polio in childhood, he was the
son of Russian immigrants (Brook was their actual name as written
down phonetically by an immigration officer, though in Russian it
was probably spelled Vryk or something like that in Cyrillic letters),
an intelligent, moody, often irascible or bitter man, and Gina was
vague and lovely and highly intuitive, and we liked one another from
the start. I had been given their names by Jan Cook in Palma, and
when I called they had thought I would be homosexual because that
was the kind of young men she usually sent around. . . . We did a lot
of poking about together here and there in their car, I serving as
interpreter when needed, and near one pretty mountain pueblo,
Chinchón, there was a medieval castle for sale cheap which Alex
wanted to buy, but didn't.

Like the previous piece on José Mut, this is from the unpublished 1950s journal,
edited with commentary in 1993.

Jan. 28, 1954, Madrid: Talking with Alex Brook last night. The deep sadness he feels as a result of aging and of the age itself, being démodé and evidently having lost confidence in his art. A fine man, but what a weak hold all artists and writers have upon solidity. His daughter is divorcing back in the States, and his money is running out. [Things weren't really all that bad, but Alex had a Russian gift for sinking into the depths and pulling you down there with him.]

April 20, 1954, Madrid, after returning from a fishing trip to Asturias: Hardly any salmon caught (none by me) but there were good people and glorious country and finally a binge in a cider mill at Gijón. . . . Brought back big centollo spider crabs and lobsters to Alex and Gina, in lieu of the salmon I had euphorically promised them.

May 28, 1955, Madrid: Alex Brook's comment on the shabby little men who stand on the long Cortefiel Sastre ribbon-sign during the intervals at the bullfights, keeping it from being blown by the wind: "They also serve who only stand and weight."

From a 1993 summary of the period from November 1955 to June 1956: Rented a house on the shore of Peconic Bay, next door to Alex and Gina Brook at Sag Harbor on Long Island, and worked quite hard, finishing by early May a retyped first draft of the novel, 441 typescript pages, though I could see that it still needed drastic revision. It was a pleasant time in good surroundings and with good friends nearby and the work mainly flowed along, with some periods of block. Few distractions beyond Alex in his more Russian periods, a girl or two, and, in the spring, fishing which has always been and remains to this late day a distraction I do not resist.

Nov. 4, 1955, Sag Harbor: I like it out here on the Island, even aside from the pleasure of being with Alex and Gina, of whom I am very fond. May settle down and take the little house next door. The city is better in terms of multiple friends and all that, but unless you have more money than I it entails a lot of grubbiness.

Nov. 15: Settled here now in the little house on the bay. [It belonged to the widow of a deceased painter friend of Alex's named Niles Spencer, well-known like Alex back in the 1920s and '30s.] It was the right thing to do. If I can keep from getting too lonesome I will get a lot of writing and reading and thinking done here this winter.

Pleasant drive back from N.Y. with Alex the other night, sipping whiskey all the way. Much friendly philosophy, and when we got here he issued a blast about contemporary painting, a protest against meaninglessness and impermanence. Some of it could be the bitterness of an old man superseded, but not all. He has dedicated himself to his art and not whorishly.

Nov. 17: Alex's parents were Georgians who came over to New York in 1886, had 8 children of which he was the youngest and the only male. Poor but cultured, good parents. They came from that region where the long-lived people are, and one of A.'s grandfathers lived to be 115. He had polio when young, drew with chalk on slate washtubs in the kitchen, pasted pieces of paper with pictures on them under the dining room table, watched his mother cook [he was himself when older a very fine cook], didn't go to school till he was 17, and then I think it was the Art Students' League. Russian ships' officers would visit his parents sometimes or invite the family aboard their vessels to eat caviar. At the moment he is painting frolicsome bawdy nudes and such, just for fun. "You know, one thing I am is a hell of a fine draftsman."

One of his old sisters, now in her nineties in a nursing home in the Midwest, gets bored in the evenings and climbs out a window and goes to a bar to drink and make friends.

Gina had a standard prosperous East Coast marriage to a stockbroker but wanted to paint. One day she packed a suitcase and got on a train to Santa Fe, changing her name en route, from Virginia back to her old childhood family nickname.

Jan. 17, 1956: And, I having refused to go to N.Y. with Alex yesterday on the grounds that I would lose a couple of days' work, he made me lose them anyhow by (1) coming over here yesterday afternoon with a bottle of Cutty Sark, (2) showing up at 11:00 today with a demand that I go to Southampton with him for oysters. What it amounts to is that he's not getting any work done and therefore by God nobody else is going to either. And yet I do have much love for the old bastard. Gina, who has coped with his ups and downs and rages and euphorias and depressions mainly by creating a sort of haze around herself, says that their path is strewn with friends discarded by him. If this keeps up, I'll be another such, because I'll blow up at him. I *have* to get to work.

Jan. 20: Alex had a kind of minor stroke last night, suddenly leaving our conversation for space, though he said later that he had retained awareness of Gina and me. It scared me a little. Him too.

Feb. 10: A moving story tonight from Gina about Alex and a pair of wire-haired terriers they had. The female got maimed and he had her put away even though she would have gotten well. Then he and the male got to where they couldn't stand each other, so he made G. have that one put away too. There had been other such things before. Probably because of his own lameness, she thinks, he can't stand imperfect creatures.

Feb. 16: Gina invited me to supper tonight and then called it off, Alex having evidently objected. It is possible that he's reacting against me as he has against so many others. When I bring my emotions on this subject into the light, I find that I give less of a shit than I previously would have supposed. Whatever his undoubted gifts and charms, he is a wearing old bastard at times and I get fed up with the way he treats G., and with being the buffer between them.

March 5: This thing will make a book, John, so on with it. I have to either go to Detroit with Alex later this week, or talk my way out of it.

1993 note: He wanted to go there — and eventually we did so — to look at an available "Brewster Ford" with a basketwork body, classic cars being one of his many passions. His main car at that time, in which we would drive to Detroit, was a 1939 Rolls closed in the rear but with an open chauffeur's seat that had only a canopy and curtains for use against rain and cold. He also possessed a 1915 Model T Ford with a gleaming brass radiator and fittings, given to him by the actor

Robert Montgomery, who had married into New York society and owned a house in nearby East Hampton. Montgomery, a very decent, slightly pompous man whom I had known passingly in California during the war, worshiped old Alex, and Alex mooched from him mercilessly. The "Brass T," a result of that mooching, ran beautifully and was lots of fun to drive through the pretty Long Island countryside, which was not very crowded then.

> *March 8*: Two good days' work behind and now I've bogged, tying flies and so on. But it will pick up and move. I managed to put Alex off for a week on the Detroit thing.
> *April 10*: Alex came over very early this morning to wake me, banging on the door and coming in and shouting jovially, "This is poetic justice!" because some drunken friends of mine had called his house looking for me at 3:30 A.M. and he couldn't get back to sleep afterward. Who called?

> *1995 note*: In late April or early May of 1956 I finished a first draft of *A Speckled Horse*. Fishing and puttering in Sag Harbor until June, I then bade farewell to the Brooks, visited Texas briefly before going on to Mexico to revise the book, and in the fall came back home to Fort Worth. There within a few weeks I met Jane Cole, a New York girl living and working in Dallas, who was a friend of the Brooks and had been told by them to look me up. And a fateful meeting that was, for Jane is my present wife and the mother of my daughters.

Over the years we stayed close to Alex and Gina in spirit if not physically, though there were some visits back and forth. I particularly enjoyed, if that is the word, a couple of longish, combative sessions with Alex here in Somervell County, not long before he died at 82. He had asked — nay, demanded — that I help him polish his memoirs, a task that turned out to be impossible. These recollections dealt with his own heyday in the art world, back in the Twenties and Thirties, and they were full of rich material. But in reflection of Alex's dark and bitter and Transcaucasian side, they were also extremely cantankerous, with such an overload of stored-up resentments and petty grudges toward contemporaries as to be unpublishable, and publication was what he had in mind. Nor would he hear any talk about subtracting those ancient rancors from the manuscript or toning them down, so we ended up just reworking the sentence structures and vocabulary and the shape of things. Maybe it is testimony to our friendship that despite much hot argument between us over the memoirs' content, he designated me as his literary executor in his will. After his death—not wanting, I suppose, to have an irascible and beloved old Russian ghost steal up behind and bite me in the butt—I resisted a strong temptation to revise the thing into something that a publisher would accept, and instead deposited a couple of copies in university library collections, where they have since been utilized by art historians.

Composed in Galliard types.

JACK STAUB

Glen Rose, August 22, 1983

Dear Alice:

Here goes an attempt at the sketch or reminiscence that you wanted for your little family book. My friendship with Jack stretched over so many years, most of them marked by colorful demonstrations of Staubishness in action, that I have a hard time picking out any single incident or episode or period as outstanding in my recollection. To me one of the loveliest things about the Horrible Doctor was the consistency of his character which, once formed in youth, never seemed to undergo any drastic changes. Certainly his knowledge and his comprehensions expanded along with the scope of those passions — medicine, birds, hound dogs, Pérez Prado, sones huastecos, pigeon shooting, bromeliads, etc., etc., etc. — that he pursued throughout his life. But essentially Jack in his later years was the same Jack that I first knew at Rice when we were both eighteen. His main qualities were present from start to finish. Since many other old friends did change greatly with time, it was always a very fine thing to know that Staub was there and was still being Staub and would keep on being Staub until the end — which, and I find myself still hating to face it, did finally come.

So choosing a tale to tell about him is a little like reaching your hand into a hatful of slips of paper. Maybe the one about his first own private hound dog Wheeler will do as well as any. This happened during the last year of World War II when Jack was in medical school at Duke and I was still in the Marines, back from overseas and in command of a demonstration battery of howitzers at Camp Lejeune on the North Carolina coast. I owned a rickety, undependable 1938 Plymouth with bad tires (they were severely rationed during the war), and used to drive up occasionally to visit him on weekends, a trip of about 150 miles as I remember it. He was in fine fettle, a ringleader and a favorite among his classmates. He had the habit that year of often speaking with a heavy accent like the Mexican who always accompanied the Cisco Kid in the movies, so the other medical students all called him Ceesco.

He was also on the brink of entering his great Coon Dog Period, having been first interested in these beasts during our college days, through black Uncle Jim Burnett on the prairie west of Houston, with whom we sometimes went out hunting at night. There at Duke his interest was further whetted by the fact that a bacteriology professor named Kyler, whom he loved and respected and who lived in a fine old rambling country house, also kept and hunted coonhounds.

As any friend of Jack's knows, he would do anything on God's earth for you that you needed done, and some things that you didn't need done. A corollary to this was that he was also likely to ask you to do anything on God's earth for him, especially if it concerned one of his current passions. Not that I ever minded much, those passions being so compelling. Hence I was not much surprised to get a letter from him saying that if I was coming up to Durham the next weekend — I hadn't known till then that I was — would I mind dropping by Hallsboro on the way and picking up a dog he had bought sight unseen over the telephone? A $75.00 check and instructions for finding this animal's current owner were enclosed.

Hallsboro turned out to be not on the way at all but about a hundred-mile detour, at least as I recall that trip. I drove there on Friday afternoon with only one flat tire en route, and had a fine extended squabble with the seller, a poor-white type who had decided he might be able to stick us for a little more than the price he and Jack had agreed on, and who only quit whining about how he hated to lose old Wheeler after I started out of the yard with Jack's check still in my pocket.

The hound I then took possession of was to my unprofessional eye a very bony and dilapidated creature, abject in manner though friendly in a slobbery way. I put him in the back seat, tethered to a door handle to keep him from jumping out one of the open windows and also from licking my neck. A few miles up the road toward Durham I picked up a couple of young soldiers hitchhiking to a weekend in Raleigh, and the one who sat in back with old Wheeler got his freshly cleaned and pressed uniform slobbered on for a while, until Wheeler became carsick and threw up all over the soldier and the seat and the floor. Since he was now a Staub dog, this seemed somehow appropriate, though I did not of course make this observation to the poor Army boy, who got sick himself and didn't look very good for the weekend even after we had cleaned him up a little with a filling-station water hose. And I'll note parenthetically that the smell of Wheeler's eruption lingered on in that Plymouth until I sold it the following winter, prompting some of the girls I dated during the period to wonder aloud what it could be.

Anyhow, I reached Durham about dark, and Jack was so delighted to have his dog, which he pronounced to be a fine specimen in good lean condition, that he insisted on going out hunting that very night. So after supper we all drove to a wooded hilltop outside the city, Jack and I and three or four of his classmates, and turned old Wheeler loose, he being the entire pack for that particular hunt. Jack slapped him on the rump and said, "Get'em, boy!" whereupon the dog uttered an eager whine and plunged into the darkness.

We built a little fire and drank some beer and listened for Wheeler's voice announcing that he had struck a trail, but no voice came to our ears. After about ten minutes one of the classmates asked, "Ceesco, why don't you call him and see where he is?"

Jack said, "You think I want to mess him up?"

"Maybe he can't bark," said somebody else. "Maybe he's got laryngitis."

"Bullshit, you dumb bastard!" Jack said in his genial fashion. "A real dog doesn't make any noise till he hits a good fresh trail."

I didn't know if this was true or not and I didn't know if Jack knew either, but it sounded good. Better than old Wheeler, who didn't sound at all. After further waiting and consumption of beer, the friend who had mentioned laryngitis said thoughtfully, "I bet that booger is halfway back to Hallsboro by now."

Jack's rage at this remark showed clearly that he had been thinking just about the same thing, as indeed we all had. He said, "The God-damn trouble is that there aren't any coons in this God-damn place you brought us to."

The friend observed that his aunt lived only a few hundred yards away on the property and had had to put chains on her garbage cans to thwart the teeming raccoon population. Jack remained silent, glaring toward the woods, while the rest of us got to talking about other things. Maybe half an hour more went by before somebody said, "What's that funny bumping noise over there?"

A flashlight was aimed in the direction of his pointing finger, and what its beam revealed was Old Wheeler in all his glory, resting comfortably on his haunches and scratching fleas. He had clearly been there almost from the start, after reconsidering his eager plunge into the dark woods. Now, exposed, he grinned at us ingratiatingly and panted and wagged his long tail.

Everybody started laughing and yelling at Jack, of course, and he finally got to laughing too after he decided there was no point in getting angry, even at the useless hound. Intense though he could be about things that interested him, he never seemed to mind much when a joke turned out to be on him.

I left North Carolina soon after that and didn't see him again for more than a year. When I did, it was in New York where he was a brand-new Navy doctor aboard the battleship Missouri at Brooklyn Navy Yard and I was in graduate school at Columbia. I believe that by then he had acquired the first of his really good coonhounds in Texas, including the superb Fannie, and had turned them over to Uncle Jim at Cinco Ranch until his Navy stint was over, but he had little to say about that first dog, Wheeler the Hallsboro Marvel.

Much later in Houston, though, he did once show me, in a Duke medical school yearbook, evidence that Wheeler had never grown any nobler than he had been that first night. This evidence was a piece of doggerel verse beneath Jack's picture in the yearbook, and it went as follows:

> *By the light of the silvery moon*
> *Old Cisco used to croon,*
> *"God damn! God damn!*
> *God damn! God damn!*
> *Wheeler got treed by the coon!"*

Much love to you and all of yours —
                                    Johnny

John Graves wrote this unpublished letter
to Jack Staub's widow, Alice Staub, in 1983.

Composed in Electra types.

BLUE AND SOME OTHER DOGS

NE COOL STILL NIGHT last March, when the bitterest winter in decades was starting to slack its grip and the first few chuck-will's-widows were whistling tentative claims to nest territories, the best dog I ever owned simply disappeared. Dogs do disappear, of course. But not usually dogs like Blue or under conditions like ours here in the cedar hills.

A crossbred sheep dog, he had spent his whole ten years of life on two North Texas country places and had not left the vicinity of the house at either of them without human company since the age of two or less, when his mother was still alive and we also had an aging and lame and anarchic dachshund who liked to tempt the two of them out roaming after armadillos and feral cats and raccoons and other varmints. This happened usually at night when we had neglected to bring the dachshund into the house, or he had tricked his way outside by faking a call of nature or pushing open an unlatched screen door. The dachshund, named Watty (it started as Cacahuate or Peanut), had a very good nose and the two sheep dogs didn't, and having located quarry for them he would scream loud sycophantic applause as they pursued it and attacked, sometimes mustering the courage to run in and bite an exposed hind leg while the deadly mother and son kept the front part occupied.

It was fairly gory at times, nor am I that much at war with varmints except periodically with individual specimens that have developed a taste for chickens or kid goats or garden corn. But the main problem was the roaming itself, which sometimes took them a mile or so from home and onto other property. In the country wandering dogs are an abomination, usually in time shifting their attention from wild prey to poultry and sheep and goats and calves, and nearly always dying sooner or later from a rifle bullet or buckshot or poison bait, well enough deserved. Few people have lived functionally on the land without having to worry sooner or later about such raiders, and the experience makes them jumpy about their own dogs' habits.

To cope, you can chain or pen your dogs when they aren't with you, or you can teach them to stay at home. While I favor the latter approach, with three dogs on hand and one of them a perverse and uncontrollable old house pet too entwined with my own past and with the family to get rid of, it was often hard to make training stick. At least it was until the dachshund perished under the wheels of a pickup truck, his presence beneath it unsuspected by the driver and his cranky senile arrogance too great to let him scuttle out of the way when the engine started.

Blue's mother was a brindle-and-white Basque sheep dog from Idaho—of a breed said to be called Pannish, though you can't prove that by me since I have never seen another specimen. Taut and compact and aggressive, she was quick to learn but also quick to spot ways to nudge rules aside or to get out of work she did not savor. She came to us mature and a bit overdisciplined, and if you tried to teach her a task too roughly she would refuse permanently to have anything to do with it. I ruined her for cow work by whipping her for running a heifer through a net fence for the hell of it, and ever afterward if I started dealing with cattle when she was with me, she would go to heel or disappear. Once while chousing a neighbor's Herefords out of an oat patch toward the spate-ripped fence watergap through which they had invaded it, I looked around for Pan and glimpsed her peeking at me slyly from a shinoak thicket just beyond the field's fringe, hiding there till the risk of being called on for help was past.

Not that she feared cows or anything else that walked—or crawled or flew or swam or for that matter rolled on wheels. She attacked strange dogs like a male and had a contemptuous hatred of snakes that made her bore straight in to grab them and shake them dead, even after she had been bitten twice by rattlers, once badly. After such a bout I have seen her with drops of amber venom rolling down her shoulder, where fangs had struck the thick fine hair but had failed to reach her skin. Occasionally she bit people too—al-

ways men, though she was nervous enough around unfamiliar children that we never trusted her alone with them. Women, for her
own secret reasons, she liked more or less indiscriminately.

She was a sort of loaded weapon, Pan, and in town there would
have been no sense in keeping such a dog around, except maybe to
patrol fenced grounds at night. But we were living then on a leased
place just beyond the western honkytonk fringe of Fort Worth, where
drunken irrationals roved the byways after midnight, and I was often
away. There, what might otherwise have been her worst traits were
reassuring. She worshipped my wife and slept beside the bed when I
was gone, and would I am certain have died in defense of the household with the same driven ferocity she showed in combat with wild
things.

A big boar coon nearly got her one January night, before she
had Blue to help her out. The old dachshund sicked her on it by the
barn, where it had come for a bantam supper, and by the time I had
waked to the noise and pulled on pants and located a flashlight,
the fight had rolled down to the creek and Pan's chopping yap had
suddenly stilled, though Watty was still squalling hard. When I got
there and shone the light on a commotion in the water, all that
showed was the coon's solemn face and his shoulders. Astraddle Pan's
neck with an ear clutched in each hand, he was quite competently
holding her head down despite her mightiest struggles. Big bubbles
rolled up as I watched with dachshund Watty dancing yet uproarious
beside me on good firm land. Grabbing up a stick I waded into the
frigid chest-deep pool, whacked the coon out of his saddle, declined
his offer to climb me in retaliation, and sent him swimming for the
other bank. But by then Pan was unconscious, and on shore I shook
and pumped the better part of a gallon of water out of her before she
started to wheeze and cough. Which didn't keep her from tearing
into the very next coon her brave, small, black friend sniffed out,
though I don't recall her ever following another one into the water.
She was not too rash to learn what an impossibility was.

We had a plague of feral housecats at that place, strayed outward from the city or dumped along the roads by the kind of people
who do that sort of thing, and a huge tom one evening gave the
dachshund his comeuppance. After a notable scrap with Pan the
tom decided to leave as I arrived, but she grabbed him by the tail as
he went. At this point old Watty, thinking in dim light that the

customary face-to-face encounter was still in progress and gaining from my arrival some of the courage that the cat had lost, dashed in for a furtive chomp and was received in a loving, tight, clawed embrace with sharp teeth in its middle. His dismay was piercingly loud and he bore those scars all his life. . . . The tomcat got away.

If my less than objective interest in these violent matters is evident, I have the grace to be a bit ashamed of it, but not much. I have friends among the hound-dog men whose main pleasure in life lies in fomenting such pursuits and brawls, and some of them are very gentle people—i.e., I am not of the school that believes hunting per se makes worse brutes of men than they already are, or ever did or ever will. Though I still hunt a little myself, I don't hunt in that way, and these home-ground uproars I seldom encouraged except occasionally much later, when Blue had become our only dog and had constituted himself Protector of Garden and Poultry. The toll of wildlife actually killed over the years was light, reaching a mild peak during the brief period after Blue was full grown and before Pan died, when they hunted and fought as a skillful team. Most chases would end with a treeing and I would go and call the dogs home with no blood having been shed on either side. But Man the Hunter's association with dogs is very very longstanding, and any man who can watch a slashing battle between his own dogs and something wild and tough, when it does occur, without feeling a flow of the old visceral, reckless joy, is either quite skilled at suppressing his emotions or more different from me than I think most men are.

There being of course the additional, perhaps more cogent fact that in the country varmints around the house and barn and chicken yard are bad news, and the best help in keeping them away is aggressive dogs.

U NABLE TO FIND any males of Pan's breed in this region, we mated her with one of those more numerous sheep dogs, similar in build and coat but colored white and black-speckled gray, known commonly as Australians. Three of the resultant pups had her coloration and the fourth was Blue, marked like his sire but with less speckling and no trace of the blue "glass" or "china" tinge that many, perhaps most Australians have in one or both eyes, sometimes as only a queer pale blaze on an iris. When the time came to choose, we picked him to keep, and as a result he turned out to be a far different sort of grown dog than he would have if we had given him away.

For Pan was an impossibly capricious, domineering mother, neurotic in her protectiveness but punitive toward the pups to the point of drawing blood when they annoyed her, which was often. The others got out from under at six or eight weeks of age, but Blue had to stay and take it, and kept on taking it until Pan died—run over too, while nudging at the rule against chasing cars. Even after he had reached full size—at seventy-five pounds half-again bigger than either Pan or his sire—he had to be always on the watch for her unforeseeable snarling fits of displeasure.

I used to wish he would round on her and whip her hard once and for all, but he never did. Instead he developed the knack of turning clownish at a moment's notice, reverting to ingratiating puppy tricks to deflect the edge of her wrath. He would run around in senseless circles yapping, would roll on his back with his feet wiggling in the air, and above all would grin—crinkle his eyes and turn up the corners of his mouth and loll his tongue out over genially bared teeth. It was a travesty of all mashed-down human beings who have had to clown to survive, like certain black barbershop shoeshine "boys," some of them sixty years old, whom I remember from my youth.

These tricks worked well enough with Pan that they became a permanent part of the way Blue was, and he brought them to his relationship with people, mainly me, where they worked also. It was quite hard to stay angry at a large strong dog, no matter what he had just done, who had his bobtailed butt in the air and his head along his forelegs on the ground and his eyes skewed sidewise at you as he smiled a wide, mad, minstrel-show smile. If I did manage to stay angry despite all, he would most often panic and flee to his hideout beneath the pickup's greasy differential—which may have been another effect of Pan's gentle motherliness or may just have been Australian; they are sensitive dogs, easily cowed, and require light handling. For the most part, all that Blue did require was light handling, for he wanted immensely to please and was the easiest dog to train in standard matters of behavior that I have ever had to deal with. Hating cats, for instance, he listened to one short lecture concerning a kitten just purchased for twenty-five cents at a church benefit sale, and not only let her alone thereafter but became her staunchest friend, except perhaps in the matter of tomcats she might have favored, which he kept on chasing off. And he learned things like heeling in two hours of casual coaching.

Which harks back to my description of him as the best dog I ever owned. He was. But it is needful at this point to confess that that is not really saying much. Nearly all the dogs I owned before Blue and Pan and Watty were pets I had as a boy in Fort Worth, a succession of fox terriers and curs and whatnot that I babied, teased, cajoled, overfed, and generally spoiled in the anthropomorphic manner of kids everywhere. Most perished young, crushed by cars, and were mourned with tears and replaced quite soon by others very much like them in undisciplined worthlessness. In those years I consumed with enthusiasm Jack London's dog books and other less sinewy stuff like the works of Albert Payson Terhune, with their tales of noble and useful canines, but somehow I was never vouchsafed the ownership of anything that faintly resembled Lad or Buck or White Fang.

The best of the lot was a brown-and-white mongrel stray that showed up already old and gray-chopped, with beautiful manners and training, but he liked adults better than children and stayed with my father when he could. The worst but most beloved was an oversized Scotty named Roderick Dhu, or Roddy, who when I was twelve or thirteen or so used to accompany me and a friend on cumbersome hunting and camping expeditions to the Trinity West Fork bottom beyond the edge of town, our wilderness. He had huge negative willpower and when tired or hot would often sit down and refuse to move another inch. Hence from more than one of those forays I came hiking back out of the bottom burdened not only with a Confederate bedroll, a canteen, a twenty-two rifle, a bowie knife, an ax, a frying pan, and other such impedimenta, but with thirty-five dead-weight pounds of warm dog as well.

The friend's dog in contrast was a quick bright feist called Buckshot, destined to survive not only our childhood but our college years and the period when we were away at the war and nearly a decade longer, dying ultimately, my friend swears, at the age of twenty-two. A canine wraith, nearly blind and grayed all over and shrunken, he would lie in corners and dream twitching of old possums and rabbits we had harried through the ferns and poison ivy, thumping his tail on the floor when human movement was near if he chanced to be awake.

With this background, even though I knew about useful dogs from having uncles and friends who kept them for hunting and from having seen good herd dogs during country work in adolescence, as well as from reading, I arrived at my adult years with a fairly intact urban, middle-class, sentimental ideal of the Nice Dog—a clean-cut fellow who obeyed a few selected commands, was loyal and gentle with his masters, and refrained conscientiously from "bad" behavior as delineated by the same said masters. I had never had one and knew it, and the first dog I owned after years of unsettled existence was the dachshund Watty, who was emphatically not one either.

He started out all right, intelligent and affectionate and as willing to learn as dachshunds ever are, and with the nose he had he made a fair retriever, albeit hardmouthed with shot birds and inclined to mangle them a bit before reluctantly giving them up. He was fine company too, afield or in a canoe or a car, and we had some good times together. But his temper started souring when I married and grew vile when children came, and the job was finished by a paralyzing back injury with a long painful recovery, never complete, and by much sympathetic spoiling along the way. As an old lame creature, a stage that lasted at least five years, he snarled, bit, disobeyed, stank more or less constantly and from time to time broke wind to compound it, yowled and barked for his supper in the kitchen for two hours before feeding time, subverted the good sheep dogs' training, and was in general the horrid though small-scale antithesis of a Nice Dog. And yet in replication of my childhood self I loved him, and buried him wrapped in a feed sack beneath a flat piece of limestone with his name scratched deep upon it.

(While for Blue, than whom I will never have a Nicer Dog even if perhaps one more useful, there is no marker at all because there is no grave on which to put one . . .)

I do think Watty knocked out of me most of my residual kid sentimentality about dogs in general—he along with living in the country where realism is forced upon you by things like having to cope with goat-killing packs of canines, and the experience of having the sheep dogs with their strong thrust and potential, never fully attained—to the point that I am certain I will never put up with an unmanageable dog again. I remember one time of sharp realization during the second summer after we had bought this cedar-hill place, long before we lived here any part of the year or even used it for grazing. That spring, after the dachshund had been thrown from the pickup's seat when I jammed the brakes on in traffic, I carried him partly paralyzed to the vet, a friend, who advised me frankly that the smart thing would be to put him away. But he added that he had always wanted to try to cure one of those tricky dachshund spines, and that if I would go along with him he would charge me only his actual costs. Though by that time Watty was already grumpy and snappish and very little pleasure to have around, sentimentality of course triumphed over smart. The trouble was that with intensive therapy still going strong after several weeks, "actual costs" were mounting to the sky—to the point that even now in far costlier times I can grunt when I think of them.

Engaged that summer in some of the endless construction that has marked our ownership of this place where we now live, I was in and out every day or so with loads of lumber and cement and things, and paused sometimes to talk with a pleasant man who lived on the road I used. He had a heterogeneous troop of dogs around the yard, some useful and some just there, their ringleader a small white cur with pricked ears and red-rimmed eyes who ran cars and was very noisy, but was prized by the man's children and had the redeeming trait of being, quote, hell at finding snakes.

One morning as I drove in, this dog was sitting upright under a liveoak fifty yards short of the house, with his head oddly high and askew. He had found one snake too many. His eyes were nearly shut and on the side of his neck was a lump about the size of his head. Nor did he acknowledge my passage with as much as a stifled yap. Thinking perhaps they didn't know, I stopped by the house.

"Yes," said my friend. "He run onto a big one up by the tank yesterday evening and by the time I got there with a hoe it had done popped him good."

"Did you do anything for him?"

"Well, we put some coal oil on it," he said. "I was going to cut it open but there's all those veins and things. You know, they say if a snake hits a dog in the body he's a goner, but if it's the head he'll get all right. You reckon the neck's the head?"

I said I hoped so, and for days as I passed in and out I watched the little dog under his oak tree, from which he did not stir, and checked with the family about him. They were not at all indifferent; he was a main focus of interest and they kept fresh food and water by him. The neck swelled up fatter and broke open, purging terrible fluids. After this happened he seemed to feel better and even ate a little, but then one morning he was dead. Everyone including me was sad that he had lost his fight to live, and the children held a funeral for him, with bouquets of wild prairie pinks.

And such was my changing view that it seemed somehow to make more healthy sense than all that cash I was ramming into a spoiled irascible dachshund's problematic cure. . . .

"Good" country dogs are something else, and are often treated like members of the family and worried over as much when sick. This is not sentimentality but hard realism, because they are worth worrying over in pragmatic terms. There aren't very many of them. As good dogs always have, they come mainly from ruthless culling of promising litters and from close, careful training, and most belong to genuine stockmen with lots of herding work to do. These owners routinely turn down offers of a thousand or more dollars for them, if you believe the stories, as you well may after watching a pair of scroungy border collies, in response to a low whistle or a word, run a half-mile up a brush-thick pasture and bring back seventy-nine Angora wethers and pack them into a fence corner or a pen for shearing, doctoring, or loading into a trailer, all while their master picks his teeth.

Blue wasn't that kind of dog or anywhere near it, nor was there much chance to develop such talent on a place like ours, where the resident cows and goats are fairly placid and few problems emerge in handling them that can't be solved with a little patience and a rattling bucket of feed. For that matter, I don't know nearly enough about the training of such dogs to have helped him become one, though a livestock buyer I know, who has superb dogs himself and handles thousands of sheep and goats each year on their way from one owner to another, did tell me after watching Blue try to help us one morning that if I'd let him have him for six months, he might be able to "make a dog out of him." I was grateful and thought it over but in the end declined, partly because I mistrusted what six months of training by a stranger might do to that queer, one-man, nervous Australian streak in Blue, but mainly because I didn't know what I'd do with such a dog if I had him, in my rather miniature and unstrenuous livestock operations. His skills would rust unused, and the fact I had to face was that I didn't deserve a dog like that.

W HAT BLUE AMOUNTED TO, I guess, was a country Nice Dog, which in terms of utility is a notable cut above the same thing in the city. These dogs stay strictly at home, announce visitors, keep var-mints and marauding dogs and unidentified nocturnal boogers away, cope with snakes (Blue, after one bad fanging that nearly killed him, abandoned his mother's tactics of headlong assault and would circle a snake raising hell until I came to kill it, or to call him off if it was harmless), watch over one's younger children, and are middling-to-good help at shoving stock through a loading chute or from one pen to another, though less help in pastures where the aiming point may be a single gate in a long stretch of fence and judgment is required. Some learn simple daily herding tasks like bringing in milk cows at evening, though I have observed that much of the time these tasks involve an illusion on the part of the dog and perhaps his owner that he is making cows or goats or sheep do something, when actually they have full intention of doing it on their own, unforced. Or the whole thing may be for fun, as it was with one old rancher I knew, who had an ancient collie named Babe. When visitors came to sit with the old man on his porch, he would at some point level a puzzled blue glare across the pasture and say in conversational tones, "I declare, Babe, it looks like that old mare has busted out of the corral again. Maybe you better bring her in." And Babe would rise and go do as he was bidden and the visitors would be much im-pressed, unless they happened to be aware that that was the one sole thing he could do and that the mare was in on it too.

On the whole, to be honest, Blue was pretty poor at herding even by such lax standards—too eager and exuberant and only oc-casionally certain of what it was we were trying to do. But he was controllable by single words and gestures and like his mother un-afraid, and in his later years when I knew his every tendency, such as nipping goats, I could correct mistakes before he made them, so that he was often of some help. He was even more often comic relief, as when a chuted cow turned fighty and loaded him into the trailer instead of he her, or when a young bull, too closely pressed, kicked him into a thick clump of scrub elm, where he landed upside down and lay stuck with his legs still running in the air. When I went over and saw that he wasn't hurt and started laughing at the way he looked, he started laughing too, at least in his own way.

For a sense of humor and of joy was the other side of that puppyish clowning streak which he always retained but which turned less defensive with time. The nervousness that went with it never left either, but grew separate from the clowning, ritualizing itself most often in a weird habit he had of grinning and slobbering and clicking his teeth together when frustrated or perplexed. He regularly did this, for instance, when friends showed up for visits and brought their own dogs along. Knowing he wasn't supposed to attack these dogs as he did strays, Blue was uncertain what else to do with them. So he would circle them stiff-legged, wagging his stub and usually trying to mount them, male or female, small or large, and after being indignantly rebuffed would walk about popping his jaws and dribbling copious saliva. I expect some of those visiting friends thought him a very strange dog indeed, and maybe in truth he was.

He was a bouncing, bristling, loudmouthed watchdog, bulkily impressive enough that arriving strangers would most often stay in their cars until I came out to call him off. Unlike Pan, he bore them no real hostility and never bit anyone, though I believe that if any person or thing had threatened one of us those big white teeth would have been put to good use. Mainly, unfamiliar people disconcerted him and he wanted nothing to do with them unless I was around and showed myself receptive, at which point he was wont to start nuzzling their legs and hands like a great overgrown pup, demanding caresses. Once when the pickup was ailing I left it at a garage in town and mooched a ride home with a friend whose car Blue did not know. No one in the family was there, and when we drove up to the house there was no sign of Blue, but then I saw him peering furtively around a corner of the porch, much as his mother had eyed me from those shin-oak bushes long before.

With his size, clean markings, silky thick coat, broad head, alert eyes, and usual aspect of grave dignity, he was a handsome beast. Having him along was often a social asset with strangers, even if it could turn out to be the opposite if something disturbed him and he went to popping his jaws and grinning that ghastly grin and drooling. One day when he was young and we were still living outside Fort Worth, I was apprehended in that city for running a red light, though I had discerned no light on at all when I drove through the intersection. I explained this to the arresting officer, a decent type, and together we went back and watched the damned thing run through six or eight perfectly sequenced changes from green to yellow to red and back again. Blue watched with us and, attuned to the situation, accepted a pat from the cop with an austere but friendly smile. Against pregnant silence I said with embarrassment that I guessed my eyes were failing faster than I'd thought, accepted the inevitable summons, and went my disgruntled way.

When I got home that afternoon, my wife said the officer had telephoned. More decent even than I had known, he had watched the light for a while longer by himself and had finally caught it malfunctioning, and he told Jane I could get the ticket cancelled.

She thought me off in the cedar hills and believed there was some mistake. "Did he have a sheep dog in the back of the pickup?" she asked.

"No, ma'am," said Blue's till-then secret admirer. "That great big beautiful animal was sitting right up on the front seat with him."

We spent a tremendous lot of time together over the years, Blue and I—around the house and barn and pens, wandering on the place, batting about in a pickup (his pickup more than mine, for he spent much of each day inside it or beneath, even when it was parked by the house), or at farm work in the fields. When young he would follow the tractor around and around as I plowed or harrowed or sowed, but later he learned to sit in the shade and watch the work's progress in comfort, certain I was not escaping from him, though sometimes when he got bored he would bounce out to meet the tractor as it neared him and would try to lead it home. Fond of the whole family and loved by all, he would go along with the girls to swim at the creek or on horseback jaunts across the hills, good protection for them and good company. But he needed a single main focus and I was it, so completely that at times I felt myself under surveillance. No imperfectly latched door missed his notice if I was indoors and he was out, and he could open one either by shoving or by pulling it with his teeth, as permanent marks on some of them still testify. Failing to get in, he would ascertain as best he could, by peeking in windows or otherwise, just where I was located inside and then would lie down by the exterior wall closest to that spot, even if it put him in the full blast of a January norther.

At one friend's house in town that he and I used to visit often, he would if left outside go through the attached garage to a kitchen door at odds with its jamb and seldom completely shut. Easing through it, he would traverse the breakfast room and a hall, putting one foot before another in tense slow motion, would slink behind a sofa into the living room, and using concealment as craftily as any old infantryman, would sometimes be lying beside my chair before I even knew he was in. More usually we would watch his creeping progress while pretending not to notice, and after he got where he was headed I would give him a loud mock scolding and he would roll on his back and clown, knowing he was home free and wouldn't be booted back out, as sometimes happened when he was shedding fat ticks or stinking from a recent battle with some polecat.

But there were places he would not go with me, most notable among them the bee yard, his first apicultural experience having been his definite last. It happened one early spring day when I was helping a friend check through a neglected hive someone had given him and Blue had tagged along as usual. The thing was all gummed up with the tree sap bees use for glue and chinking, and the combs in the frames were crooked and connected by bridge wax so that we had to tear them when taking them out, and on that cool day all thirty or forty thousand workers were at home and ready to fight. They got under our veils and into all cracks in our attire, and those that didn't achieve entry just rammed their stings home through two or three layers of cloth. They also found Blue, a prime target for apian rage since they all hate hairy things, probably out of ancestral memory of hive-raiding bears. With maybe a hundred of them hung whining in his hair and stinging when they found skin, he tried to squeeze between my legs for protection and caused me to drop a frame covered with bees, which augmented the assault. Shortly thereafter, torn between mirth and pain, we gave up and slapped the hive back together and lit out at a run, with Blue thirty yards in front and clouds of bees flying escort. And after that whenever he saw me donning the veil and firing up my smoker, he would head in the other direction.

He did work out a method of revenge, though, which he used

for the rest of his life despite scoldings and other discouragements. Finding a place where small numbers of bees were coming for some reason—a spot on the lawn where something sweet had been spilled, perhaps, or a lime-crusted dripping faucet whose flavor in their queer way they liked—he would stalk it with his special tiptoeing slink and then loudly snap bees from the air one by one as they flew, apparently not much minding the occasional stings he got on his lips and tongue. I suppose I could have broken him of it, but it was a comical thing to watch and for that matter he didn't get many bees in relation to their huge numbers—unlike another beekeeper friend's Dalmatian, afflicted with similar feelings, who used to sit all day directly in front of a hive chomping everything that emerged, and had to be given away.

Maybe Blue considered bees varmints. He took his guardianship of the home premises dead seriously and missed few creatures that came around the yard. Except for the unfortunate armadillos, which he had learned to crunch, the mortality inflicted on their ranks was low after Pan's death, as I have said, for most could escape through the net yard fence that momentarily blocked Blue's pursuit and few of them cared to stay and dispute matters except an occasional big squalling coon. We did have some rousing fine midnight fights with these, though I suppose I'd better not further sully my humanitarian aura, if any remains, by going into details. During the time when cantaloupes and roasting ears were coming ripe and most attractive to coons, I would leave the garden gate open at dark and Blue would go down during the night on patrol. There was sometimes a question as to whether a squad of coons given full license could have done half as much damage to garden crops as the ensuing battles did, but there was no question at all about whether the procedure worked. After only two or three brawls each year, word would spread around canny coondom that large hairy danger lurked in the Graves corn patch and they would come no more, much to Blue's disappointment.

I TALKED TO HIM quite a bit, for the most part childishly or joshingly as one does talk to beasts, and while I am not idiot enough to think he "understood" any of it beyond a few key words and phrases, he

knew my voice's inflections and tones, and by listening took meaning from them if meaning was there to be had, responding with a
grin, a sober stare, melting affection, or some communicative panting, according to what seemed right. Like most dogs that converse
with humans he was a thorough yes type, honoring my every point
with agreement. Nice Dogs are ego boosters, and have been so since
the dim red dawn of things.

I could leave him alone and untied at the place for three or
more days at a time, with dry food in a bucket under shelter and
water to be had at the cattle troughs. Neighbors half a mile away
have told me that sometimes when the wind was right they could
hear him crooning softly wolflike, lonely, but he never left. When I
came back he would be at the yard gate waiting, and as I walked
toward the house he would go beside me leaping five and six feet
straight up in the air in pure and utter celebration, whining and
grunting maybe but seldom more—he saved loud barks for strangers
and snakes and threatening varmints and such.

Last winter I slept inside the house instead of on the screen
porch we shared as night quarters during much of the year—unless,
as often, he wanted to be outside on guard—and I hadn't moved
back out by that March night when he disappeared. He had been
sleeping on a horse blanket on a small unscreened side porch facing
south, and I had begun to notice that sometimes he would be still
abed and pleasantly groggy when I came out at daybreak. He was
fattening a bit also, and those eyes were dimmer that once had been
able to pick me out of a sidewalk crowd of jostling strangers half a
block away in town, and track me as I came toward the car. Because,
like mine, his years were piling up. It was a sort of further bond between us.

He ate a full supper that evening and barked back with author-
ity at some coyotes singing across the creek, and in the morning he
was gone. I had to drive two counties north that day to pick up some
grapevines and had planned to take him along. When he didn't answer my calling I decided he must have a squirrel in the elms and
cedars across the house branch, where he would often sit silent and
taut for hours staring up at a treed rodent, oblivious to summonings
and to everything else. It was a small sin that I permitted him at his
age; if I wanted him I could go and search him out and bring him in,
for he was never far. But that morning it didn't seem to matter and I

took off without him, certain he'd be at the yard gate when I drove in after lunch, as he had invariably been over the years.

Except that he wasn't. Nor did a tour of his usual squirrel grounds yield any trace, or careful trudges up and down the branch, or a widening week-long search by myself and my wife and kids (whose spring vacation it used up and thoroughly ruined) that involved every brushpile and crevice we could find within half a mile or more of home, where he might have followed some varmint and gotten stuck or bitten in a vein by a rattler just out of its long winter's doze and full of rage and venom. Or watching for the tight down-spiral of feeding buzzards. Or driving every road in the county twice or more and talking with people who, no, had not seen any dogs like that or even any bitches in heat that might have passed through recruiting. Or ads run in the paper and notices taped to the doors of groceries and feed mills, though these did produce some false hopes that led me up to thirty miles away in vain.

Even his friend the two-bit cat, at intervals for weeks, would sit and meow toward the woods in queer and futile lament. . . .

I ended fairly certain of what I had surmised from the first, that Blue lies dead, from whatever cause, beneath some thick heap of bulldozed brush or in one of those deep holes, sometimes almost caves, that groundwater eats out under the limestone ledges of our hills. For in country as brushy and wrinkled and secret as this, we can't have found all of such places roundabout, even close.

Or maybe I want to believe this because it has finality.

And maybe he will still turn up, like those long-lost animals you read about in children's books and sometimes in newspaper stories.

He won't.

And dogs are nothing but dogs and I know it better than most, and all this was for a queer and nervous old crossbreed that couldn't even herd stock right. Nor was there anything humanly unique about the loss, or about the emptiness that came in the searching's wake, which comes sooner or later to all people foolish enough to give an animal space in their lives. But if you are built to be such a fool, you are, and if the animal is to you what Blue was to me the space he leaves empty is big.

It is partly filled for us now by a successor, an Old English pup with much promise—sharp and alert, wildly vigorous but responsive and honest, puppy-clownish but with an underlying gravity that will in time I think prevail. There is nothing nervous about him; he has a sensitivity that could warp in that direction if mishandled, but won't if I can help it. Nor does he show any fear beyond healthy puppy caution, and in the way he looks at cows and goats and listens to people's words I see clearly that he may make a hell of a dog, quite possibly better than Blue. Which is not, as I said, saying much. . . .

But he isn't Blue. In the domed shape of his head under my hand as I sit reading in the evenings I can still feel that broader, silkier head, and through his half-boisterous, half-bashful, glad morning hello I still glimpse Blue's clown grin and crazy leaps. I expect such intimate remembrance will last a good long while, for I waited the better part of a lifetime to own a decent dog, and finally had him, and now don't have him any more. And I resolve that when this new one is grown and more or less shaped in his ways, I am going to get another pup to raise beside him, and later maybe a third. Because I don't believe I want to have to face so big a dose of that sort of emptiness again.

First published as "Ol' Blue" in *Texas Monthly* (December 1977), "Blue and Some Other Dogs" appears in *From a Limestone Ledge: Some Essays and Other Ruminations about Country Life in Texas* (New York: Knopf, 1980; Austin: Texas Monthly Press, 1985; Houston: Gulf Publishing Company, 1991). This version is published in book form, *Blue and Some Other Dogs* (Austin: Encino Press, 1981). Reprinted by permission of Alfred A. Knopf, Inc.

Composed in Goudy Old Style types with Matura Scriptoral Capital initial.

Elsewhere

THE GREEN FLY

I N THE ONE-ROOM COTTAGE
he had taken at the rear,
near the stream and the steeply rising green mountainside, Thomas
Hilliard awoke each morning early, sometimes at six with the clean
tolling of the bells in the village below, often before. An old man
named Celestino brought fruit and rolls and coffee from the kitchen
at the main house of the hacienda. After breakfast Hilliard would
walk for a few minutes along the stream, watching for fish, and
then he would go back to work at his typewriter until one o'clock
and the midday meal.

In the thin, high, foreign air, undistracted, his mind moved
spiderlike, weaving and linking ideas and words with a precision
that he had not really expected, and the work went well. Although
he had half agreed, laughing, when Wright Forsythe had told him
that Mexico was a hell of a place to go to finish a dissertation in
English literature, it went smoothly and fast. Within a few days his
existence at the hacienda had shaped itself into a life. A backwater
life without conflict or crisis or betrayal, one that would last only
until Wright and Deirdre drove down to join him later and to take
him back northeastward, but a life nonetheless, full enough.

There was the fishing. In the afternoons Hilliard went to the
stream, because for anyone who cared for trout it was lovely fishing,
the best he had ever known. It flavored that life indispensably, and
when old Dr. Elizondo came, it was through the fishing that they
met at the start, and the fishing gave their meeting its meaning. In
the rich cold water of the rapids and the stairstepped pools, and in
the small dammed lake at the stream's end where it plunged to the

valley below and the river, the trout lay thick among broken walls and aqueducts and enigmatic masses of stone that had had usefulness in a vanished feudal time. The prosperous Mexican families at the hacienda, paying guests like himself, used heavy lines and worms to take small fish by the basketful, but in the smooth water of the poolheads the big rainbows waited haughty and selective. Hooking them required a well-chosen fly on a long fine leader, cast carefully and stealthily from downstream.

No other Americans came to the hacienda, and Hilliard did not mind that. Within the formal limits of his acquaintance with them, he liked most of the well-mannered Mexicans vacationing in the other cottages and in the rooms of the main house. In the evenings by the fireplace in the big sala they would talk, quietly and with their friendly foreign distantness, to one another and sometimes to Hilliard, enduring with grave humor his faulty Spanish and the incomprehensible fact that he spent long hours of each day wet to the knees, flourishing a caña de pescar over running water.

They came and vacationed and left, and others took their places. One evening in Hilliard's third week a new man appeared at dinner, graying and baldish, alone, with a strong Iberian nose and light-brown shapely eyes that gazed, afterward in the big living room, with remote gentleness into the fire while the others around him talked. Then the next day Hilliard, casting into white water where the stream debouched from a jumble of huge weathered building stones into a pool, glanced up to see him watching from the bank. In that moment the line twitched and Hilliard raised his rod tip against the tug of a stout fifteen-incher that thrashed up and down the pool before coming finally exhausted to the net.

"Bien hecho!" called the man on the bank.

Smiling, Hilliard wet his hand and held the trout up for a moment for the other to see before he shook the fly from its lip and slipped it back into the water. For a moment, spent, it hung there and then with a drunken flirt of its body rode the current downward and out of sight. Hilliard waded ashore.

"You released it," the man said, in the flat courteous Spanish manner that was neither statement nor question. In the sun he looked quite old, his face hollow, leathery wrinkles radiating from the corners of the alert almost golden eyes. He was dressed to fish, in a tie and a rusty black coat and patched wading boots, and in his hand was an old-fashioned long English bamboo fly rod with closely spaced silk windings. Looking at that battered old-world formality of gear and attire, Hilliard in his dripping khakis and with his glittering American equipment, felt suddenly both shabby and crass.

He said, "I let most of them go. What I care about is getting them to take the fly."

The old man nodded in approval. "They are noble fish," he said. "Permit me. I am Juan Elizondo."

Hilliard took the old, slim hand and then, with the ease of strangers who share an enthusiasm, they talked for a while. The doctor—he said that he was a doctor, and that he got to fish little nowadays—asked politely in measured Castilian about the personality of the stream and its trout. Of specific spots and fly patterns he said nothing, and Hilliard, watching him finally trudge off downstream, comprehended the painstaking pleasure he would derive from learning those things for himself.

And from that meeting—because, as the doctor remarked later, no one else at the hacienda was crazy enough to possess an afición for real angling—a mannered mild comradeship sprang up between them. On the water when they happened to meet they would sit down and smoke and talk, nearly always of trout, and the evenings by the fire were the same. They traded some flies; the doctor tied his own, whipping them together deftly and with care, European patterns strange to Hilliard. "Esta!" he said once with love, holding up a gaudy tuft of tinsel and peacock herl. "This one. She did much killing on the Gallego. My colleague Aguirre used to call her the Green Traitor."

The friendship broadened gradually without effort from either of them. From the copious morning gossip of old Celestino, Hilliard learned that the doctor was a Spanish Republican refugee, which explained the coolness and the distance that were apparent between him and the upperclass Mexican guests. Having listened well when the señora, his employer, talked to those other guests, Celestino knew also that the doctor had once been a surgeon very noted, señor, but now, with exile and political discredit, was lucky to have work in the infirmary of a tile factory in Puebla. Staunchly Catholic, the old servant clearly took pleasure in the doctor's poverty, and in the fact that his wife and daughter in Madrid, adherents of the Franco regime, were said not to communicate with him at all. They did not write so much as a word, señor. . . .

Hilliard said severely that morning, ashamed to have listened, "All this is none of my business, or the señora's, or yours."

Celestino, making the bed, patted a bolster. "Pues, maybe not," he said equably. "But the suitcases of this Red doctor, how barbarous and mutilated. You should see."

In conversation with the doctor himself Hilliard had other glimpses of a past that had been obviously busy and full of accomplishment. Vienna-trained, he had traveled through much of Europe as a surgeon, and had fished in a number of its countries. "Medicine and sport were companions," he said smiling. "Sweethearts. Where the scalpel went, so did the rod."

It did not bother Hilliard that with their increasing closeness the other guests' coolness toward the doctor came also to envelop him. He understood it well enough that when the señora, the diffident patrician widow who owned the hacienda, approached him about these matters he almost avoided showing irritation. Almost but not entirely.

He liked the señora and the quietly gracious way in which she operated her family's onetime home as a lodge. She had asked him into her office, a tiny room baroque with the sculptured and embroidered furnishings of Porfirio Díaz's day, and had tried unskillfully to draw him into talk about the doctor. Hilliard said in a tone that brought apprehension into her velvet-wrinkled face that he had no intention of gossiping about a friend. Had the doctor done something to disturb her or the other guests?

"No, señor, nothing yet. But his politics . . ."

Hilliard, opening the office's carved door, said, "He has not even mentioned politics to me, señora, and neither will he mention it to your guests. To tell the truth, he is more of a gentleman than anyone else I've met here. They won't suffer."

"I meant only . . . You're American. You can't know."

"Yes, I can," he said. He had seen a couple of bitter squabbles in Mexico City cafés, with Spaniards shouting "Reds!" and "Fascists!" at one another, and had felt the acrid hatred still knife-sharp in them a dozen years after their war had ended. He had read a good bit about that war and thought he had sensed a little of its complexity. He also comprehended the señora's sequestered, conservative fearfulness about such things, but when they touched the doctor they made him angry. "Con permiso, señora," he said with finality, and as he passed through the door she answered with the automatic, "Pase usted."

It aligned Hilliard. The doctor had begun—when, he had not noticed—to address him with the familiar "tú," like a son. They ate together now at a corner table in the dining room, and without always being able to say how, he knew a great deal more about the old man.

The Forsythes had been good friends to him. Wright Forsythe, seven years older than he, was one of the young emergers on the university's faculty, and it had been gratifying to Hilliard that someone of that caliber should have taken keen interest in him, almost as gratifying as the fact that a warm and graceful woman like Deirdre Forsythe had made him welcome always in their home. They were intelligent, alive people who balanced each other in a life built around the quiet, unexuberant luxury of inherited money and the pull of scholarship and the arts, and they had treated Hilliard like a younger brother.

Yet he had never really thought of them apart from the university and its town, so that when their letter arrived a few days before the doctor was due to leave, it came as a mild shock into the hypnotically pleasant regularity of life at the hacienda, with its work and fishing and friendship. It was as though he had forgotten them, as in a way he had. They were already in Mexico City, and he sent a wire over the hacienda's rickety telephone, asking them to drive up immediately. At lunch he told the doctor.

"I am content to know it," the old man said.

"You'll like them."

"I'm certain. And for a change you'll have some fellow countrymen."

It was somehow an odd thought. "Yes, I will, won't I?" said Hilliard.

That day became entirely remarkable when in the afternoon the doctor, as a climax to his vacation, took an incredible seven-and-three-quarter-pound trout, having stalked it laboriously in the spot where he had first seen it weeks before, teased it to his gaudy peacock fly, and played it with a half-century's skill on the delicate old English rod before dipping it at last from the water. He quit fishing then and came almost running up the streamside path to where Hilliard was wading. His usual reserve was drowned in tremendous pleasure.

"She is handsome, no?" he demanded, holding the big trout across his palms, its living iridescence not yet dulled. "She is noble?"

"Beautiful," Hilliard agreed, as happy about it as his friend was, for he knew what the fish meant to the old man, and would mean later in memory. When they had weighed it on the doctor's worn brass scale, he wanted badly to offer to have it taken to the capital for mounting. But it was not the kind of thing he could offer to the doctor, not conceivably, so they carried the great trout to the charcoal-pungent kitchen of the hacienda, where the fat head cook Félix bellowed in unaffected astonishment.

And that evening at dinner when Félix had brought it in on a plank, with ceremony, its smoky pink flesh perfectly baked, and had offered it around at the tables, even the wary, cold-eyed Mexican bankers and lawyers smiled to the doctor and raised their glasses in congratulation. He was quietly triumphant and nodded in acknowledgment of the toasts. In the trout's honor Hilliard had ordered a bottle of wine and afterward, instead of his usual single thin, dark cigar, the doctor smoked two.

"An insanity, to excite oneself with the murder of a trout," he said. "But she was big, no? On the plank? I wish your friends had arrived in time to see her."

Hilliard grinned. "They aren't fishermen. The little ones will be good enough."

"People of intelligence," the doctor said. "Commonsense Americans, not like you. Caray, what a fish!"

Nor in truth were they like Hilliard, the Forsythes. He felt it more strongly than he ever had, the next afternoon when they emerged from their car into the quiet air of the old courtyard. They were like a robust and alien breeze, handsome blond people, congenitally crisp and northern. But he found himself glad to see them. On the long tiled gallery of the big house, when he had introduced them to the señora and they had seen their rooms, the three of them talked.

"You look healthy," Wright Forsythe said. "You also look unscholarly as hell."

"I've worked," Hilliard answered. "I've gotten a lot done."

"I wouldn't," Deirdre said, gazing with pleasure out across the stone-walled courtyard with its trickling, carved fountain, a gnarled ahuehuete tree clinging to life and two brown children scrambling obscurely against the far wall. Her small, sandaled feet rested on the gallery's railing, a pose that looked odd to Hilliard after weeks of being around decorous Mexican ladies, but like everything else he had ever seen Deirdre do, it also looked fitting.

She sighed, making a face. "Work, in a place like this? Not I. How did you ever find it?"

"You'd better reserve judgment for a while," he said. "For one thing, the plumbing's haunted."

Wright wore a checked gingham shirt and flannels and looked inevitably like the scholar that he was. He grinned, poking with a twig at his pipe bowl which he held three inches out from his face because he wasn't wearing his glasses. "In regard to plumbing, we had a couple of years of Italian pensiones, after the war," he said. "What gets me is how you've stood the solitude."

Hilliard said that it wasn't exactly solitude. There were people, and fishing.

"Fishing," Wright said with a grimace. "Your letter mentioned it. I did bring a pole, for trolling if they've got a lake."

"They do, a small one," Hilliard said, with a smile because Wright, who knew the right names for all things, had used the word "pole" with deliberate amateurism, to bait him. Nor did he say anything about the trolling, which he viewed with the illogical slight disdain of a fly-fisherman, for he had learned long since that that particular ritual was no more defensible than any other. "I know a Spaniard here," he said. "You'll like him."

"I might, if he speaks English."

"He doesn't," Hilliard said. "Or very little. He's a refugee, or was."

Wright lifted a humorous eyebrow. "A kumrad?"

"No, I think not. It wouldn't matter, anyhow. He's a doctor."

"Doctor, smoctor," Wright said idly. "It matters, all right." He regarded a pair of vultures wheeling in the domed mountain sky. "Have you read anything decent, in between fish?"

"Not yet, please!" his wife said. "It's too nice here. Let's just talk a while about things that haven't been printed on paper."

"As though anything worth talking about," Wright said, "hadn't been printed on paper."

The doctor smiled warmly in the dining room that evening, bowing to Deirdre. His English was labored: "How do you do? It is good."

"It is good, indeed," said Wright in tweeds, with grave irony as to an Indian chieftain.

Hilliard said, "I spoke to the señora. We're all going to sit together."

Comprehending, the doctor touched his arm. "With permission, I prefer that you eat with the friends, alone." Nor would he reconsider, making the gentle semicircular gesture with a palm outward that was polite but firm refusal. "You three have enough to say," he said. "For knowing one another there will be time."

Wright grinned after the doctor as he moved toward the corner table where he and Hilliard had sat together. "Exclusive old bird, isn't he?"

"It's not that. He didn't want to be in the way."

"He's fine, Tom," Deirdre said. "Like someone from a long long time ago."

"So long ago that it might not count," said her husband. "He looks like the emperor Vespasian, on a coin. Maybe with a hammer and sickle on the obverse. Let's sit down."

Quite simply it did not work; the chemistry was wrong. After dinner, by the fire in the big sala, the doctor for the first time since Hilliard had met him seemed awkward, not self-possessed. He sat for a time listening with courteous incomprehension to their conversation in English, and once he and Wright exchanged a few remarks in French. But it had no warmth and Hilliard knew that it was not going to work. When finally, earlier than usual, the doctor had excused himself and gone to his room, Wright chuckled.

"With all due respect, Tom, I'm afraid your old revolutionary is something of a dud," he said. "Or maybe —" for they had spoken of the doctor's big trout—"maybe he's still dazed from wrestling that seven-pound whale."

Deirdre said, "He's only shy."

Hilliard, flipping a chip of eucalyptus into the fire, did not want to discuss the doctor. He said, "He's not shy, just hard to know, I guess. He's all right."

"De gustibus," said Wright.

Hilliard grinned wryly. In his life he had tried before, and had failed, to bring people together when things would not work. "De gustibus," he agreed.

He did not try to mix them again. During the following week he spent most days wrangling over his dissertation with Wright, who liked it, or wandering with Deirdre around the hacienda's environs, gossiping about Mexico and the university town that was home. But on the two afternoons when he slipped away to the stream, the doctor was as gentle and friendly as ever, glad to stop fishing and to talk for a time while sitting on old stones or the soft grass of the bank. He asked courteously after the Forsythes but avoided them, either going to his room early in the evenings or reading alone in a corner of the great sitting room.

The señora approved of the Forsythes, especially Deirdre, and grew friendly to Hilliard again. Wright developed indigestion from the seasoning so that his food had to be cooked separately; Deirdre tumbled harmlessly from a burro on a trip to the Toltec pyramid around the mountain; and Hilliard's work began to take final shape. Then suddenly it was the Saturday before the Sunday when Dr. Elizondo was to leave, to go back to his work in the tile factory's infirmary and whatever existence he had there.

Hilliard felt relief when Wright, who had wandered along with them to the stream with his spinning rod, grew restless and said that he was going to try fishing from the battered canoe in the lake.

"Leave a few," Hilliard said.

"I intend to wipe your puristical eye," answered Wright over his shoulder. "Trolling."

"How says the friend?" the doctor asked, looking up from a knot in his leader. Hilliard translated and the old man laughed. He was in a fine humor, buoyant, as though the imminence of his departure made the day not worse but better. "Some troll," he said.

"Some pull nets like Saint Peter, but you and I, we fish with reeds and spider threads. Pues, who is crazy?"

They worked the stream together, alternating, watching one another cast into the stairstep pools. Unroiled by recent rain, the water was beautifully clear and the fish were feeding well, with just enough caution to compel stealth. They stopped and rested and talked often, and before it was at last time to stop they had between them caught and freed nineteen heavy healthy trout. Never, the old man said as they walked in the gathering dusk toward the hacienda, not anywhere had he known fishing like that of this stream.

"Not even on the Gallego?" Hilliard said, teasingly because the doctor had always shown special reverence when speaking of the Pyrenean rivers.

The doctor grunted humorously. "Bueno, not even there. No."

The afternoon had been fine enough to make trivial its finality, its flavor of farewell. When they were nearly among the first cottages, Wright's voice called to them from ahead and they saw his white shirt luminous against the hacienda's old dark wall. He was walking toward them with Deirdre behind, and as they approached Hilliard saw that his left hand was wrapped in a handkerchief.

Wright said with a slight twist of pain on his mouth, "The trout rodeo is over. I need your friend."

Deirdre held a bass-stringer festooned with small dead trout. She said, "The fish weren't big enough, so he decided to catch himself."

"What a comic!" Wright said, removing the handkerchief. Pendant from the fleshy web between his thumb and forefinger dangled a red-and-white trolling spoon, one point of its treble hook embedded above the barb.

Carefully the doctor leaned his fly rod against a bush, and taking the hand examined it. He looked up into Wright's face and smiled, touching with his finger a small white scar on the back of his own left hand and then another on his cheek, near his eye. To Hilliard in Spanish he said, "The mark of the angler."

"It's nice that everybody gets such a boot out of this," Wright said.

"All right," said Deirdre. "Who stuck that thing in you?"

The doctor had brought from his pocket a pair of long-nosed pliers that Hilliard had seen him use as hook disgorgers with the trout. "To pull it now will relieve him sooner," he said. "This will serve as well as any instrument I have."

"Yes," Hilliard said from personal suffering with hooks, and then without hesitation, moving surely, the doctor grasped Wright's wrist in his left hand, seized the hook at its bend in his pliers, and with one strong pull drew it free.

Wright, who had not expected this, wrenched his hand away and glared at the doctor. He said, "Good Jesus Christ!"

The doctor smiled uncertainly at Hilliard. "Tell him . . . there had to be pain. At the hacienda we will clean it."

Watching Wright, Hilliard said, "Take it easy. You have to pull hooks that way. Or push them through and cut them."

Pale, his friend didn't answer. No one spoke as they went up the hill to the main house, and Wright said nothing until the three of them stood waiting in the courtyard while the doctor went to his room for antiseptic and a bandage. Then, whimsically, he eyed Hilliard. "You said he was a bone specialist?"

"I think so," Hilliard said shortly.

"T-bones," Wright said. "He's a pure butcher, that old boy."

Silently Hilliard occupied himself with dismantling his fly rod, and when the doctor returned he cleansed the wound of its black crusted blood, bandaged it, then glanced up at Wright, who had not winced, with a slight quirk of his mouth. "Así se hace," he said. Thus it is done.

"Good as new," Wright said. "Barring gangrene."

Hilliard said to the old man's questioning eyes, "The friend thanks you."

Dr. Elizondo nodded politely and for a moment, on the ancient weed-tufted paving stones, they stood awkwardly, without speaking. There seemed to be nothing to say, until Wright, twisting to reach his hip with his right hand, brought out a wallet. Hilliard saw suddenly that he was very angry.

Deirdre said, "Wright!"

The doctor looked at the billfold and at the sheaf of money that Wright's finger had brought half into view. Hilliard said sharply, "Put that away!"

The corners of Wright's mouth turned downward in perverse amusement. "I pay my way," he said. "Ask him how much."

Even as Hilliard spoke, he felt the hurt shock in Deirdre's eyes as they swung to his face. He knew that it was the end of something and he didn't care. "You bastard!" he said to Wright. "You complete and arrogant son of a bitch!"

Staring back, Wright was not grinning now, but after a long moment he lowered his eyes, slipped the wallet into his side pocket, and stood looking away, strumming the thumb that stuck out of his bandage against the fingers of his left hand, in an odd gesture that Hilliard had seen him use in classrooms.

To the doctor finally, who had watched all of this with stoic perception, Hilliard spoke quietly: "There was a lack of comprehension. The friend . . ."

"I am sure," the doctor said.

But the politeness was in language only. It was not in his tone, or in the tawny-golden eyes that moved from Wright Forsythe to Hilliard now, and to the pretty woman beside them, flicking all three with condescension. In the eyes was the end of something else, a rebuff of sympathy and of friendship, old pride that had stood for long years alone and would stand again alone for the years that might remain. There was no anger. The doctor picked up his rod from where it stood against the ahuehuete tree, then leaned slightly toward the three Americans in a half-bow that conveyed not courtesy but dismissal.

"With your permission," he said, using the formal pronoun.

"Pass," Hilliard answered mechanically.

Without glancing at him again the doctor turned, and the three Americans stood silently watching as he walked away toward his room and the meager packing he had to do, the delicate, long, antiquated rod in his hand waving up and down with the slow rhythm of his old-man's stride.

"The Green Fly" was published in *Town & Country* (May 1954) and reprinted in *Prize Stories of 1955: The O. Henry Awards*, Paul Engle and Hansford Martin, eds. (Garden City: Doubleday and Company, 1955). Reprinted by permission of *Town & Country*.

Composed in Walbaum types with Engravers Roman initial.

THE AZTEC DOG

WHEN, ON SANDAL-SHUFFLING FEET, the young Indian maid had taken away the last plates, the two of them sat at the table smoking. The boy was reading a book, as he had been doing throughout the meal. The old man's bored forefinger made squares and triangles of crumbs of tobacco. The dining room was wide, floored and wainscoted with patterned green tiles, its three windows mullion-paned, but it had no ceiling and the roof that showed dimly above rough-milled rafters was of corrugated steel. Of furniture it held only the heavy table and the unmatched chairs in which they sat. In a corner, where the old man had tossed it before dinner, lay a quirt.

He had a gray mustache, cold dark eyes, and the face of a falcon, and wore a gray short riding-jacket and a white shirt buttoned at the throat without a tie.

He said distantly, "Would you want a game of checkers?"

The boy raised book-focused blue eyes. It was poetry, the old man knew. He had glanced through the book where it lay on a chair that afternoon and had seen that it was poetry, in English. Not even good poetry, as far as he considered himself qualified to judge . . .

The boy said in formula, "No. No, thanks."

He had been living at the hacienda for six weeks and had learned nearly all of his Spanish, which was good enough, in that time. It was one of the reasons given for his being there, to learn Spanish. When his father came again he would perhaps notice its excellence, not that the old man, whose name was Fernando Iturriaga, cared greatly.

Nor did he care about the checkers; the invitation was a nightly convention. At the beginning of the six weeks while feeling each other's temper they had played every evening. Later less, and later still not at all . . . But he went through the ritual of the invitation each night because irony and formality made living with the boy possible. He would have enjoyed carrying the formality to the point of coffee and cigarettes in the salón de estar, but that was not feasible because the salón, like the rest of the house except the dining room and two bedrooms and a kitchen, was without even a steel roof above it. Raw edges of mortared masonry left white marks on your clothing if you walked much about the unfinished parts of the house, which had been unfinished for eighteen years. The porch lacked railings, and outside the back door gaped a staired, never-covered cellar entrance into which a hog had once fallen to break three of its legs. Much pork, that had been . . .

Rats danced sometimes in the moonlight on the tiles of the salón de estar. Fernando Iturriaga had seen them dancing there. It had seemed well.

The boy coughed and lit another cigarette. The old man went to the window and swung it open and looked out in the late dusk at his flower garden beneath old aguacate trees. Pallid small roses speckled the gloom and he smelled them. From a hole in the great wall beyond the garden, water he could not see trickled audibly. He was reassured by the roses and the sound of water running from a wall his people had built two hundred years before, and by the knowledge that among the roots of the aguacates violets bloomed as they had since his mother's time.

For a wife his father had gone to Spain—to Asturias—and she had brought the gardening with her to the moist valley where the hacienda spread, big in those days. His father's family had been hard, harsh, rawhide people, precipitate in pleasure and in work, and it was only now, after nearly seventy years of living, that Fernando Iturriaga could feel a little of his mother in himself.

When the boy came back with the blue-glass liter bottle of aguardiente it was his turn to be ironic. He set it on the table and asked Fernando Iturriaga if he wanted a drink.

As always, the old man refused. He drank, sometimes too much, but not with the boy. He valued the formality too highly.

The boy's father planned, or said he planned, to make the hacienda into a guest ranch. Fernando Iturriaga believed by now that the boy, who was there because he had slapped a professor, or had fecundated a girl, or something of that sort, was the only guest this particular guest ranch was ever likely to have.

Not that he wanted more.

Watching the boy pour yellowish liquor into a glass, he said, "You rode into the upper valley today?"

"Yes."

The boy took a piece of bread and soaked it in the liquor. Fernando Iturriaga heard a quick tapping of claws on the tiles.

"You shouldn't," he said. "I've told you, with the elections coming on. You went into the cantina?"

"I do every day," the boy said. "Vidal! Look, Vidal!"

"You shouldn't," the old man repeated, risking a loss of formality in the irritation that cooled his belly when he thought of the boy speaking with the peasants of the upper valley in a brushwood bar, about Fernando Iturriaga.

The boy said indifferently, "Oh, it's all right. I get along with them."

The dog barked, dancing on quick white feet. It was tiny, brindle above and white below, with fragile legs and shadings of black about its muzzle and eyes. Before the American boy had come, the dog had never entered the house, though Fernando Iturriaga had played with it on the veranda in the afternoons, quietly, and had dropped bits of tortilla and meat to it out of his dining-room window when it begged from the the garden. It was two years old and he had named it, whimsically, Vidal, because in his country's capital there was a street called that where the French mistress of a friend of his had once lived. It was of the ancient breed of alert Mexican mongrels from which the Aztecs had bred their even tinier bald dogs, and was symptomatic of a gentleness that had troubled him now for five or six years.

He had never seen gentleness as desirable, except in women. Insufficiently gentle, his own wife had left him eighteen years before, taking his sons, when the house was half-rebuilt and the money had run out and she had found out about his relations with the cook they had had then.

He conceded now that there had been enough for her to be ungentle about. But he had several grandchildren whom he had never seen.

"Stand up," the boy said.

Fernando Iturriaga watched as the dog skipped on two legs before the boy. It snatched the piece of liquor-wetted bread from the air when he dropped it, gulping without chewing.

"Salud," the boy said sipping from his glass and grinning. "Salud, Vidal."

The old man said stubbornly, "They're troublesome people. Sooner or later you'll meet one of them drunk."

"One?" the boy said and laughed, glancing at him. "The half of them always are. They let me shoot a pistol at a cactus today."

"Sons of whores!" Fernando Iturriaga said forcibly through clamped teeth.

And wished that he had not, since it only meant that the boy had once more broken through the formality. He sat for a moment swallowing anger like spittle, then went to his room to change his slippers back to half-boots and to shave. When he passed through the dining room twenty minutes later the dog was drunk. It had no capacity for the liquor. Neither had the boy, who crouched laughing on the floor, teasing it. It ran in short circles about him, yapping and dashing in to snap at the flickering hands.

Fernando Iturriaga thought that it was much like the rats' dance in the drawing room.

In the moonwashed court before the house a fresh horse stood saddled, as it did every night whether or not he wanted to use it. From the great wall's shadow two Indians' cigarettes pulsed; they murmured inarticulate courtesies and he grunted back in the same spirit. Leading the horse through the gate, he mounted in the road by the river. The horse shied, bouncing under him, a gray he had not ridden for several days. As he reined it into darkness under the cottonwoods along the little river, he was conscious of the valley's wide concavity to either side, more conscious than he had usually been when it had belonged to him. He had been there only occasionally during most of that time. At the valley's mouth, below the town toward which he rode, the earth fell away two thousand feet to malarial jungle, where the river ran turbidly wide to the sea. On clear days, from the flat top of a granary at the hacienda, the old man had often seen the shimmer of sun on salt water a hundred kilometers to the east.

Inland, the valley rose and flattened into a grassy bowl beneath the high peaks. His family's cattle had grazed there for seven generations, but now it was checkered into the irrigated holdings of Indian agrarians. In the days of the change he had killed one of them. That had cost him a good part of the money he had had left, and they had nearly killed him later, skipping a bullet off one of his ribs as he passed a canebrake, six months before his wife had left him.

In the mornings the miserable dog had hangovers. Like a Christian, with thirst and groaning, and when you rolled back the thin black lids the balls of its eyes were laced with blood.

He thought the gringos had begun to spawn rare ones, finally. Maybe they always had, but before, except for their nervous accessible women in the capital and the resorts, they had sent usually the meaty big ones like the boy's father, who knew cattle or oil or cotton or some other one thing completely and whom Fernando Iturriaga had always disliked a little, because they profited from change and he did not.

But without obsession. Without what he thought of as the national obsession . . . He rode along on the pleasantly tense gray gelding toward the town where he would clatter dominoes and sip habanero with a drugstore owner and a grain dealer and a fat incompetent doctor who—though, with less reason than he, they shared his political bitterness—were not really friends of his. The kind of people he had chosen for friends lived in France, or the capital, or New York. Or were dead. He had not chosen well; he recognized that. Even the survivors had comfortably forgotten him when he had left that world.

But he had lived for five years in Paris and had known how to eat and drink, and had bayed after actresses and gringas and such quarry, as a man of his background had been expected to do, and had spoken good English and French.

The gringo boy and his father did not know about all that, not even about the English, which he had never spoken with them. They thought of him, he knew, as decayed local gentry left over from feudalism.

That kind of feudalism had not existed since Iturbide, or before. But the old man granted that he was, at least, sufficiently decayed.

Riding, he thought without obsession about the gringo boy, and the dog, and gringos, and actresses with generals in long touring-cars riding out to bull ranches, and how there ought to be green peace in the valley when, finally, you wanted peace.

DRINK MADE THE BOY DIZZY. He did not especially like it. It was a thing to rasp the old man's feelings with, like speaking of the cantina in the upper valley. His name was John Anders and he was at the ranch because he had driven a pink unmuffled sports car into a culvert rail near Amarillo, on his way to Hollywood with money from a considerable check forged in his father's name.

He had not known why Hollywood. . . . An unpleasant hitch-hiker with a ducktail haircut, sitting beside him, had died in the crash but the boy had waked up on his back among prickly pears, with a state patrolman bending cold-eyed over him and nothing at all broken in his slight body.

"No," he said to the dog sternly. "You've had enough."

He put down the book. It was Dylan Thomas. The boy's mother had had two tense short stories published when young and all his life, in lieu of comprehension, had besieged him with literature. Some taste for it had stuck. He was nineteen, with one expulsion from college behind him and another school to try in the autumn, four months ahead, and for two or three years poetry and kindred queernesses had been serving him for armor in prep schools and around country-club swimming pools, where he did not fit well. Queernesses and a willingness to fight.

His mother had wept emptily in her dove-gray bedroom and he had watched her, not for the first time or the fiftieth, and afterward had listened to his father's bellowing querulity in the same mood, and had ridden with him on the peremptory trip down into Mexico, not-listening all the way. He had learned to do that before he had been twelve.

When he got up from the table he found that the raw aguardiente had him in the legs, if not in the head. He lurched; the quickly counterpoising sole of his half-boot screeched in unswept grit on the tiles. He stood, resisting the sudden idea of going out to see the Indian maid in her room beyond the laundry court.

Foggy guilt swirled in him when he thought of the maid, and he cursed aloud.

Turning, he walked through a hall to the old man's room and snapped on its light. It was monastic under the bare bulb's glare—a blue floor, a dresser of scarred oak, a table, a bed made of scroll-bent rods of tarnished brass, and a little wall-Virgin. The boy stood resenting the room. The old man's dignity was there like a smell, but did not explain itself. On the dresser stood a silver-framed photo-graph, cloud-haired, of an actress he somehow recognized to be Jean Harlow. It was a publicity picture of a special vintage, but was affectionately inscribed and signed. It did not fit with anything else that was there. He stared at it.

It stared back.

Him, the old bastard, the boy thought—but principally with puzzlement.

In the beginning he and the maid had talked at night in the laundry court outside her door. She was shy, and alone a good bit, and giggled at his ragged confident Spanish, correcting him. Her people had worked there always and she would not talk to the boy about Don Fernando. She was not unhappy. She had a young man in the upper valley who possessed some education and would one day, maybe soon, be a power in the ejido there. But she saw him only on Sundays; Don Fernando did not encourage the upper-valley people at the hacienda.

"You have no life at all," the boy had said to her roughly, three nights before. He felt his own sophistication to be relative wisdom, and was enraged that ignorance and immobility could so brace the contentment she professed to feel.

"None of you do," he said. "The ejido! Maybe they'll let him weigh sacks of grain."

"Maybe," the girl said, placid in the dim light that came through the open door of her room. "Maybe so, señorito," she said. "But he won't end in the cantina, waving a machete with shouts. And there is no hurry . . ."

Feeling wise still, and miserable, the boy said, "There's always a hurry."

"Not in the valley," the girl said quietly.

She was young, with the Indian shyness and a round, brown,

velvet face. Abruptly he put his hand up to her cheek. She sucked in breath sharply through her teeth and ran inside, closing the door behind her.

That had been all, but it had shamed him; he had not wanted to be alone with her since.

He made a big embarrassed X-mark with his finger on the glass that shielded inexplicable Jean Harlow against the eatings of time, and left the room, the little dog's claws clicking along behind him.

He would apologize.

You rode the bay horse (your father having paid for it sight unseen when Don Fernando had said someone was offering it for sale) hard up the valley by the river, under the big cottonwoods, and then left the river before you reached the cantina, not wanting to go there first. Rising, the horse's flanks straining against your calves in labored effort of ascent, you passed ox-carts and strings of timid people with loads on their backs, in a roadlet that ran between ter-races of irrigated grain and fiber, green. The world there smelled of green, and leather, and dung, and of woodsmoke and toasted maize in the huts between the fields. On the higher mountains, mists lay. The boy had not in his life known a freshness like that of the green upper valley as your horse mounted its side toward the mists.

When you were under the mists but not in them, you came to an almost vertical belt of cactus and stone and gray-green clawed plants, and trails were there that led to villages in the sierra. Clank-ing, clicking shout-harried burro trains came along them. One trail ran simply parallel to the river, far below you now. Taking that trail, you stopped somewhere along it and dismounted and sat on a rock, the cold feel of the mists above you on your neck, the horse tearing irritably at clumps of inedibility among the stones, the quilt-patched sunlit green of the valley troughed below you, smoke-tufted, split by the roving line of the river's trees.

Sometimes he would sit there for hours smoking Elegantes, coughing-strong. Once he yelled aloud in ferocious exultation of aloneness, "By God!"

The upper valley was, too, the brushwood cantina on the way home, and the taste of tepid black beer with loud peasants crowding toward his oddness. They liked him. He liked them, or thought he did, and was a little afraid of them—it was the main reason that he went there. He would not talk to them about Fernando Iturriaga, toward whom they felt the frank reflex hatred of crows for a crippled owl. They asked him about the States United, and the flogging of wetbacks, and told him with pride that they were Reds. Once, when a stumbling-drunk Red with a drawn machete had cursed the boy and had gone outside to ride the bay horse away, one of the others had knocked him from the saddle with a shovel and had courteously tied the horse again to its post.

"It is that at times, one drinks," the courteous Red had said.

"It is so," John Anders said with the solemnity of that dialect, and they laughed to one another to hear their intonation in his mouth, and slapped his shoulder.

Sometimes he ran the bay horse all the way back to the hacienda, a long, pounding lope downhill, and walked him cool in the courtyard there, and rubbed him slick with a cob.

The fact was, he liked living in the valley. It was a recent admission, and it had had no effect on his pricking-war with the old man, who perplexed him. He had been at war with many adults, but had managed to touch most of them more painfully than he could touch Fernando Iturriaga.

Maybe, he thought, it was because the others had given a damn.

He paused in the open back door, blinking against night's dark assault, and saw a yellow line beneath the maid's door. When he started down the unrailed steps, the aguardiente took him to the right. His foot pawed vacancy. Blackness jerked him cartwheeling down into the unroofed cellar-pit; he landed among shards of bottle-glass, right-side-up and sitting, his right leg twisted back under and behind him.

At first he felt only the shallowness of force-emptied lungs, and fought to get his breath. Then a knowledge of the leg ascended through him like nausea. In sick shock, he knew that he was about to faint, but the little dog's whine cut into his ken and it was jumping at his face, licking. He took it in his hands and held it, speaking to it as it squirmed and licked and the sickness went down. Then he waited while the dull but sharpening pain rose.

His hand was bleeding. The Indian girl was standing above him at the edge of the hole, uttering a mooing sound. He supposed he had made noise.

"Look for help," he told her.

She went away, still mooing. Without shifting, the boy held the dog and met the leg-pain full-face and decided that it would probably be bearable. She came back with the gardener Elifonso. Elifonso gritted down the steep steps of the pit and loomed over the boy, smelling of peppers.

"If this is bad, señorito!" he said. "If this is very bad!"

"Don't touch me yet," the boy said.

But Elifonso grabbed him by the armpits and yanked upward, and the boy yelled and struck at him, and when Elifonso let go the hurt was twice what it had yet been. The boy's hand touched a stick; he flailed out with it and Elifonso went back up the steps. The boy shouted upper-valley words at him and the maid and they murmured between themselves in the darkness, above him. He quieted, ashamed but still angry. After a time he asked the girl to bring the bottle of aguardiente from the dining room, and when she gave it to him he drank five gulps, cold and oily, without stopping. It warmed him and pushed the pain down for a while, and he drank some more. Then he vomited, and for a long long time sat coldly full of pain while the quiet Indian voices murmured on above him.

Finally a flashlight glared down into his face, reawakening dull rage. Fernando Iturriaga held it.

After a moment he said quietly to the boy, "You are a disaster."

John Anders said, "You aren't going to touch me."

"Go for the doctor Rodríguez," the old man told Elifonso.

Walking around the pit and down its steps, he knelt beside the boy and played the flashlight on the leg.

"How handsome," he said.

"Don't touch me," the boy said, and raised his stick.

Fernando Iturriaga took it from his hand and dropped it among the broken glass.

"Boy, I will touch you," he said. "I will hurt you too. Shut up. You, Luz, come."

They were careful, but the pain was a twisting shaft up inside him, though it seemed that when the responsibility was no longer yours maybe the pain was not yours either. The maid mooed all the way. When they had him on the bed in his room and had cut away the trouserleg and were waiting for the doctor, the leg as straight as they had dared to put it with the big splinter of bone sticking through the flesh above the knee, the old man said matter-of-factly,

"It will have hurt like ten demons."

The boy rolled his head negatively.

"Don't lie," the old man said. "I know hurts. It will have hurt."

He considered, hard eyes candid. "Fat Rodríguez will hurt you more when he comes," he said. "He drank a lot this evening."

Weakened by the bed's comfort against his back, the boy began to cry. He cried because he hurt, and because the doctor would hurt him again, and because the old man clearly did not give a damn about him, and because he was a thousand miles from even a home that he despised—having, therefore, no home—and because the green pleasant foreign valley had turned on him and bitten him and was foreign now altogether, and hateful. He laid his forearm across his eyes and sobbed.

Astoundingly, the old man was patting his shoulder.

"Child, child," he said. "It will pass."

The boy stopped sobbing, and after a time uncovered his eyes. The formal hawk face was smiling gently at him.

"I suppose it will," he said.

"Yes."

"All right," the boy said.

HE WAS LISTENING.

"At least a telegram," the boy's meaty father said earnestly, down-wiping sweaty hands against the front of gabardine trousers. "Don Fernando, a letter that sat in the club in Mexico City for three weeks was . . ."

Fernando Iturriaga dropped his shoulders, flashed the cupped palms of his hands briefly upward, and turned away, unapologetic. He felt some pity for the big man, but he felt a little bit nationally obsessed, too. He considered that a telegram would likely have cooled in that club for three weeks also, awaiting the big man's arrival, and even had he known how to telephone him he doubted that he would have tried to do so. The bone had been set.

Crookedly, yes, healing with a bend like a pruned tree-fork. Fat Rodríguez, gold-spectacled, standing nervous now against the whitewashed wall while the slim young doctor from the capital felt with long fingers the boy's humped femur—Rodríguez had thought of a thick fee but had not earned it. But Rodríguez had been all that there was; even the boy had understood that.

The slim capitaleño did not glance toward Rodríguez as he spoke to the boy's father.

"It will need re-breaking," he said. "There is also infection. A question of various months."

"Like hell they're going to bust it again," the boy on the bed said in English.

"Close your mouth," his father said. "For Christ's sake, you make any more trouble now and I'll . . ."

"I'm not going to let them," the boy said unemotionally. "I watched them with Phil Evridge at school and he still limps."

The big man's voice shrilled. Rodríguez, his nervousness requiring expression, said to the slim doctor, "It is that sometimes, despite what one can do . . ."

The slim doctor turned on him for an instant two liquid slits, said, "Sí, señor!" and looked away, closing thin lips in punctuation.

Fat Rodríguez shuffled.

Fernando Iturriaga grinned and turned to go outside. My nationals, he thought. But the slim contemptuous capitaleño was one of his nationals, too. Did he mean, then, those of his nationals who would end in a place like this valley?

Maybe.

On the gallery he dropped into a big hard chair of aguacate-wood and the little dog's nose shocked cold against his dangling hand. He caressed the bulb of its head and not looking felt its warm eyelids with his thumb.

Changing, he, gentling. A week after the boy's fall, three agrarians from the upper valley had come to the hacienda. With some pleasure he had gone out to tell them to go away again. But in their stubbled faces before he spoke, and in their politeness, he saw an actual concern for the boy. He had not expected that. Quietly, he led them himself to the boy's room, and afterward spoke to them about the year's crops.

You are effeminated, he told himself.

Prepared for the big-meaty-gringo anger, he was a little disappointed when the father came out, alone, with cold control on his face.

He said, "Don Fernando, it was not well done."

"No."

"I don't mean that fat fool!"

His voice trilled at the end and Fernando Iturriaga glanced up hopefully, but the control was still there. The blue capable eyes glittered down at him like tile-chips.

"There will not be a guest ranch."

"No," the old man said, and sighed courteously. Even in his childhood, the line of the mountains where he was now looking had seemed to have the shape of a woman lying on her side. As a boy he had ridden there, on the high rocky slopes under the clouds, and the young gringo had told him of doing the same.

Gently he pinched the small dog's ear.

"What a very great shame," he said in exact British English.

"By God!" Anders said, and stood above him for a moment longer, and then went out to the long brown-and-cream car to bring back a blanket.

The old man watched as all of them, the maid and the gardener and the slim doctor and even still-hopeful Rodríguez, bore armloads of books and clothes to load them into the luggage compartment. At last the capitaleño and Elifonso brought the blanketed boy between them through the door. They paused with him beside the chair.

"Well," the boy said. "Many thanks."

"Nothing, son," Fernando Iturriaga said. "May they make you a good oilman."

Crooked amusement split the boy's face and he said a word from the upper valley that caused the gardener to laugh and Fernando Iturriaga to smile. They carried him to the car, and the old man watched still while the father strode past him unspeaking and managed to direct them into ramming the boy's head into the car's doorpost and the back of the front seat. At the end, the maid Luz ran out with the whittled crutches that she had bought for the boy in the village, but which he had refused to try.

By then, however, the car was moving; the maid stopped behind it holding the crutches and began foolishly to weep. Fernando Iturriaga saw the flash of the boy's face turned toward him from the back seat. In the narrow gateway of the wall a stone tilted the big car's rear, and he felt a reprehensible surge of national pleasure as its finned fender scraped against the arch.

Fee-less, fat Rodríguez stood in the courtyard with the maid, his hands clenching and unclenching at his sides. Then he walked with head down and wagging to his old Ford, and drove away in it.

"Well, then," Fernando Iturriaga said aloud and for some reason in French.

He stared across the sunlit, slab-paved court at a section of wall where, mixed among the pocks of revolutionary bullets which in 1911 had killed his brother and a cousin and the peons who had stuck by them, were newer gray marks where he and the boy's father had held pistol practice some months before, speaking of the grandeurs of guest-ranching while they fired. It gave him satisfaction to remember how easily he had outshot the big American; then it disturbed him to recognize the satisfaction.

You are becoming nationally obsessed, he told himself.

He felt quite alone. Diffidently, the Indian girl Luz came and asked if he would want his midday meal. He said that certainly he would. Hearing his calm tone as permissive, she said, "They left an envelope with money. The big one said it was for room and food."

"Shut up," he said.

"Caray!" she protested.

"Shut up. What was he doing there in the laundry court that night, beside your room?"

Offended, she went back inside. He was half-certain she was his daughter, the child of the cook who had cost him his wife and sons. The cook had died quietly and quickly one winter, after the way of Indians, and the child had grown up here. He would give her something when she married her prim young man from the ejido.

Not much. There was unhappily little to give.

The old man walked to his room, looked about it for a moment, and in leaving lightly, affectionately, flicked the picture of Jean Harlow with his forefingernail. He had not known her. The picture had been some sort of joke from a friend, its point now lost. Or maybe he had bet and won it.

He went around to the shaded garden between his breakfast window and the wall. At its gate he examined the small perfect roses with pleasure, and he moved into the green gloom of the great aguacates slowly, so that hens in the path edged aside with only ritual noises. He would tell Elifonso that the violets needed water; the outlet in the wall when he looked at it was closed with a whittled plug. Diverted river-water, cool and vocal, ran in all the circumference of the peripheral wall. Two centuries before when his people

had raised it—first, his father had said, the wall first of all, for protection—the old Moorish water-love had caused them to build conduits within it that ran to the houses, the gardens, the laundry court,
the stables. As a child he had leaned against the wall and listened
while the water spoke its words.

Now he went to it again and put his ear against it, and heard
the water. In the pigpens these days there was only a drip from hairy
green slime; he had meant for years to have the conduits cleaned. A
man lived in the town who could do that, somehow, with hook-
ended wires.

Beside him there was a sound. It was the dog, squatting, one
foot held delicately before it in the air as though in supplication. Its
bright dark eyes were on his face.

"Vidal," the old man said.

The dog yipped in answer to its name.

Fernando Iturriaga said, "You miss him. Poor Vidal."

The dog whined and pumped the air with its foot, and sat up
as it had been taught. Commandingly it barked. The old man leaned
down and picked it up, stroking its head as he glanced about.
Against one of the aguacates leaned a section of rusted pipe. It had
a familiar look. Holding the dog gently in the crook of his arm he
walked to the tree and picked up the pipe, half a meter long, heavy,
plugged with dirt. They had used it one year, he recalled now, as a
stake for strung sweet-peas.

He hefted it, and then in one deft motion, with Indian grace,
he swung the little dog downward, holding its hind legs together in
his left hand, and even as it yelped in surprise he hit it a swift un-
cruel blow on its skull.

At the base of the tree he laid the dog and the pipe down beside each other, beyond the violets his mother had brought from
Asturias, and rubbed the palms of his hands horseman-wise against
his hips.

Now, he thought. Now maybe we will have peace here.

Written in 1954, "The Aztec Dog" was published in Colorado Quarterly (Summer
1960) and reprinted in Prize Stories of 1962: The O. Henry Awards, Richard Poirier,
ed. (Garden City: Doubleday, 1963).

Composed in Fairfield types with Legend initial.

IN THE ABSENCE OF HORSES

AUTHOR'S NOTE: *During the winter of 1954–55 I lived on Tenerife in the Canaries, and after I left there in April, heading toward England and the States, I stopped in Madrid for a while, saw some old friends, and attended the San Isidro corridas, having during the past two years developed a sort of standard foreigner's fascination with bullfights. I had written only two or three pieces on the subject, however, and wasn't very fond of any of them, including the one below. In part this was because I didn't trust whatever there was in me that liked bullfights, and in part also because to write about such matters in English positions you within the immense shadow of Papa Hemingway, not a comfortable place to reside, at least for me.*

    The dollar-peseta exchange at that time was such that even an impecunious type like me could afford a couple of barrera seats for all seven of that festival's corridas, and a tauromaniacal American girl, a friend of long standing, went to them with me. One afternoon we were privileged to witness the single loveliest faena I have ever seen, performed by a scrawny ill-favored Venezuelan named César Girón, who at one point brought a fine honest bull clear around himself with four separate, timed, graceful passes of the muleta, never moving his feet. That faena was a stroke of felicity since to my recollection I never saw any more bullfights anywhere after the ones that week. Maybe all the good, miserable, or indifferent corridas I had attended in Spain, and the interest I had expended on that bloody art, were justified by my being able to see the perfect beauty of Girón's achievement that day, or maybe not.

    Incidentally, when Girón made his triumphal tour of the ring after killing that bull cleanly on his first thrust with the sword, holding up the two ears he had been awarded, and people were tossing roses and hats to him, my fair friend in exaltation took off one of her red shoes and threw it. Girón picked it up and grinned broadly at her and kept it, so that later we had to go to his dressing room to retrieve the damned thing—she wouldn't go alone as she was expected to do.

That embarrassment I later tried to set down in a short story but it didn't come out right.

The story that follows grew out of the only occasion on which I witnessed anything even faintly resembling the old brutal and dangerous village bull-baitings which had pretty much disappeared by the time I got to Spain but had flourished in earlier times. I used to have a little 19th-century book called Las Capeas *in which a number of those gory affairs were rendered in all their awfulness and grim humor; I intended at one time to translate it for Knopf, but never got around to doing so.*

The sketchily depicted girl character in this story has some things in common with the one who threw that red shoe. . . .

HE LAND WAS WIDE AND BROWN and rolling and touched here and there with the wind-stirred green wheat of early May. We turned into a dirt road through an irrigated valley with a few peasants grubbing in garden patches, and at the river some unhopeful Sunday anglers standing along the bank. From the ridge beyond the valley I counted five castles at one time, all far away. The wind hissed at the tops of the closed car windows, and my older friend who was driving, a painter, muttered once or twice when gusts made the heavy car rock.

Loeches had its own castle, a small broken one above the pueblo that was spraddled up a slope. We came at it from below and saw no bull ring, and I remarked that the place didn't look large enough to have one.

The girl stated with certainty, "There *is* a ring. They said so."

She knew the people who were going to fight the bulls. Once in the village, we had no need to ask about the ring. At the main plaza oxcarts blocked the street, the gaps between them filled with upright peeled logs lashed together. People stood around talking and from inside the plaza came the noise of a crowd and a brassy blare of band music.

A brown-faced, hatless man in a black suit came toward us with a pad of tickets in his hand and I got out of the car to meet him. "How many?" he asked.

"Three," I said. "They're having the corrida right here in the plaza?"

"That's right. It's a miserable wind for the bulls, isn't it?"

It was. It whipped at the dresses of the women on the carts and they squinted into it. When my companions emerged from the car the ticket man eyed the girl, startled, and asked if we were Americans. When I said yes, he said, "There are special arrangements. Will you follow me?"

We walked behind as he ducked through a narrow gap between carts, the burly painter with his stiff leg squeezing through with difficulty. The plaza was wide and unevenly sloping, its bare, rocky dirt troughed by rains. There were sidewalks in front of the houses that lined it, some scattered small trees in bud, and in its center a stone fountain and drinking trough with a concrete angel's statue holding a tilted jug from which, however, no water flowed. All of the tributary streets were plugged. In one side street a truck holding three of the big boxes in which fighting bulls are transported was backed up to the square. Women jammed the carts and the windows and balconies of the houses facing inward, and out in the open ground bereted male villagers and peasants stood around in loud groups. Nearly all of them looked happily drunk, or nearly so.

Leaving the girl and the painter to wait beneath the decorated balcony of the Ayuntamiento, the ticket seller led me to another side street where stood a wooden box office.

"Three," he told the man inside. "Three Americans."

The man fished up three large rectangles of white invitation cardboard. In English they announced themselves as subscription tickets for a special novillada featuring Alberto Díaz, nicknamed "Madrileñito," and the American Harry L. Whitney. In a lower corner was the price, one hundred pesetas.

At the Plaza Monumental de Toros in Madrid, where that afternoon we had passed up one of the first regular bullfights of the season because the girl knew Harry L. Whitney, you could buy a very fine seat in the shade for less than a hundred pesetas. It was not a village price. I began to have the trapped sensation you get when you're being fleeced in a foreign country. Among Spaniards it was a feeling that came only rarely, but it turned up sometimes. The first ticket seller was watching me with concern, and I frowned for him.

"Listen," I said. "Three hundred is a little heavy. What goes on?"

"It's a subscription," he answered more loudly than he had to, and glanced at the man in the window, whose eyes had gone a bit steely. "It's that the bulls cost a lot. The seats are special, you know, on the balcony of the Ayuntamiento itself."

"They dreamed it up," said a young man in a tweed jacket, in English. He indicated the man in the booth. "It was this manager's idea."

I said, "I only meant . . ."

"I know," he said. "It's to pay for the animals, but damn few Americans showed up. Listen, give him a hundred and fifty. Give him two hundred. You know."

I didn't know, but I'd begun to feel cheap and dug out a couple of bills to shove them through the window. The steely-eyed type protested, and the American told him nervously, in bad Spanish, that it was enough. "Where are your people?" he asked me. "Come on, I'll show you where you sit. Stand, rather. Frankly, this is all an unholy mess."

"You're Whitney?"

Staring, he said, "Hell, no, I'm Judd Thomas. Harry and I went to college together." A hard puff of air thrust at our backs and he took out a comb to smooth his hair. "Look at that damn wind," he said. "I didn't know it was going to be like this. Harry didn't either. He thought there was a regular ring. There aren't even going to be any horses, to wear the bulls down for the kill."

When we found my friends under the Ayuntamiento's balcony the young man gaped at the girl in recognition, and groaned. He said that since she had been personally invited we weren't supposed to have to pay for tickets at all. But he didn't say anything about getting my money back, and I surmised that he didn't want to face the steely-eyed box-office man again.

He led us upstairs and out onto the long iron balcony decked in red-and-yellow bunting, where a little band was braying out pasodobles and jotas. Among a sprinkling of other foreigners and a good many well-dressed Spaniards we found standing room beneath the faded, red-painted arrow-sheaf of the Falange that marked the building as an official place. The wind assaulted the balcony and plastered our clothing against us. In the plaza below, it raised dust devils, darkened the green water in the fountain's drinking trough, and buffeted the noisy groups of men. Leather winebottles circulated among them, and other people passed in and out of little bars in the side streets.

Strangely, many of the local men carried cut lengths of green cane. Young ones, some of them clearly not villagers, took turns running at one another like bulls. Those being charged made awkward verónicas with raincoats, or putting sticks inside their jackets executed brave muleta passes. A middle-aged local in a purple shirt, very drunk and with a half-inch of black beard, grabbed somebody's raincoat and essayed a farol, a swirling, upward lighthouse pass, but the raincoat got wrapped around his head and he tripped, sitting down hard in a puddle of mud beside the fountain. Younger men ringed around laughing and pushed at him as he tried to get up.

Thomas said, "How the hell are you going to have a bullfight in a mess like this?"

The girl said, "If you don't know, who does? What's holding things up?"

In answer, a drum rolled and the band gave a blare and flourish of the kind that is supposed to start things moving. Nothing else happened and the people in the square kept milling.

I asked Thomas how long Whitney had been fighting bulls.

"Couple of years or so," he said gloomily. "But the others were in rings, with horses and picadors. Some kind of a ring. Not like this. He's killed seven or eight." Suddenly he pointed to a side street where several men stood in trim, tight-fitting Andalusian country costume, fighting capes over their arms, faces shaded by flat-crowned, flat-brimmed Cordovese hats. "There he is!" Thomas said. "In the light-blue suit. Hey, Harry!"

His voice was lost in the din from the square, but a moment later Whitney glanced up of his own accord and waved, a tall young man, blond and lean and unsmiling. Two American-looking youths with complicated cameras were taking pictures of him. I said it looked as though we had press coverage.

Thomas answered darkly, "They *say* they're press. You wouldn't believe all the freeloaders . . ."

Frowning, he excused himself and left. The band blared and flourished again, and two Civil Guards with slung rifles started trying to shove the crowd out of the plaza. But there were too many of them, and finally the guards made gestures of futility toward the mayor on the balcony, and the band repeated itself. Workmen put a ramp up to the bed of the truck that held the bull boxes and started hammering at one box's latch, whereupon panic flowed and the crowd began to melt.

In the rush for cover, those who were too boiled to react were dragged along by their friends, and the center of the square emptied except for a few people in trees and a clot of them perched on the plinth of the fountain's concrete angel. Men were jammed under the carts and some clung monkey-like to window gratings. However, things relaxed for a spell when Alberto Díaz "Madrileñito" and Harry L. Whitney made their processional march to salute the mayor, squads of subordinate costumed peones at their shoulders. Then they disposed themselves about the margins of the square. Somebody's flat-brimmed Andalusian hat blew off and rolled like a tumbleweed in the fierce wind. The trumpet for the bull sounded.

Judd Thomas reappeared, sad-faced. "Harry lost at least three hundred bucks," he told us.

The painter said, "How? A pickpocket?"

"On tickets," Thomas answered impatiently. "They had to buy their own bulls and a fighting cow for the town."

Things began to fit together and I felt a little guilty, having believed it was to be a regular fight administered by the town. I apologized to Thomas for complaining about the price of the tickets.

"I told you," he said. "You weren't supposed to pay anything. Christ, what a botch this whole thing is."

With her eyes on the men trying to open the bull box the girl gestured angrily at us. She worked for the American Military Mission in Madrid, and had gone to the summer university in Mexico while in college, and she took all bulls with a seriousness that could scare you sometimes. "Here he comes!" she now said. "You two shut up."

He came out nicely, skidding a little on the board ramp but recovering to charge the cape of a nearby waiting peon. Though small, a standard three-year-old novillo, he was tightly proportioned and had good horns. He circled the plaza on quick trotting feet, head high, led on by the caping peones, and the crowd shouted happily. At a house window a covey of young girls squealed each time he drove at a yielding cape, but even with the peones, who didn't take unnecessary chances, you could see that the wind was making trouble. As the bull ran at them the wind would often flick the gaudy swirling cloths against their bodies so that they had to leap backward.

Thomas said, "Frankly, I'm nervous as hell."

Madrileñito came out with a cape, a slight, dark, good-looking boy whom I had seen fight in a regular novillada the year before. He shook the cape at the bull and shouted, "Ha, toro!" But the animal had taken a dislike to the yelling men on the fountain, and running there he thrust up at their legs with his horns. They clustered on the other side of the angel and kicked at his nose. The young girls squealed in unison.

Cape ready, Madrileñito advanced toward the fountain. The novillo charged him hard, then turned and charged again, and several times more, so that there was a series of pretty verónicas, with applause, before a gust of wind caught the cape and flattened it against the torero, forcing him to skip away from a vicious diverted stab of the horns. Moving in to help, his peones worked the bull toward the lee of a large house on the square's windward side, but when Madrileñito came there and waved them off and planted himself for more caping, the beast charged a group of arm-waving Castilians fifty yards away. Having emerged from beneath carts or inside them to watch, these gentry now scuttled back to refuge and the bull tried to follow, getting his head under one cart's bed and hooking, while men above him inside the vehicle whacked him with lengths of cane until he backed away.

And so it went, with scissor-kicking villagers dangling from tree limbs and getting the bull to charge so that they could swing up and then kick his departing rump as he passed beneath, and the Civil Guards trying vainly to move people back to safety. Finally, after missing one drunk by inches the bull caught another one on a sidewalk, bowling him over and then probing with his horns. But before he found flesh another man grabbed his tail and made him whirl until Madrileñito's peones came running with their capes.

Beside me the girl was weeping with laughter. So was nearly everybody else except Thomas, who said, "They had to buy the town a cow. They bought them two God-damn bulls too."

"Somebody's going to get hurt," the painter said in a somber voice, though he had been laughing as hard as anyone. The girl glanced at him strangely before turning back to watch the mêlée.

There was plenty more of the same. The peones managed to put in five pairs of banderillas and one of the American photographers got chased around the fountain by the bull and broke his camera. Madrileñito watched the whole thing sadly, then began his doomed faena, the final stage of the fight. Aside from the furious wind that destroyed his passes with the red muleta on its stick, and the crazy crowd, his bull was still too fresh because there were no picadores, and by now had established querencias, preferred spots in which to make a stand. The mud puddle by the fountain was his favorite place, and there the torero finally went in with his sword to kill. Killing in a querencia is dangerous and hard. Madrileñito tried four times as correctly as he could, hitting bone, waiting while the bull made side-charges at villagers. But at last he got the blade in, and the novillo staggered across the plaza to lie down on the sidewalk just below us, head nodding, and die.

Though the crowd was in high good humor, applause was short because most of those who might have applauded were headed for the dead animal to jab at him and flog him vengefully with canes. Small boys poked their fingers into the gaping sword holes and squabbled over banderillas. Shooing everyone off, a butcher in a white apron cut the bull's throat and exercised artificial respiration to squeeze out its blood, which flowed in a stream to the cobbled gutter and pooled there.

Thomas said, "Good God!" An American lady and her blonde daughter left the balcony with set faces. When I looked at the painter he was staring down at the red pool in the gutter. A sensitive and kindly man, almost too gentle, he shook his head at me with a worried grin, and the girl began to laugh at our expressions. She laughed more than seemed necessary. In the absence of horses or mules, the butcher and four peasants dragged the dead bull with a rope to the side street where our car was parked. Stirring, Thomas told us he had to go and make sure that all the meat got saved for the two toreros, to whom it belonged. The public refreshed itself from leather bottles or in the bars. Admiring and envious groups formed around those individuals who had managed to grab the bull's tail or to get their clothing torn.

They were reluctant to disperse when the trumpet brought in Whitney's novillo. It was smaller and more ungainly than Madrileñito's, but vigorous, and knocked over three locals in quick succession. Whitney's caping and that of his peones was perfunctory and wind-blown and devoted mainly to the salvation of peasants, and then Madrileñito placed four pairs of banderillas beautifully, citing the bull arrogantly while bouncing up and down on his toes, running diagonally across the animal's line of charge, rising and turning to plunge the gaudy barbed sticks vertically into the hump. It was so good that it shocked the crowd into silence for a moment and brought a stir of appreciation.

But the dusty shouting men with canes did not intend that the bull should be taken from them. Raucous, they moved in along the wind, and Whitney's faena had not a prayer. He got to work his bull perhaps a little more than the most active of the locals, but not much more. The two Civil Guards moved about the plaza hopelessly, whacking peasants with canes precisely as the peasants were whacking the bull. Disgust settled visibly on Whitney as he trudged along behind the confused bull, occasionally managing to divert its attention with his red cloth. Thomas mumbled beside me in sympathetic rage, and a nearby elderly patrician Spaniard, chuckling, said that it was all a great shame. He said the pueblo people were accustomed to the old illegal bull-baitings called capeas, and hated to see a beast wasted on just one man.

Finally, because he had no choice, Whitney decided to kill. The other torero and the peones offered him much friendly advice about it. He listened impassively, went to the bull, struck bone twice and was knocked down, and on the third try, despite a longlegged peasant who came looping in at the "moment of truth," got the sword in from the side. The novillo clung to life and he dispatched it with the stiff, short descabello sword, villagers panting down his neck.

Whitney was elevated to men's shoulders and given a severed bull's ear, and the throng whirlpooled around the plaza. Thomas went off to keep vigil on the butcher again. When someone on the balcony gave the painter and me drinks from a flask of brandy, it went down so pleasantly that we descended to one of the side street bars for more.

In the bar the painter said, frowning, "I don't . . . It's the part of human nature that I despise." When I didn't answer, he added, and it was the root of his anxiety, "The trouble is it's funny. I never saw anything half so damned funny in my life."

I said I'd bet the cow would be a real howl, with scythes or whatever they were going to use on her. He looked more worried still.

Hearing us speak English, one of Whitney's peones, still in his Andalusian suit but without his flat hat, invited us to the table where he sat with a friend, a clean-cut serious youngster with a muleta who had ridden all the way from Madrid on a bicycle, just for the chance of fighting the cow. This boy intended to ask the mayor's permission to kill her properly, with Whitney's sword. This conversation ceased abruptly, however, when a roar outside jammed the bar's door with departing patrons. . . .

When we reached the balcony they had begun on the cow, a lean, long-horned creature with her left eye pearled over. She was older and wiser than the novillos and saved her strength, singling out individuals from the shifting thin ring of people around her, keeping after them until deflected by a raincoat or somebody hanging onto her tail. Because there were now no peones with capes to divert the animal, fewer and braver members of the local public were willing to get near her, but she was what the serious young outsiders had come for. In a short time three or four of them with improvised capes or muletas got spilled, and one of them had his newly pressed trousers split from knee to belt, touching off general mirth. The drunk in the purple shirt, standing well out on the perimeter, panicked without being charged and dived under a cart. But it was all getting a little old.

Thomas appeared, having just left Whitney and Madrileñito at the inn where they were resting. He said, "Harry doesn't think he did well. He feels bad about it."

"I'm starting to feel bad about something, myself," the painter said. "Or tired. Don't you think it's about time to leave?"

"No," the girl said flatly without removing her eyes from the cow and its assailants, and the painter shrugged.

The boy with the muleta whom we had met in the bar managed to corner the cow in a windless spot and after four naturals he performed a breast-pass that was as good as anything Whitney or Madrileñito had managed. Then another young man with a cape made the mistake of working the cow from her blind side. The left horn ripped into his side and flipped him backward and she was on him as he fell. When she had been hazed away people lifted him and carried him out of the plaza with a red hole in his abdomen and what looked like another in his thigh.

Grimness moved in. Braver with anger, locals ringed the cow and rained strokes of their canes upon her as she whirled about in confusion. One man was methodically using something that looked like a hoe handle, and in somebody's hand I caught the glint of sharpened metal.

The painter said matter-of-factly, "I'm going to Madrid."

The girl spun around. "Please, no!" she said. "Why don't we watch it to the end?"

"Because I've got to live with myself," the painter said.

They had not known each other well before and were angry now, but I felt detached from their disagreement, and very detached from what was happening in the plaza. The boy from the bar presented himself formally before our balcony, standing erect with the borrowed sword laid across his arm on the folded muleta. He was petitioning the mayor to be allowed to kill the cow, and when the mayor refused him with an outsweeping waggling gesture of his hands, the boy lifted both arms high, in protest to Heaven.

"Come on," I said to the girl. "The next thing you know they'll bring out the butcher knives and axes."

"If they do, I want to see it." She glared at the painter. "If it's part of the whole thing, I do. Do you think not watching because you've got a weak stomach changes anything?"

"Yes," said the painter, turning to leave. "Yes, it sure as hell does."

I took her arm and she came reluctantly with us toward the balcony's French windows, but just then, shockingly, a shot sounded in the plaza. Turning, we saw the cow near the fountain, facing one of the Civil Guards and bucking against the pain of a bullet in her shoulder. He raised his Mauser and put the second shot between her eyes. She looked at him as though puzzled for two or three seconds, then stiffened her legs outward, bucked once more, and crumpled to the ground.

"Thank God!" the painter said.

The girl looked disgusted as well as angry. "You see?" she said bitingly as she squared her shoulders and moved toward the French windows. "You big weak sisters didn't have anything to be scared of after all, did you?"

"In the Absence of Horses" was written in 1954 and published in *Escapade* (June 1961).

Composed in Stone Sans and Stone Serif types with Raffia initial.

A VALLEY

U P THE COBBLED STREET in which the bus stopped I could see the head of the valley, a notch in a rugged stone mountain wall that rose from pine forests, snowstreaked and austere above the green ridges on either side of the village. The other side of the mountains would be France. The late-afternoon air at that altitude was cool and my light tweed jacket felt right for the first time that day.

A Civil Guard with a slung Mauser checked the other passengers' safe-conducts and my passport. He said I was the only American he had seen in the valley that year, and instead of telling me where the inn was he took the trouble to show me to it. Soldiers in groups lounged about the streets, and some were leading mules down to the river to drink. The Guard said that a regiment was having its maneuvers in the valley that week. He didn't think they would disrupt my fishing. "They go up into the sierra," he said and then, with pride, "There are even airplanes, from Huesca."

At the inn the landlady, plump and dark with a spoon in her hand beside a great wood stove, told me that the only bed left was in a room with an army lieutenant. It didn't seem to matter much to her whether or not I took it, but she said in a slurred dialect, hard to understand, that the lieutenant was a sympathetic person and the price would be forty pesetas a day, meals included.

After I had carried my things up to the room I walked between stone housewalls and lush vegetable gardens down to the water. Small trout were rising to a hatch of fly. Here and there against rocks and snags were jammed pieces of trash—a broken wagon wheel, half an oaken barrel, a boot—but it was clear, cold, strong water and the fish were there as I had been told they would be. I watched the river until nearly dark, and at the inn when I returned, people were sitting out in front on two benches. In the short lull that I brought to their talk I sat down, feeling their eyes, in a chair on the other side of the door.

Two of them were army officers and the rest civilians. They were teasing a tall man with a heavy French accent. It had to do with the Frenchman's having strolled into the mountains without his passport and meeting a Civil Guard, and with an audience he worked up a good show of indignation. He said, "I told him, listen, I'm not Spanish. I don't have to carry papers in all my pockets!"

Everyone except the senior officer laughed. A pretty girl with yellow eyes and a husky voice said, "And he told *you*, come along to the calabozo, eh?"

"The franchute!" said a stout older man beside her. It is a derogatory word like our "Frog," but he said it genially and the girl had used the friendly familiar "tú." Sitting apart from them beyond the door I felt for a moment very alien and alone.

Supper was announced by a small shy girl and more people appeared, all Spanish. The family groups and couples went to a dining room upstairs, and in a smaller one below I sat down with the two officers, a lieutenant and his junior alférez, and with five brown-faced men in shirtsleeves who looked like technicians of some sort. Alert beside the lieutenant's chair lay a great wolfish pup. On the table were two bottles of wine and two pitchers of water, and in the moments before the small shy girl brought in a big bowl of boiled potatoes and green beans anointed with olive oil, all those present amused themselves by staring at me and saying nothing.

The food gave them something else to look at and think about. The lieutenant, a dark man with a melancholy face, crossed himself and served his plate, then he and his junior officer started talking, as did the men in shirtsleeves, who spoke the same fast dialect as the landlady.

The lieutenant was telling the alférez that he treated a certain sergeant with too much familiarity.

The alférez laughed. He had ruddy clear skin, curly brown hair, and a strong nose and chin, and he didn't look much older than eighteen. He said, using the familiar pronoun, "You don't know—he's all right. It's only that we're both from the North."

"Vascos!" said the lieutenant. "Without Basques and Catalans this country might function. You'll see, about that one."

It sounded like conversations that I remembered from my own military years. There was nothing delicate about the food but there was plenty of it. We ate through a salad with black olives and chunks of tuna, and into a course of mutton chops with tomatoes, the little girl bringing more heavy purple wine as the bottles emptied.

The wolfish pup came over beside me and put a broad paw on my leg, begging, and his master said, "López! López, come here!"

Glancing at the lieutenant, López stayed where he was with his tongue hanging out, and one of the shirtsleeved men chuckled slyly. I said, "It's all right. Can he have the bones?"

Briefly the lieutenant's sad face smiled; he said yes, and thanked me. "You're Spanish?" he asked, which is a polite Spanish way of inquiring just what the hell you are.

I answered, the shirtsleeves silent now and listening, that I was a norteamericano and had come to the valley to fish and, when asked, that I spoke Spanish because I was long ago from a place called Texas, near Mexico. This met with interest. Texas was, was it not, a former Spanish possession now noted for its motion-picture industry, and their major had a great enthusiasm for fishing, having caught three weeks before ("It was a month and a half," interjected the alférez, and was told, "Shut up. It was three weeks ago, when the dun horse broke its leg") a trout of two and a half kilos.

I concurred in the general opinion that this was quite a trout. How were their maneuvers progressing?

"They're not ours," the lieutenant said. "We're stationed here. But truly, you should speak to the major about the fishing."

The alférez, good-natured and loud and irrepressible, voiced a belief that the major caught fish not usually with a rod but by dropping hand grenades into the river's pools, a bit of disrespect that produced snorts and nudgings among the shirtsleeved gentry.

"Tú!" said the lieutenant, dropping the subject. The other men left with toothpicks in their mouths—electricians, I was told, who had come to overhaul the village's lighting system. The Basque and I smoked hand-rolled cigarettes and drank more wine while the lieutenant, a Huescan who used neither tobacco nor alcohol, asked me about military things in America, such as how frequently officers got promoted—a young enlisted man in the Civil War and a cadet at the academy in Zaragoza later, he had been in his present rank for eight years—and how much they were paid. Nor did my answers elate him.

Followed by his great pup he departed—to visit with his fiancée who was vacationing in the town in order to be near him, according to the young alférez. They had been engaged for years without hope of the money they would need for marriage. For himself, the alférez ("Ángel Iturriaga, at your orders") said that the military was a foolishness. He was from San Sebastián and was doing a part of his obligatory service during university vacation. In time he intended to enter his father's shipping business, to sail Star class sloops in Sunday regattas, and to breed new generations of seaside Basques who would torment professional soldiers when the time came to do their service. His family was good at that, he said. In the war his mother's people had been Republican and his father's Nationalist, both equally a hindrance to their factions.

In the bedroom upstairs, I was still awake when the lieutenant came in with claw-clicking López, but he did not turn on a light even after I spoke, undressing in the chill darkness to avoid disturbing me, or perhaps from modesty.

❧

In the morning I went downstream alone, not yet ready to look up the local fishing druggist to whom I had a note of introduction. His cousin in Barcelona, who had written the note, had described him as an ardent angler but a little bit chiflado, or touched. This first time I wanted to try the stream alone, but I slept late and missed the morning hatch if there was one, and the good dry-fly fishing before the sun grew strong on the water. A mile below the town I started fishing upstream beneath a small high stone bridge. Peasants working in grainfields paused to watch me, and once Spanish troops in German helmets passed, marching up the road.

Occasionally I sat on the bank to rest and smoke and warm my unbooted wet legs. The July sun was high and hot and no fish wanted my dry flies, though I saw at least two good ones rising. When I switched to a sunken hare's-ear nymph I caught a series of bright fingerlings and then finally, below the town just before one o'clock, two hard-bodied vigorous twelve-inchers, which I returned to the water alive.

After a stupefying midday meal the alférez and I sat outside the inn and watched the little cobbled sun-shocked plaza and two yoked oxen across the way, waiting patient under the hot sun and the attacks of biting flies. Some of the other residents joined us—the franchute, the portly old gentleman who was, it seemed, a livestock inspector, and the handsome, husky-voiced, yellow-eyed girl who was his daughter. The Spaniards understood impractical addiction, afición, but the Frenchman eyed me askew and I divined that he had the French bug about Americans. "All that distance?" he said. "Only to kill *fish*?"

When I asked how long he had been there he said with rude shortness, three months. The yellow-eyed girl, whose name was Maribel, laughed. "Philippe is a practical man, unlike you. He is looking for Visigothic words. He is a . . . what is it that you are, Philippe?"

"A philologist," Philippe said sullenly, not looking at me.

"With a university?" I asked.

"No, I work for myself."

And before I could find out specifically how a philologist worked for himself, he left. The girl's stout father, Don Martín, took a silver watch from his vest and said that it was imperative that he go to examine some pigs. As he and the girl walked away the young Basque alférez gazed after them wistfully.

"That old one won't even let me stroll with her," he said. "He doesn't trust me."

"With reason, maybe," I said.

"Maybe," he said, and grinned. Don Martín was a Navarrese Carlist, he said, which perhaps explained his suspiciousness, Carlists having been losers for a hundred years or so, clear through the Civil War after which, although they had fought on the winning side, they were quite shabbily short-changed by the Falangists.

❧

My Barcelona friend's druggist cousin was in the café where I had been told I would find him. He was playing chess with a bereted farmer, and lifted a cautionary finger when I spoke to him, his eyes still on the board. As I watched he countered his opponent's efforts with a series of quick, confident moves and finally slammed his bishop into checkmate position.

To the farmer he said, "You want to know what you did wrong?"

The farmer told him to go to the carajo.

"Ha!" said the old druggist. "Listen, you've been binding too many sheaves, Tomás. Wheat dust has entered your head through the nose. There's a long winter coming; you'd better improve."

He was still chuckling as he shook my hand and scanned the note from his kinsman. It pleased him and he shook my hand again. "Wonderful!" he said. "Stupendous. Someone who knows fishing. We'll show these Aragonese yokels something about science."

The farmer Tomás said, "This Cándido has much science, yes. Only four days ago he came home with five entire trout the size of my little finger."

"Ka!" the druggist responded absently, then to me, "Listen, you've eaten? Have coffee. We'll go fishing this afternoon, won't we?"

❧

Soldiers were encamped on the hillsides above the town. Young conscripts, lean and healthy and sweat-stained, they were bathing in the river, and tending mules, and cleaning mess kits, and wrestling in crisp stubblefields. In one field four of them were helping a farmer scythe and bind and shock the last of his wheat, one skinny soldier singing a hard-voiced, high, sad jota. To get beyond all this activity we had to go far upstream from the town, leaving the main road finally below a ruined castle to walk by the river in a flagstoned lane that Cándido Montjuich said dated from the Romans, so that it was late when we started fishing. But we caught a rise, and I took eight small trout on dries while the old man horsed out three somewhat better ones with a bent stubby cane pole equipped with a rickety French spinning reel, making great double-handed efforts to hurl his devon minnow twenty-five feet or so.

All of our fish looked very runty when a countryman came along with a hook-jawed creature that measured fifty-six centimeters by marks on Don Cándido's rod. This angler had a reel-less fifteen-foot pole that looked as if it had been made from the instructions in Izaak

Walton, and one big brown chicken-feather fly at the end of a thick line. When he had left, the druggist and I sat down and smoked, the rise over, and he said in a discouraged tone that the campesinos did know the river, and where the large trout lived. Though without science, they fished every day, and trout were sometimes foolish.

There on the river he sounded much less scientific than in the café, but it is a common failing. He admired my equipment—the enameled English silk line and the light fiberglass rod. Yes, he liked living in the valley. "Vaya," he said. "Confess that it's beautiful. And the fishing. The winters are long with much snow, but we've got the café, and chess, and I read."

"What kind of books?"

"History, mainly," he said, and smiled. "The Moors and the great Christian warrior kings and the days when Spain meant something. And Dumas—I have read *El Conde de Montecristo* eleven times."

He also played chess by correspondence, often five games at a time, living with his sister in the tiny old house I had seen when we went there for his tackle, dark inside with small windows, his little botica in the lower front room, with its flasks and tins of chemicals, its patent medicines, its herbs and powders and roots and even dried reptiles.

When I asked what had brought a Catalan to this corner of the country he was silent for a moment, then asked me if I knew much about the war in Spain, which he did not call by the winners' term the Movimiento but simply, the war.

Not a lot, I said, far less than I had thought I knew before I came here.

"You'd know less still if you were Spanish," Don Cándido said. "It was a filthiness, that war, and from both sides. At the beginning I was in the territory of the ones they call the Reds. I had a big botica in a good town and I was doing well. You wouldn't believe it about the denunciations and the brutish killings, and later, when the others came and even if you weren't political, it was the same. A pig filthiness."

The subject made him nervous. He cut the devon minnow from his line, wound the line onto his reel, and rose. "Do you know it's getting dark?" he said. "Listen, I don't think much about all that, thirteen years in the past. We had the whorish war, but you can't always look at what's bad. I've never seen the use in that."

๛

One afternoon we had company, a vacationing doctor from Zaragoza who did not like foreigners. When I asked him if he thought
the river water was safe to drink, he hissed in contempt and said that
Spaniards had been drinking it since their days in caves. Shortly afterward he made a few remarks about the new Castellana Hilton in
Madrid, whose Hollywoodish opening had enraged practically all
Spaniards from the far right wing of the Falange to the exiled Red Re-
publicans who fulminated on Radio Moscow. Then, after making sure
I was watching, he drank a quart or so of river water. It seemed we were
not destined for warm friendship, and I found myself hoping that he'd
sucked in a dysentery amoeba or two.

By nature the doctor was not a fisherman but a hunter, a nervous
active man who after two hours of uneventful angling put down his
borrowed rod and went scouting restless over the hills and through the
fields. The afternoon was glaring and old Don Cándido and I caught
nothing until finally, in a narrow deep shaded pool at the foot of a cliff,
I saw a good one rising, stalked him on hands and knees, and laid an
almost-floating pheasant-tail nymph lightly in his feeding lane. He
took it and fought hard and I lost my footing once on slippery stones
and got very wet, but it was all right. The old man shouted bad advice,
got in the way when I was beaching the fish, and was enchanted.
"What a love of a rod!" he said. "It doubled completely, I saw it!"

When the doctor came back with a cut alder staff in his hand, he
glanced at the trout and told the druggist that once, in Panticosa,
he had seen seven in a creel all bigger than this one. The mountain-
guards there knew how to fish, really fish.

"Man," said Don Cándido, "so does this American."

The doctor's eyes flicked me with distaste. "Listen, old one," he
said. "Haven't you had enough cold water?"

Old one hadn't and neither had I, but the doctor was a force and
Don Cándido seemed a little afraid of him, so we headed homeward
with the sun still above the mountains. Later in the café with me, the
old druggist said, "Listen, he isn't a bad person, this médico. He gives
free treatment to the people here during his vacations. He saw much
of the war and is very Falangist, and I believe that he thinks of Ameri-

cans mainly as members of the Abraham Lincoln Brigade. You have to understand that."

I said that I did, and he looked relieved.

❧

My time in the valley went smoothly. The doctor did not come fishing again and once when we passed each other in the street he looked away. In the mornings the old druggist tended his botica and I fished alone, but in the afternoons we angled together upstream and down, quite happily though we caught few trout, comforting ourselves with the semi-fiction that the best of the season had passed. Because I did not again make him nervous by asking questions, I never learned more about his exile from Cataluña, or about the reasons for the sadness that lay not far beneath his enthusiasms.

In the evenings at the inn the Basque alférez held forth on sailboats, the livestock-inspector made speeches about what it would mean if Spain had real Catholic kings again, his daughter laughed huskily, the Frenchman got around to telling me with embarrassment, as a compliment, that I did not seem American, and if the food remained indifferent and plentiful, the purple wine remained good. One day the big pup López badly bit a soldier of the maneuvering regiment who was teasing him, and my roommate, his master, exchanged blows with the officer who came to complain about it. He was a reserved man, decent but hard to know and usually away in the evenings with his fiancée. The fight had upset him, and that evening after we were in bed he wanted to talk. In reflected moonlight I could see him dimly, hands locked behind his head against the long bolster, elbows spread like wings. In a corner López scratched himself thumpingly.

The lieutenant said with unexpected bitterness, "What a life you have, eh? Traveling and fishing and spending dollars."

I answered uncomfortably that I didn't always travel and fish.

"I know it," he said in quick apology. "It's only that . . . It's a dirty mess here, isn't it?"

"The valley?" I said. "Maybe, to live here. But it's good to visit."

"The valley, the country. Spain. You can't make any money. You can't marry. You can't live."

I thought about the blonde novia and the twisted hopeless conversations they must have night after night, about his attachment to the big awkward pup, and about his usual reserve that had now cracked open. I said, "Look, I know. I've seen. But it will have to change. It's a good country, with good people."

"Man, do I need a foreigner to tell me that? I fought for Spain, for my side of it. I would again. But change? Mierda! You don't leave the army, because after all these years . . . And if you did leave it, there's no money outside either. None. What do you do?"

He didn't expect an answer.

On my next-to-last day it turned rawly cold, raining in the afternoon and badly wetting us two ardent anglers. The following morning was gray with a hard rain-flecked north wind blowing down from the mountains, but because I would likely not get to fish for trout again for nearly another year, I went as usual to the river. No one was working in the soggy fields beside it and no soldiers were maneuvering. After two hours of having my line and flies whipped back into my face by the wind, I saw a thing in one long pool that looked like a human skull, bobbing shiny down toward me in the current. When it drifted near I saw that it was a sheep's stomach, attached intestines trailing below. With cynicism I cast to it and startlingly, silhouetted in the water beneath that obscene train of guts, a great dark trout rose from the river's depths. For a long moment the big trout examined the fly, then sank back down into grayness without taking. Chilled and somehow depressed, I wound my line onto the reel and headed toward the inn.

That night they gave a sort of farewell party for me. It was a little embarrassing and very pleasant, with cigars and brandy furnished by the young Basque alférez, who always had money. When the brandy had warmed everyone, my melancholy roommate the lieutenant performed deft sleight-of-hand and card tricks for over an hour, his blonde novia sitting beside him and watching his face with adoration. Even the Frenchman seemed happy. The old Carlist livestock-inspector slapped the table in appreciation of the lieutenant's tricks and roared above the laughter of his yellow-eyed daughter, "How about that, norteamericano? You never saw that before, eh?"

It was hard to remember that I had once felt alone and alien among these people, and in the end they all embraced me and gave me visiting cards, and I wrote my address for them on slips of paper, the alférez pounding my shoulder and making me promise to go sailing with him at San Sebastián in the spring. Finally through thin cold rain I walked Don Cándido home.

In his doorway he tried to give me money for some devon minnows and other lures I was to send him from Barcelona. I didn't tell him that I intended to send some more things too, among them a decent spinning rig. I said, "I don't know what they cost. You can pay me back next year."

"Ka! You won't come here again."

"Almost certainly," I said. "I'll write."

"Try," he said. "And think about an old chess-player from time to time, who reads about dead kings while the snow descends outside." He gripped my shoulder and shook it, then pushed me out into the rain. "Think about him. May it go well for you, young one."

Sports Illustrated magazine bought but never published "A Valley," which was written in 1954.

Composed in Utopia types with Neuland Inline initial.

A SPECKLED HORSE

AUTHOR'S NOTE: *I put in the better part of two years of work on this failed, partly autobiographical novel, which is one of my two efforts at long fiction—the other one never got finished—a form for which I seem to be definitely unsuited. My New York agent, John Schaffner, was horrified by the novel when I sent it to him. I had in part expected this reaction, because he was gentle, civilized, and effete, and the book was quite masculine, with hard edges. It also lacked political correctness, and although the growth of that mutation of puritanism into a reigning force was still in the future, its rudiments were active back then, especially in the Northeast.*

But Schaffner's distaste started me to reexamining the novel, and in the end I became dissatisfied with it myself because of its occasionally clumsy dialogue and characterizations, its extremely jumbled chronology (caused in part by an addiction to the work of Faulkner and of Ford Madox Ford), and its heavy overload of asides incorporating what must have been damned nearly a majority of the thoughts and feelings I had had up to that point in my life. Therefore I did not try to peddle it anywhere on my own, even though somebody would possibly have been willing to publish it. Rather bitterly, I viewed the time spent on it as totally wasted.

I modified that judgment later, though. What those two years finally appeared to have been was the culmination of a miserably protracted apprenticeship, and in writing the novel I seem to have sloughed off some old limitations. Much of what it had to say was not startlingly fresh and some was not even clearly presented, but I suppose that all of its defects represented tendencies I needed to get out of my system.

In rewriting and rearranging the following excerpts for use in this anthology, I have done away with certain stylistic mannerisms of which I was overfond at that time, have cut out or altered some plain bad writing (though I fear not all of it), and have put the excerpts into mainly chronological order, with some connective bits added. Despite such adjustments, however, I have not really tried to render the novel's narrative burden, to tell the story that it tells. It does not tell that story well, and maybe the story wasn't worth telling anyhow.

It is worth noting that I afterward stole and rewrote bits and pieces from A Speckled Horse *for use in other writing, one example being the segment concerned with a young marine's death in a hospital tent one night on Saipan, used here in more or less its original form. An old war-veteran friend of mine once got angry when I told him I had adjusted that incident to make it fit better with the agricultural slant of my book* Hard Scrabble, *in which a slightly different version appears.* * *He said I had no right to tinker with such material and he may have had a point. But now perhaps he will be mollified by the fact that the conversation in this novel excerpt comes closer to what was really said in that dark and dreamlike canvas shelter.*

Saipan, Marianas Islands, June 1944

RICHARD HILL CAVITT'S WAR had ended as he was moving through a stubbled rust-red canefield littered with dead and wounded Japanese. It was early in the morning and he was forward-observing artillery fire with a platoon of infantry, and the dead and wounded people were those who had tried to surfdive two crisscrossed lines of machine-gun fire in a crazy charge at gray dawn, forty-five minutes earlier. Because the platoon was behind schedule they were going through the canefield standing up. It was jumpy, with snipers on the hill beyond and people beside you shooting suddenly down into bodies that had moved, or that they thought had moved. With his carbine Hill shot one that did move, horribly, and never afterward forgot it. . . . Then he moved on, carrying the big radio because

*See *Hard Scrabble*, Chapter 8.

his corporal radioman had boils where the straps had chafed him. They were all filthy by that time. He remembered worrying that he might get boils, too, from the sweaty straps that had rubbed the corporal's boils.

He had probably been thinking too, a part of him, about his friend Willie Calloway who had been killed two nights before, in darkness and accidentally, by one of his own men at the batteries. Either Willie or the corporal's boils, he must have been thinking about, because if there was any one thing you could look out for, a little, it was a grenade in broad daylight. A man who had seen it had told him much later in a hospital in Long Beach that he had seen the Jap roll it out from under himself where he was lying, playing dead. Someone yelled at Hill, and yelled again, and he stood there for the better part of a long second, knowing with certain instinct that it was close but unsure which way to dive, and then a thin fountain of rusty earth rose at him from the left, and he saw in sudden brightness a web of red before his eyes that seemed to mean something, that seemed to mean everything, superimposed and brightly red against the canefield, against the slope ahead down which small slant-eyed men had swarmed that morning, screaming. The crazy hopped-up poor little bastards . . . And the black came down, and the simplicity of war went away and never came back.

He awoke in the hospital at Aiea on the high mountainside above Pearl Harbor, with the big hole behind his ear. They said he must have been hit by the fuse assembly because Japanese grenades usually broke into tiny pieces. And they told him he could not have been conscious before, but they were wrong. He thought they were wrong. Because he had waked first, or thought he had, on a cot in a tent on the island where he had been hurt, and in that tent he had helped a boy die.

The boy's voice was thickly, gently Southern. Hill did not know what he looked like or how he was hurt, because the darkness in the tent was absolute and for some reason Hill could not move his head. The boy talked in the dark. He was half Italian, he said. He came from a part of southern Alabama where Italian farmers had settled seventy-five years before, black dirt and liveoak country, and he had joined the service thinking he was getting into the merchant marine, not knowing what that was either except that it paid better and his mother needed money if he was to be away. . . .

It seemed to Hill that the boy had been talking when he awoke. Hill remembered saying things too, but not what they had been. The talk seemed to have had no beginning. The boy said, "My name's Cavitt. What's yours?"

Hill said in the great rotating dark where he had no weight and nothing had beginning or meaning, "Cavitt."

"Yes," the boy said. "What's . . ."

But it seemed to be too much trouble, as it was for Hill.

"God, it hurts," the boy said.

No beginning, and a great dizziness.

It was an Army tent hospital, the boy said, speaking again. He had been there since the afternoon, and when they had brought him in he had thought Hill was dead on the other cot. He said he was glad that Hill was a southerner and a marine, not a soldier. And alive. He couldn't have taken it if Hill had turned out to be a soldier or a Yankee. Couldn't have stood it. He said all of this with a strained urgency, and it did not have to make sense any more than the dizzy darkness made sense.

He said, the boy, "You want somebody that knows what you're talking about."

Hill said, "That's right."

"Listen," the boy Cavitt said, sounding very young. "Hold my hand, you mind?"

Hill reached under the mosquito netting toward where the other cot had to be, feeling with the movement for the first time the great bandage on his head and the firm objects on either side that wedged it in place.

The hand met his and clenched it, a thin hand, a hard rifleman's hand. Hill could hear the boy's shallow breathing.

"Thanks, Mac," the boy said, and clenched Hill's hand harder still, and died.

Then Hill went to sleep again, or whatever it was.

Goodbye to Negras, February 1952

AGAINST THE THOUGHT of his wife, or rather ex-wife, Hill hurled his oaken stick at a striped lizard that was rounding a turn in the graveled walk so fast that he was slewing. He missed, of course, and the stick broke, dry-rotted inside. In the old days he and the Thomason boys and his cousin Bert had killed a cruel number of that lizard's ancestors with catapults, which they and everyone else had called niggershooters. Had killed jack-daws and doves too, and cottonmouthed moccasins at the river, in the black mud of the bank. He recalled the feel of bare feet in that mud, and the expectant fear of snakes, and poison ivy.

The Thomasons both ranching these days, married with children and prickly toward outsiders, including Hill whom they now saw as foreign, rightly he supposed. Bert dead for eight years, blown to small pieces at the Rapido.

Walking in the yard of the big gingerbread house that had been his grandfather's, where his father now lived alone, Hill reflected on the town of Negras as it had been during his childhood and youth, when he had spent the summers there. He had grown up mainly in a city to the north where his father had a law practice, but the father had wanted the son to know what he himself had known, so that for the two or three months of each year that he was allowed to stay there with relatives, Hill had been not of the city but of this older, slower, richer place.

You had known where you stood. Long generations of people had fitted life's complexities into a jigsaw that seemed to make sense, and the seeming itself was what had mattered. Negras told you what was good and what was bad, and by the time you learned that good and bad were not that easy, you had at least the strength of having seen them starkly clear when you were young.

He knew that many people in the town kept on seeing good and bad starkly clear all their lives, and that it could be a narrow and unpri-vate place that would strangle a man like a rag. His father had known this too, and had left there when young, not to return until retirement.

That did not change the other.

Nearing the vegetable garden behind the house, next to where the burned-down stable had stood, Hill heard the thunk of a cotton hoe striking mellow soil, and entering, got into an argument with old Hooper about the name of the horse his grandfather had been riding when at a highway crossing he had collided with a speeding car and had been killed. His grandfather having held to the monolithic belief that if you did not look at automobiles they could do you no harm. That had been fifteen years before.

Hooper said, "It were Bolivar. You think I ain't aware the name of all them horses? Twenty-five years feedin' out crack oats?"

Hill said, "It was Pip. You're getting old and foggy."

It had been Pip, too, a big starred nervous bay that a good many younger riders would have been careful of, Hill among them. Though Grandpapa's skull had been smashed on the pavement, Pip, because he had reared, had only gotten a cut across the belly.

"Old's foot!" Hooper said, dropping his hoe. "You mean devil. Loses your wife. Quits your work. Comes loafin' 'round here stompin' on my ongions and callin' me old. You get outa my garden patch."

They were very fond of each other. For a short time after the war Hill had tried to be sentimental and liberal about Hooper, but you could not stay sentimental for long about anybody that crusty. Twenty years and more ago Hooper had made fine niggershooters for him, calling them that, and they had always ended up arguing, about anything. . . .

And when it came time, just before he left, to speak more fully to his father, Hill found that he did not have much to say. His father listened stoically, gray head tilted, cigar gone out. Though he was not deaf, he tilted his head as Hill did, but to the right. Maybe it was having seen him do that all your life that made you tilt yours, when you had an excuse. Hill knew that the stoicism meant little. Both he and his father were externally taciturn, though probably more than normally soft inside. The deadpan tradition that trickled down from ranching and feuding forebears.

Finally his father said, "It's a long time that I've watched you, boy. I don't know, but it looks like you're always doing things the hard way."

"There must be an easier one," said Hill.

He did not point out that his father had often done things that way also. Signing for instance a note for a friend during the Depression, whereupon the friend had died and instead of taking bankruptcy Hill's father had spent six lean years paying off the note.

He liked being kin to his father. The only trouble with it was that later on you could not blame a father like that for the messes you had gotten into. Made, rather.

"You were going to be a civil engineer," the older man said, relighting his cigar. "Then a doctor. So you went into the Marines at precisely the time you could have been sent through medical school free. After the war you started studying history in graduate school and were going to stay single so that you could get a better start with the teaching. So you got married and had a child. Then your baby died and you're not married any more, and just this side of the Ph.D. you quit teaching, and now you're talking about the New Mexico mountains, and after that Spain. You see what I mean?"

"Sure," Hill said miserably. "You think I get a kick out of it?"

"I'm not condemning," his father said. "I, least of all."

Hill said, "I'll finish the doctorate, just for the hell of it."

"In Spain?"

"I guess, Papa. There or somewhere else."

Musing, his father said, "What will you do when you find out you don't like it over there?"

There was no answer to that. Hill looked out of the window where liveoak limbs were swaying in a breeze.

His father said, "You've got brains, and people like you. You could have had anything, done anything. Maybe I should have pushed you."

"No. It wasn't you, Papa. Maybe it was partly the war. I guess I never told you about that."

"Telling me now?"

"Not really. When I came home I thought I was going crazy. I had hammers in my head, where they put that plate."

"The war," his father said, shuttling a penknife among his fingers like a baton. "Wars."

"You went to one. You had to go see."

"Yes. And I wouldn't feel the way I feel about you, if you hadn't had to go see too."

It was the nearest Hill had ever heard him come to criticizing his other son, Hill's brother, currently a wholesale appliance dealer in the city to the north, who had found a pleasant Navy staff job in Washington during the war years.

His father said, "So how do you feel about things in general now?"

Hill said, "I don't feel worth a damn."

Life in the Valley, New Mexico, Winter–Spring 1952

IT TOUCHED ON DEATH, the thinking in the mountains. It was with him that what he might be going toward instead of redefinition was oblivion, and that was all right. That was the least hard thing to live with.

That'll redefine you, he told himself. That'll redefine you all to hell.

There was food to cook, and cleaning up, and chopping pine slabs for the stove at the abandoned sawmill site behind the hill, and water to carry in buckets up from the creek. He walked in the mountains, sniping sometimes at jays or crows or stumps with a twenty-two pistol but not often—never, in fact, after the first two or three weeks. The noise was wrong, and the idea of killing inedible creatures, though he had seldom hit anything but the stumps. The season moved on in the manner of seasons, the snow grew infrequent and melted as it fell, and Hill often sat in pale early-spring sunlight on the creek bank and watched in pools the clean small trout that later he would fish for with his friend John Fly, who owned the ranch and was known as the Horse. In the middle of the day the trout were feeding even then, but they were for later. From under stones he took nymphs and creepers to study, and in the cabin tied imitations of them out of fur and thread and feathers, for later. At this altitude the bugs ran small, nearly all of them of the size for a number fourteen or sixteen hook.

He had begun writing the dissertation when he moved into the cabin, working two or three hours each morning from research notes he had made long before. He had a very detached sort of interest in it, and it wrote itself smoothly and made a nucleus for each day, separate from the life there and from his other thinking. Finishing it and getting it approved were the only things that stood between Hill and a doctorate, and although becoming a doctor of philosophy seemed faintly ridiculous at this point and in this place, the writing moved along.

Jays and owls and juncoes, and a pair of mallards nesting down the creek at a swampy spot, and a little later band-tailed pigeons and in the greening, drooping grasses and bushes along the water the redwings with a song like a rusted hinge, as well as tiny arrivers of a number of species whose names he told himself he would learn someday. Time for everything. He had to speak seldom, except once in a while to the ranch's caretaker Bill Topperman, who lived in a back room of the main lodge far up the creek and would sometimes ride his horse down and try to persuade Hill to drive him to Pecos across the mountains, so that he could restock on the sweet wine that sustained him from day to day. Or to old Juan and his sons who lived quietly across the property line downstream.

"Buenos días, Don Juan. Qué hay?" Knowing that nobody, probably, had ever called the old man Don before, but knowing too that he liked it. The easy formality of Spanish . . .

"Hombre, no le vi. Qué tal?"

And they would look at each other for a moment as though trying to think of something more to say, but they were not. That was enough. Juan had lived all his life in the valley and had raised a family there and was unused to talking. His boys were the same, even the bitter-mouthed one with a twisted leg from the war, Elisario, who invited Hill to come along in May when he drove the family's cows to the high aspen country where the elk lived, and where, since a cold snap had put the trout down, they ate porcupines and a blue grouse that Elisario killed with a thrown rock.

Someone had told Hill that old Juan was also one of the area's bloodiest and most dedicated Penitentes, at Easter. It did not square, but what ever did, about people?

As he walked one day in the mountains a bear passed below him, lean and furious with the stored-up hunger of hibernation. They both stopped.

"Bear," Hill said absurdly. "Don't look at me slanch-eyed. I'm meaner than you are."

He was not certain that he believed this, but it was nice to feel that way after so long. He narrowed his eyes into the slitty eyes of his ancestors, and spat. The bear looked up misanthropically at Hill where he stood on the trail, and wheezed, and took off loping on four feet.

In the beginning he had left the valley only to go to Pecos for groceries, driving on chained tires every few days up and over the hump with its frozen slush and down the switchbacks on the other side, and loading up at the store-and-bar where they had a Doberman with his teeth worn to stubs from fetching rocks that the loafers threw for him. Later, in April, when snow was gone and flowers had come to the valley, he began to drive to Santa Fe for supplies, and to see Horse Fly, and to sit with him sometimes in the afternoons in the bar at La Posada, talking and watching the ranchers and the pseudo-ranchers and the fairies in foulard neckcloths and the sunbrowned Eastern divorcees. Some of the women were handsome, but when Hill felt a tightness inside of him, looking at them and having them look back, he looked away again. Just then he didn't want even casual encounters with women, not that he believed any longer in the possibility of casual encounters, for him.

Occasionally he stopped overnight with the Horse and Vickie in town, but in May when the fishing picked up they began coming regularly up to the valley, bringing their children, and he quit going to the city. A good spring, a good summer. Time went, and one day in July Hill noticed consciously, with surprise, that he was . . . not happy, exactly, but there was a healthy scab now over the troubles, and if it would have to be lifted later, to look, that did not yet make any difference.

New Mexico, August 1952 *(originally the novel's opening scene)*

IT WAS LATE SUMMER in the Sangre de Cristos, and afternoon, and no wind blew through the valley. A man knelt in the middle of the small clear creek. Watching him, Hill Cavitt lay propped on an elbow in tall grass, drowsy, smelling sunwarmed clover. Hill's face was browned, and loose now with directionless thinking. In a flannel shirt and khakis his body lay slack down the waterside slope in the sun.

Because he had been in the valley that year since the winter before, living in a one-room cabin down the creek a way, Hill felt that it was something he deserved, the sun. It fell yellow on the bright-green clover in the bottomland field, and on the dark pines and spruce of the ridges that held the valley. And higher up, he wondered, would it be melting away the last of the tightpacked snow in the aspen country, where the herds of elk lived? He had not been to the high country since early May, when he had ridden up with Elisario behind a motley bunch of cattle for which that family held grazing rights.

It was said that the elk were more evident in the fall of the year, when they came a little lower down, to be shot through telescopic sights by people who had paid a lot of money for a permit granted through a sort of lottery. Then when you had killed your elk you often had a hell of a time getting him back down from the high country, where now the sun, perhaps, was finishing off last winter's snows. Or maybe the snow would already have started to fall again up there, though Hill thought not.

They would have brought down the cattle, if so.

Since neither he nor the man in the creek wished to kill an elk, they were not going to enter the lottery. Hill Cavitt lying on a flexible spine considered elk, and the fatal periodicity of their apparition, and the facts of the sun and the snow, and the stealthy actions of his friend in the flowing cold shallow water.

He did not consider women, or wars, or any of the other complications of being a man, because the sun made it unnecessary to do so. He acknowledged their existence, merely. Like liquor, the sun allowed him for then not to give a damn.

Out of bushes abruptly, a sneak attack, a black dog ran with swift determination to the streambank. He stopped with his front paws in the water at a point where the kneeling man after many maneuvers had just flicked a trout fly, and began barking. The kneeling man cursed; Hill's searching hand curled over a round stone and he threw it. Faint guilt twitched in him, for in the little world of his childhood there had been a dishonor in throwing rocks at dogs.

You feel bad about too damned many things, he told himself, and threw another one.

But it was a game anyhow, with known rules. He aimed wide and the dog, a cocker known as Eugene, loped off with stub tail low, having won that round. To keep him from winning you had to throw the rock before he made his charge. Eugene belonged to the ranch's wino caretaker Bill Topperman, and was with sufficient reason a little bit crazy. Besides stalking trout flies he also tried to make love to shoats, who naturally objected. It made for quite a sight, one which Bill Topperman if he was not too drunk was likely to call upon you to come and witness.

The man in the stream stood up, immensely tall, and looked down at his dripping trousers. The Horse, he was called, or sometimes The Human Cannonball, for a trick he could do in bars, running up a wall and kicking the ceiling. He did this less often nowadays than when they had been younger. . . .

"God damn him," he said. "They broke like quail. There was one at least twelve inches and it was a good cast."

Hill rolled up to a full sitting position, his head as always rotated a little to the left because of the entire deafness of that ear. He watched his friend slosh ashore and in the Texas intonation of their youth which, without noticing, they both used more strongly when speaking to each other than with other people, he said, "It was all right. It was going to drag."

Horse Fly leaned his rod into the unresisting leafy twigs of a bush beside Hill's, squeezed a wet package of cigarettes until it dripped brown, and threw it away.

He said, "The hell you shout, Alistair."

"The hell I don't, Alistair. You didn't give it any slack."

The big man said, "Can't hook them if you do."

He sat down heavily and rubbed huge wet legs. Hill gave him a dry cigarette and took one himself. They had begun smoking together one winter when they had both been sixteen years old. Which, since they were now both thirty-two, was a reasonable number of years to have been smoking. A good bit of tar on the old . . . bracheoles? Bronchioles?

No. Something-oles, damn it.

There were things that Hill would have given a great deal to be able to place sixteen years away from himself, though being young was not one of them. But he didn't mind thirty-two. He was a little beat-up, but thirty-two was all right.

Physically, it was. . . .

Tracheoles?

He leaned over and scooped a palmful of cold trout-water onto his face to shock away the sun-thinking. Horse Fly stretched long cheeks in a yawn. His skin was browner than Hill's because he was naturally dark. An Indian streak probably; someone had once nicknamed him Comanch. They had always been slapping nicknames on one another. Alistair had been a sort of generic nickname for the bunch they had belonged to in those highschool times, back before college and the war.

The Horse's face was longly oval, pleasant, and looked in reality slightly equine. He glanced at Hill with his dark eyes watering from the yawn and said, "I could eat a roasted baby."

"How old?"

"Oh, six months," the Horse said blowing smoke. "Seven. Around there."

Without at first knowing why or having felt it coming, Hill flinched and dropped his eyes, half-closing them. It came from deep inside and was uncontrollable, like what had been called in the Marine Corps, delicately, a piss chill, and it passed as quickly as it had come.

Looking at him closely, the Horse said, "You can stop that, damn you. Right now."

Hill said, "Stop what?"

"Damn you," his friend repeated, looking at a little cloud above the high horizon of pines.

"Damn me."

"I was thinking . . . That night down in Santa Fe . . . You didn't mean that, about being to blame when the baby died?"

Hill didn't answer. The feeling was gone, and in its place he could sense the numb cape of calm that had covered it over. But the lazy sun-thinking was gone too. A trout's dimpled feeding ring spread over the smooth upper stretch of the pool that the Horse had been fishing. Without getting up Hill reached around for his rod and unhooked an artificial nymph from its keeper-ring above the grip.

Al . . . Alveoli, by God! Relief warmed that former-biology-lab-assistant's part of his mind that had been searching for the word. Hill had formerly been a number of things, though he was nothing in particular at the moment except an ex-husband and an ex-father and a doctoral candidate in history with a dissertation nearly completed.

He said examining the nymph, "I wish I'd had better glue when I tied these things last winter. They're coming to pieces."

The Horse said, "They're good bugs. Better than the stores sell. You keep your dirty fly line out of my pool."

"Take him, then."

Skidding downward stealthily over the long grass, rod in hand, the big man said, "Have no fear, Sir Alistair."

Then for a moment he paused and looked back stubbornly at Hill. "Listen," he said. "I want to know. You meant it, about blaming yourself?"

Hill said, "It's none of your damned business. The drinking gave me a loose tongue that night. I meant it, but you don't need to worry about it. It's something I've got to work out for myself."

A Death, New Mexico, October 1952

IT ENDED.

That afternoon on the Colorado highway a flatbed truck loaded with migrant workers had smashed into a canyon wall and it was a busy night at the little hospital. Periodically as Hill and Philip Allison waited a siren would whine mosquito-like in the north, approaching, and as the sound swelled nuns and interns moved toward the emergency entrance, rockfaced against whatever was inside them. From beyond the door where they disappeared came women's screams and high-pitched Spanish gabble and once, returning from another of the pointless trips to the room on the third floor, Hill passed a senior sister on the stairs, going up with a limp child in her arms, its features Indian and undistorted by pain, but its eyes clinging unbelieving to his own as they passed.

In the room upstairs they had the Horse's body in a wicker basket that looked like one of the Navy stretchers for hoisting the wounded aboard ships during the war. The first time Hill went up he pulled back the sheet, but the face was swollen and scratched and meant nothing, which was like the war also.

"Anyhow I got to talk to you," Hill said to his friend's body. "Big man."

In the lobby Philip sat broadshouldered, waiting silent with his hands on the arms of the easychair. Shortly after nine Hill said, "One of us could go get gas, and the chains put on the car."

Philip said stubbornly, "The plane's not due till ten-forty, Alistair. We've got to wait here till the man comes. We promised Vickie."

"You stay here then," Hill said. "I'll come back and get you."

But Philip didn't want that either. He didn't want anything. He was at the point of wanting to do things one at a time, and deliberately, and not alone. Not by any chance alone. Hill understood it. There was in him a little of the same, but being with Philip made him feel it more. He was edgy. He did not know what had happened to Philip during the war, nor did he want to know. He knew only that Philip made him edgy now. And because Philip had known the Horse's father better than Hill had, when the plane came and if it could land in the snow it was Philip who would have to speak to him, the Horse having been alive when the father had boarded the plane in Texas. They waited in the lobby in the long rhythm of the sirens and the screams.

They said that from the marks in the dry red mountainside, among the piñones five miles up from Pecos, it looked as though the car had rolled over six times. Had nearly gone over the edge once before being yanked back to climb against the cut dirt and stone on the inside and then had bounced outward and over. The Horse had been thrown clear finally and had lain there a hundred yards below the road, his spine gone in two places, one of them with a vertebra shoved aside like a coin out of line in a stack, so that not wanting to the doctors had had to operate in the afternoon even with the crushed chest and the pelvis and the shock.

Having lain there from four in the morning or whenever it had been, through the iron-cold mountain night, calling maybe sometimes because he was conscious and a little delirious when a Mexican rancher came along at eight-thirty in a pickup and found him, and later waited beside him for all the time it took an ambulance to come.

Hill, having driven out of the valley and along that road four hours later, wondered how the rancher had seen anything. He himself had not even noticed marks.

When they had let Hill into the room, with Vickie, the Horse under drugs had grinned up at him with the corner of his big mouth that he could still move.

Hurting, Hill said, "Hell, Alistair, you're all right. In a month you'll be doing the Human Cannonball."

The Horse said laboring hard, "You know . . . something?"

"What?"

"Don't ever try to cannonball a mountain," the Horse said. "It's rough."

The nurse pulled Hill away, and outside in the corridor Vickie Fly took Hill's upper arm tightly in her hands and began to cry against the hard point of his shoulder. Soon she stopped, and did not cry again. Hill gave some blood, and then on the operating table the big man died, and her face when Hill looked at it again had been elongated and solemnly ugly and he could not meet her eyes. When he had looked out a window, it had been snowing.

The plane could not land and went off to the south. And now, through falling snow, Hill and Philip Allison drove in Hill's car slowly to a filling station on the highway. It was not the nearest station or even on the same side of town as the airport, but it was the one they had always used. As they got out the station's owner, Remigio Segura, came toward them.

"I hear about that," he said. "I'm sorry, you know? He was a good man, Mr. Fly."

"Yes," Hill said, watching Philip who was watching the snow drifting down out of the north into the light under the station's white-painted arcade, pushed by a faint cold wind from the mountains.

Hill said again, "Yes."

"Say they have to operate."

Hill said, "That's right. Want to sell us some gas?"

As the clicking hum of the pump filled the silence, two brown men watched impassively from the station's doorway, and by the ladies' room sat a little tan-and-white mongrel with a pinched alert face.

Hill was thinking with clarity that it was the end of a time. He did not think his mind had ever been clearer in his life.

The little tan-and-white dog got up and trotted across the driveway into the snow and the highway, and a truck ran over him. It happened. A yelp, and into the snowflecked edge of light that spilled from beneath the arcade the dog tumbled, not even on his feet, scrabbling, the feet uncoordinated but each foot when it somehow touched ground pushing him farther from the thing that had happened. He fell kicking into the lighted patch of gravel and when he stopped the high rhythmical screams began, a crazy quaver at the end of each.

Philip said slackly, "Oh, Jesus. Jesus."

As though thoughtfully, the truck slowed for a few yards and then the bass of its exhaust sounded as it picked up speed. One of the men in the doorway walked over to the dog.

"It's Andrés's, all right," he said. "It belongs to Andrés's kid." He reached down but the dog twisted up at his hand like a snake, still screaming, and the man jerked away. Looking toward Hill and the others he laughed. "The son of a bitch," he said. "He nearly get me."

"Why don't they kill it?" Philip said, weaving and searching the gravel with his eyes. "For God's sake I'll kill it."

"Easy," Hill said. "Take it easy, Philip."

From behind them a little boy came and stopped beside Remigio Segura at the pump, looking toward the dog.

Remigio said, "Es tuyo?"

"Sí."

He was eight or nine years old and though his dog was dying there was nothing in his face. He wore a rubberized jacket with a corduroy collar and creamy cotton-flannel lining.

Against the dog's high screams Philip Allison began suddenly to yell, and Hill slapped his shoulder hard. The slap and the immediate stony pain of Philip's fist against his cheekbone, and being flat on the gravel, had the clarified feel of a thing that had been meant to happen for a long long time, the feel of a thing in a dream dreamed twice.

Philip's eyes as he looked down toward Hill were unseeing because he was weeping. He said, "I'm sorry, Alistair. I'm sorry."

Getting up, Hill touched his arm and said, "It doesn't make any difference."

The dog stopped screaming and died.

Mallorca, March 1953

THAT FIRST TWO WEEKS on the island he had been living in a hotel and had known no one, not yet having used the notes of introduction to people there that a friend had given him. It had been lonely in the way of new places to which you had transplanted yourself, a way he was beginning, a little, to grow used to but not to like. Traveling, he saw people frequently who seemed to move into new places easily, speaking with the fluidity of friendship to new people in bars and hotel lobbies. He had never been such a person nor would he ever be. The shades of John Wesley Hardin and of Hill's ranching, feuding ancestors grew tight-lipped around strangers, and suffered loneliness.

It was another of the unforeseens that took away some of your hunger to devour the wide world, and although you could carry stacks of books around with you in emulation of the English ideal of the lone traveling scholar, and could even read them with comprehension, the books did not help much when you saw, on a beach, a young Frenchman caressing a curve in his wife's back.

He had rented a motorcycle for two days to look around the island and on the second day, lacking the right clothing, had in a rainstorm in the rugged mountains along the north coast caught a deep chest cold that turned into flu and put him to bed for six days, with fever and a cough and sinuses that felt as if they'd had thirty-two pounds of air pumped into them and the cap screwed on. And the yellowbrown taste of sickbed spittle and loneliness and the hot guilt which came into him when he was alone and weak and which in the seven months of working in North Africa was what the numbness of New Mexico had become.

It was rough, lying guilty and ill, to try to see yourself as a brave lone wanderer visiting places with beautiful names. He was now in a place with a beautiful name because, more or less, it had looked magical to John Fly under moonlight from a PT boat during the war, and they had always intended to go there together. And what he felt now was the pointlessness of being there alone, and all the evil he had done, and it tasted like hell in his mouth.

The second afternoon after getting up, still weak and moody, he had gone to a little British lending library and had taken out Huxley's *The Devils of Loudun*, and had carried it into a bar called, for God's sake, Pete's Tavern, to read in it while down the bar from him some resident Americans had been joking among themselves in the manner of people who knew each other so well that they could find two words, meaningless to you, funny enough for long minutes of laughter.

They had seemed pleasant enough, interesting, as people often seemed when you were by yourself and did not know them. Later he came to know all of them, and the man who owned the bar, but he didn't know them yet, so for then they seemed interesting.

Mercy had been one of them, looking younger and fresher that day than he had ever seen her since, which had been only his aloneness looking at her. She had said in that New Orleans voice with a Spanish edge to it, "I *had* to lock him out. You can only get so many into a bedroom at one time."

They laughed and someone said, "Where the hell did he find a ladder?"

Monstrously alone, Hill was unable to find anything but melancholy, slightly pompous wisdom in the last chapter of *The Devils of Loudun*, which he read first. Paying for his beer he stuck the book into his coat pocket under curious glances from his compatriots down the bar, and walked a long way out along the villa-lined coast to beyond the end of the trolley line and past the Hotel Maricel to a section of gray rocky shore below scrub pines, where there were no villas. An empty green Volkswagen was parked under the trees at the end of a dirt road. Hill sat down with his back against a rock near the water, but Huxley did not read any better there. No one was in sight. Weak from the time in bed, he had sweated walking and felt chilled now in the damp breeze off the water, though there was sun. It was not yet fully spring and he wondered what the hell he was doing there.

A tallish young woman in red shorts and a halter and alpargatas came at a fast walk from around a point, picking her way through jumbled rocks as she headed for the green Volkswagen, looking back toward the point from time to time. When she saw Hill she turned slightly to make a half-circle around him, watching him as he pretended to read. He heard her stop to his right rear.

"Oiga," she said. "Listen."

Though he had been away from the language for a good while before coming there, he was fairly sure that the intonation was not Spanish, and when he looked around he was certain. She was darkhaired and brown-eyed, but Spanish women did not carry breasts like those around under only a halter, in public.

He said, "Sí?"

She moved three or four steps closer, breathing hard from having hurried. The large breasts rose and fell. She said, "Listen, I just hit a man with a stone!"

It sounded like a threat, with heavy French "r"s, and Hill started laughing. "Where?" he said.

"In the stomach," she said, looking relieved and a little cross-eyed but it was only that the brown eyes were close-set. "Or lower down," she said. "He was . . . how? Exhibitioniste."

Hill said, "Good. But I meant where was he?"

The girl said, "There he is!"

Hill looked toward the point fifty yards away and behind its boulders saw the head and shoulders of a man with tousled black hair and a stubbled face, frowning at them.

The girl shook her fist at him. "That's right!" she called in French. "You stop, cochon! I have more stones here!"

The man scowled at them for a moment longer, then turned and disappeared behind the point. In profile, staring after him with a full lower lip projected in anger, the girl was handsome.

Hill said, "Well, he's gone. Sit down and rest."

"Spaniards!" she said furiously. "They wait to find a girl alone, to molest. Filthy, all of them."

Hill said, "You don't want to generalize too much."

It was one of the hard words for him in Spanish and his tongue stumbled on it. The girl glanced down at him, her long tanned face still angry but not at him. She wore her hair parted in the middle and pulled back under a kerchief, and it looked good. Without his willing it Hill's eyes flicked down the length of her body and back up again to her face momentarily, and something moved far down inside him. It had been a long time.

He knew that she knew the thing had moved inside of him, and he knew that she liked that. All in a moment. He looked away toward the rocky point.

She said, "You're not Spanish."

"No."

"English."

"American," Hill said.

"Merde," the girl said. "I don't like Americans."

He said, "That's too bad. You must pass it pretty black, having to go around disliking so many kinds of people."

"I wish I could speak Spanish like you," she said. "What are you reading?"

"A book about what the French do to people they don't like."

She smiled with long white teeth and said, "You don't sound American."

"That's a miserable enough compliment, if you're trying to make compliments."

"Maybe I am," she said. "I think so, yes."

But all of the words were only a careful, dog-like circling around the knowledge in both of them that something had moved inside Hill and something inside the girl had responded to it. It had been a long time for Hill, because after New Mexico there had been work in Morocco with Arabs peeping out of doorways, and a brief touristic turn around the peninsula from Algeciras to Cádiz and Sevilla and Granada and Valencia and Barcelona, looking at churches and going to early-season bullfights which, like one he had seen here in Palma, were very bad. And unless you liked to go a-whoring, as a stranger you were out of luck on the other in the Arab lands and in peninsular Spain, pretty much celibate.

The sun and maybe his thoughts had warmed him under his coat and he began to cough. The French girl said with concern that it was a bad cough. He said that he had been sick but wasn't any longer. Eventually they went to the Volkswagen and drove down to Cala Nova to sit drinking white wine and talking. They tried French, and English, and ended up again in Castilian. Hill soon shut up and listened to her flow of accented bad Spanish, which he found charming, then. She spoke a lot of it, the girl Simone. Two or three months before she seemed to have had some of the kind of bad luck that foreign women had with Spaniards, and the loneliness that Hill knew so well was in her too, coming out now as talk. She was divorced like him, and living on the island because here, you saw, within her income she could have a seaside villa and a nurse for her child and a pair of servants, besides the sun and the beaches, and for all that in France it would have been needful, you understood, to accept help from her parents, who had vineyards. . . .

She had gotten in the God-damned vineyards, right away.

Her former husband, you would not believe, had been perverted and had wished to intromit another woman into their bed. . . .

What is the seventy-two? Hill was thinking. It was an old joke of John Fly's. Oh yes, he said, he knew of such things. Sympathy flowed between them.

The Germans during the war had been very gross pigs but the Americans when they came, though she knew that many were different, had been nearly as bad, and she was twenty-eight years old and in those moments when she could bear the Spanish she liked Mallorca very much. . . .

Still heavy-headed from the illness Hill was a little bewildered by it all, but not much. He knew where it was going, and it charmed him. Even the close-set intense brown eyes charmed him. How would they not, above such breasts?

She said, "We have confidence, I feel it. You feel confidence in people."

And Hill, who if still simple in some ways was mature enough to doubt that what he was feeling strongest was the confidence between them, said that there was no question about it. The next day they drove across the island to the Formentor peninsula and had lunch at the big hotel, and lay around on the beach afterward, Simone talking still, he mainly listening. In the sun his cough got worse, so that when they got back to Palma that evening she insisted that he move out of the hotel to her villa because he needed care.

Some care that had turned out to be. He wondered who had told her about that as treatment for a cough. After half a bottle of Martell late that night on sofa cushions before an olive-wood fire, all of it tangling deliriously with his inflated sinuses, a force of good, dirty, instructed passion that simulated love and was stronger than it for then, because he needed the passion badly and did not need or want love. . . .

Mallorca, Summer 1953

IN THE RANK stood six taxis, the first a shiny Citroën. Out of principle Hill took the oldest, a Huppmobile from about 1928 with an almondshell-burning gasogene on the back, although this day it seemed to be functioning on gasoline. Or would have been if it had been functioning. The driver, a sourfaced old man with yellow eyes, went to the front and cranked it twenty times or more, pausing to rest between turns, and then came back to the window to look in at Hill.

"No anda," he said unapologetically.

Hill said, "What's the matter with it?"

"What do I know?"

Hill got out and took the shiny French one. It carried him smoothly into the Paseo Marítimo and past spread fishing nets to the door of the Little Club Náutico, which was the same club as the Big Club Náutico except that different kinds of members chose to hang out in the two different parts, a situation resulting from an old, not quite perfect fusion of two former clubs. Hill paid the driver and scanned the street for green Volkswagens, as he did all streets now.

There were none. He had lately moved from his little rented house near the Plaza Gomila to a furnished room downtown, partly to get away from his newly acquired American and English and Scandinavian friends' daily bacchanals, and partly to elude Simone. He had made the mistake of going to France with her and meeting her family and seeing their vineyards, and at some point she had decided she was going to marry him, which had had a remarkably chilling effect on his feelings toward her.

Passing through the club's entrance into its patio and the locker-house, he spoke to two bellboys who grinned up at him from wicker chairs, undaunted. He had seldom managed to daunt people. During the war this had given him trouble as a second lieutenant, before he had learned the essential automatic nastiness that could get things done. Back then it had been often necessary to want to daunt people, because there were things to be done. . . .

At his locker he changed to shorts and a sweatshirt and alpargatas, and heaving the heavy sail-bag onto his shoulder walked in white sunlight along the quay past parallel slips and their aligned white boats. He saluted a doctor, a small official of the Armed Police who was tinkering with a contraband twenty-five-horse Johnson outboard, and a group of young men in swimming trunks who were sitting at the edge of the quay and dangling their feet toward the water, while they waited for vacationing foreign girls, preferably French or Swedish, to show up and manifest a desire to go sailing. Their talk was usually of conquistas. They were nice kids and most of the conquests were incomplete, though there was a good bit of biology in their descriptions. Near the Big Club Hill turned onto a slip to walk between the tall masts of Star Class sloops to where the Germá and the other Hispanias were moored.

He stopped for a moment before boarding to enjoy looking at his boat. She was twenty years old and had rotten garboards, but you could not see that. When he had come back from Bilbao and France he had spent a week refinishing her, and though a series of owners had neglected her badly since the days before the 1936 war, there was no way anyone could have told it except with a knifeblade, probing. Smooth brilliant white, with good German varnish on the mahogany brightwork and a red waterline and blue mercury antifouling paint on the bottom that an American on a yacht had given him.

From the concrete slab of the slip Hill dropped into the center of the afterdeck, steadying himself against the boat's slow answering fall and rise with a hand on her boom in its crutch.

Odd, to think of a boat as "she" that was named the Brother. Mainly he just said "it," though in Spanish it had to be "he." His friend Rafael, a young local doctor, scowled whenever anyone spoke of his seven-meter Uliso as a female, which meant that it was a small boat, a plaything, not a ship.

By God, it had looked pretty small, the Uliso, off Ibiza one night, running in. Small enough. They had not slept in twenty hours, and had run in toward the Tagomago light with a quartering easterly gale behind them kicking up phosphorescent waves that looked as high, bearing down from behind, as the Uliso's mast, and while alone at the helm in the darkness with the deadly drowsiness on him, and nothing but the light that he could see, Hill had had a vision of a peasant family grouped around the light which had become a candle on a table, all of their faces distinct, and had listened to their talk. And had shaken his head and come out of that dream barely in time to prevent a broach that would have sent them to the bottom.

Rubbing his eyes, Rafael had come up from a doze in the little cabin to relieve Hill. He looked astern at a huge hissing wave that lifted them a split second before it was ready to break over the stern. He had said, "We do it a little for the wrong reason, you know? We do it to scare ourselves. There is something wrong in that."

No water in the Germá's bilge. He took an esparto mat from under the afterdeck and unrolled it along the floorboards, and then kicking off his sandals moved swiftly barefoot to bend and hoist the jib and the main. Because the normal wind did not strike in that corner behind the Big Club, you could do pretty much what you wanted with your sails at the mooring. Hurrying because he did not want Simone to catch him there, he jerked angrily when the boltrope, damp from the day before, stuck in its groove along the boom, and retaliating, the boom crutch buckled and fell and the boom swung away to return and swat him, nearly spilling him among fruit peels on the water's iridescent scum. He got the sail set finally and ran it up, proudly tall and flapping gently in the head, where ragged breeze fragments touched it. A good sail, new the year before, the only thing not old on the boat when he had bought it.

Loosing the stern bridle he ran forward to cast off the bow line as the Germá surged toward the pull of the mooring buoy's chain, then back to the tiller to turn smoothly toward ruffled water beyond the tip of the Big Club's pavilion, the boat coasting slowly and awaiting the wind's thrust. At the corner of the pavilion it came, stronger than he had thought it would be that early, and the mast creaked in its step as the sail filled in a deep curve and leaned cleanly down, water boiling along the rail as he came up into the diagonal push of the wind.

He jammed the arches of his bare feet against the coaming and leaned out on the weather deck and sucked the hard breeze in. The boat would sail. By God it would sail.

Madrid, 1953-54

IT WAS NOT that he was always by himself, that first winter in Madrid. It was only that he thought of it that way, that he preferred it that way, a chosen solitude.

Abie Elmore from Morocco was there, worried over six years of his savings tied up in asphalt for paving the proposed new air bases, and in the daytime Hill worked with him and worried with him too, from friendship. The agreement had been signed putting hydrogen bombs behind the Caudillo and legitimatizing him internationally, so that the newspapers were polite to the United States that winter. Big muscled Americans from the Morocco projects peopled the cafés, not speaking Spanish or needing to, waiting for the work with big machines to begin, teasing with the highgrade café whores over prices. They had jobs in prospect, or deals such as Abie hoped to have, and it was pleasant enough to sit with them sometimes, the big men with a pride in the work they knew how to do. After the idle, hard-drinking expatriates in Palma he found a cleanness in them.

But much of the time Hill was alone that fall and winter among Spaniards he did not know, reading, writing letters to old relationships, waiting like the big men for the hard work to begin, with something like hope. Because work made sense by itself, which was the sole and sufficient wisdom of the big Anglo-Saxons.

He lived in a good little hotel in the Gran Vía that he had lucked into and never afterward escaped, the chambermaids having become motherly toward him. Most nights he ate supper alone, resentful if anyone threatened the aloneness, sitting with a book propped before him against a winebottle in a little restaurant in a sidestreet near the Ministry of the Army. It had marble tables and good pueblo food, white beans with sausage, and lamb, and kidneys in sherry and veal milanesa like chicken-fried steak but ten times better, all washed down with the red Valdepeñas a little too sweet but good of its kind. Nearly all the people who ate there were men and a number ate alone like Hill. Some were vaguely literary, and young bullfighters showed up from time to time and made noise to cover the fact that they could not afford a gaudier place. Before the Civil War García Lorca had come there often and the woman who owned it, gentle-faced, remembered him reciting poems to his friends and that he had always eaten raw garlic with whatever he ordered. She did not think Castilians would have shot him, not even Castilians of that special sort. . . . Andalusians, had it not been? Her own man a Largo Caballero socialist—dead, yes (musingly) dead.

Hill came to know the faces of the other regulars who ate there as he knew faces in other parts of the city that season, without knowing or wanting to know names to go with them. They nodded when he came in, and everyone wished everyone else good appetite. He had never seen any of them recite poetry or even eat raw garlic, and there was a sadness over the place that suited him, a sadness of García Lorca murdered perhaps, a sadness of widowhood, a sadness of sweet Spanish solitude. The fine baby lamb chops fried in deep oil, a broad pile of them with salad and the Valdepeñas, and boiled coffee afterward that wasn't much good but it didn't matter, and when you had finished eating you could sit there smoking harsh black tobacco and sipping wine till midnight if you wanted, writing letters and reading. He wrote many letters that season, and thought of others that he did not write, and knew the taste of solitude and found that it was a taste he had never before known, not really.

He had the not-desperate feeling that it was possible he would forever be hanging between things that did not make sense. If so, he would be able to stand it. He learned that. He read George Borrow and Richard Ford and Gerald Brenan and Madariaga and Azorín, and fought through a little of Unamuno in Spanish, and Juan Ramón Jiménez and Barea. All in a kind of lone celibacy that had nothing to do with, that was not touched by, the occasional evenings in the big cafés with Abie and the teasing girls who all tried to use an andaluz accent to excuse, a little, what they did, and the big laughing men who did not speak Spanish.

Federico Castaño de las Heras, who claimed to be positive that no God existed but who might still have been a university professor and a statesman instead of a garage attendant, had not his defunct government seen fit to buck the earthly representatives of one of God's many manifestations, sat down at Hill's table in a sidestreet café, shabby though fully dressed in coat and tie and with a frayed overcoat over his arm.

He said, "Hola, Yankee. How goes the construction of bulwarks against the Marxist hordes?"

"It doesn't go."

"Less bad," Federico said, hissing at a waiter for service. He was in a stimulated humor because he had talked with a former colleague, still a professor because when the war had come he had gone Right or at least Not Left, and the colleague was entirely pessimistic about doing any worthwhile work, as things were.

Federico said, "Naturally they can't. Do you know that in every classroom there are tattlers to run with talk if you speak some faint truth or another?"

"What is truth?" asked Hill in the vein of Pontius Pilate. "The Russians are worse."

"Maybe so," Federico said, for a moment depressed and forgetting to be happy over the troubles of the enemy.

"George Orwell says that Spaniards do not have the efficiency to be totalitarian."

"Nor republican," Federico said. "Nor anything but medieval. But a foreigner has no right to say it. Who is he, this wise man of yours?"

He was ready for argument as he always was. Hill had looked up the old man two or three months before, bringing a letter from a senior teaching colleague named Jerry Robertson, who had known Federico in Republican times. Hill had gone two times to the address Jerry had given him, a furnished room in a filthy little street in the Cuatro Caminos district, without finding Federico, but the second time he had cornered a child in the hallway who was not too suspicious, Cuatro Caminos being still rather solidly Red, to admit that he knew that the viejo worked in a garage somewhere near Juan Bravo. When Hill had found the garage, it was close to the Military Mission and many of the cars belonged to American officers.

Federico in a blue garage attendant's monkey-suit had listened gravely as Hill introduced himself. He took the note from Jerry and read it. His cheeks were long and sagged like a hound's at the jawline. White hair rose in wisps above.

He said, "Yes, Robertsohn. He has written before, and sent clothes. I gave them away."

Hill grinned, and Federico said, "He is a good man, Robertsohn. Why did he send you to a remnant like me?"

"I suppose I'm a kind of remnant, too," said Hill.

He was fierce and frail and gentle, and after a couple of evenings together arguing in cafés he was willing to have Hill around and began to call him tú, though Hill still used the respectful third person to him. He was ineradicably political and objected to Hill's military countrymen who came in their De Sotos and Buicks demanding washings and greasings in unintelligible Spanish, and who had not come to the aid of the Republic in her hour of desperate need. . . .

Now, in the sidestreet café, he probed further about the mysterious George Orwell but got only a little response from Hill, who was not feeling up to their usual arguing that day. After a time they left the café and walked, muffled in their overcoats against the sharp Castilian wind. They were not going anywhere. It was not believable how far you could walk with a Spaniard, talking, good weather or bad, the slow steps carrying you God knew where, through poor neighborhoods and rich neighborhoods and down alleys and bare business streets until at last you were somewhere a fat taxi-fare from home, not knowing just how you had gotten there. When Federico got warmed up he would take your elbow in his hand and jiggle it up and down for emphasis while he waved the other hand before you.

Hill let him talk on and felt bleak. That day he would have preferred the silence of emotionally bottled-up Anglo-Saxons.

They came to a shopwindow with housewares. A few were of the silky-soft greasy-feeling plastic of which at home they now made sickroom drinking glasses and douchebag tubes and shakers for frozen orange juice. It had only recently appeared in Spain, at high prices.

Federico stopped to look at the plastic and said, "There is in it neither sweat nor dreams nor skill. Nor human thought except for the engineer who drew it once on a piece of paper. That is your world, North American, a plastic world. What is it made of? Of coal? Of petroleum? Of milk?"

Somehow he gave "milk" its dirtier meaning. Hill, enraged, loved the old man but was not in a mood to defend polyethylene. He said only that he was not guilty.

"You are a displaced person," Federico said. "You don't know what you are. If you reject plastics you are nothing."

It was the kind of thought that in another time Hill might have had about himself, but not now. Soon afterward they found themselves on the Castellana, not far from the Café Gijón. In the bleak mood still, made bleaker by irritation, knowing that Federico hated and avoided the Gijón, Hill steered him vengefully through the revolving door without letting him object, saying that there was possibly someone in the café whom he needed to see.

It wasn't true. He himself disliked the Gijón, a gathering place supposedly for people with interest in the arts or intellectual matters. It had about it the mist of sour jealousy that seemed to hang over all European groupings based on art and thought. That wasn't fair, of course, but the Gijón was a café for winners who had not won much. At that hour it was jammed with successful intellectuals and show people and such members of the aristocracy as believed themselves to have afición for either the intellect or the theater, or simply for actresses.

All of them stared through layered tobacco smoke at each new arrival. The three or four times Hill had gone there before, he had been with an Argentine girl who lived in the little hotel on the Gran Vía and sang tangos in nightclubs. She had dragged him along to the big café to listen to the narcissisms of actors she knew, while aristocrats with afición gaped from nearby tables at her breasts and legs. She had enjoyed it, of course. . . .

Iron-jawed, Federico stalked to an empty table and sat down, still in his frayed overcoat. So did Hill.

Federico said, "I don't suppose there are more than fifty or sixty here whom I know. All of them I hate. Would you believe there was room for that much hate?"

"I'm sorry," Hill said. "It was a bad idea to come here."

"You're full of bad ideas."

"We can leave. Let's go."

"Why?" Federico said. "It is a café. Any café whatsoever. Those who don't want me to be here, I shit on their fathers!"

He said this loudly, and a man sitting at the next table with a woman turned to look and turned away again. Federico, his silky white hair tousled from the north wind outside, glared at the man's back, then glared around at a few other people, and at Hill. "Take off your overcoat," he said. "Demonstrate the gracious suit with a split tail like a maricón's. Be at ease."

Contrite, Hill did not answer. In a few minutes most of the café's eyes moved from them to a Cuban music-hall star who came in, Carib-eyed and sinuous of tail, and though Federico was slow to forgive they began to talk a little over a half-bottle of manzanilla. Federico was still on nationality, and Hill listened now without irritation.

It was necessary, the old man said, to be what you were. Hill said that covered a lot of ground in any one nationality.

"Yes. Look around you here."

"I'm not talking about politics."

"I am."

"You usually are," Hill said. It was true and he was tired of politics, though without rancor now. He said, "I'm going home in the summer."

Federico registered surprise and asked when he had decided that.

"I don't know," Hill said. "It's about time, I think. I've been writing letters about teaching jobs."

A tall man with a gray mustache, of the deep-voiced Moor-eyed macho type, was standing before their table holding out his hand to Federico. He had a good voice, restrained and resonant. Federico took the hand but fended off a cross-table embrace. The man said, using the *tú*, "I've asked about you. Someone had seen you. Man, you ought to have looked for me."

Federico said, "I've been busy. Before that I was . . . away."

"I heard. How long were you . . ."

"Eight years."

The tall man shook his head and sat down as Federico watched him sourly. The man said, "All for a little bit of opinion that . . . What do you do now?"

"I'm a mechanic."

He did not know a cam from a piston rod. He was worse at machinery even than Hill, who had never understood anything since the Model T Ford, and not even the ignition system of that. But in a society where manual labor was in low esteem, you might degrade yourself more thoroughly by laying claim to such skills than by calling yourself a garage attendant.

The tall man looked gloomy. His manner was like Rafael's, a doctorly manner.

Federico said bitterly, "Oh, I was a Red, what they call a Red. What *you* call a Red."

"Man," the other said. "I didn't . . . That's all finished."

"All finished. Stupendous."

"Come to see me," the tall man said sharply. "Don't be bruto. We can do something."

Federico said, "It is necessary to understand one thing. I am *still* a Red."

The tall man would not be offended, and tried for a time longer to get Federico to promise to come to his office, and left. Despondently, Federico watched him go.

"That is a decent man," he said. "One of the best of them. Everything he has done in his life has been intelligent and honest."

Hill stared at his glass half full of manzanilla and reflected on the absurdity of politics which had somehow made it impossible for Federico, who hated communists with good reason, to keep on being friends with a conservative who like himself was intelligent and honest. It did not make any sense, but then no politics had ever made much sense to Hill.

Federico was nodding at someone, even smiling. Hill was glad, and when he leveled his eyes along the line of the old man's gaze it was the girl he had talked to at the party in Palma and had glimpsed at the pigeon-shooting club north of Madrid not long before, the long-waisted girl with an oval face out of a portrait. She was smiling to Federico from halfway across the big café, and when she saw Hill the smile drew in and grew puzzled. After a moment she turned back to the older woman who sat with her.

"The stupendous," Federico said as though to himself.

Hill said, "I met her once."

Federico looked at him unpleasantly.

"At a fiesta of Americans and English and others, in Palma," Hill said. "We talked a little."

Federico said, "She is an angel. I was her tutor before the war."

"Tutor? You?"

"Her father was one of the best friends I ever had," Federico said. "There were two children, she and an older brother, in a big house near Serrano. I taught the two of them in the evenings after English tea. Because I had no children of my own . . . She would sit on the arm of my chair in a starched frock and the brother would walk up and down before me, arguing. About anything. He was very intelligent and he was killed at the Ebro when he was eighteen. They were monarchists, and the father died too."

He paused, thinking. Hill said to keep him talking, "In the war."

"Clearly in the war," the old man said irritably. "Everything died in that funereal war. *I* died. The mother with the children was in Ávila when it began, with her own family. He had to hide in a neutral embassy here in the city. I didn't know where he was. We were so close that if he had been a pure Falangist I would have hidden him if I could have. One night he tried to slip out, to go north, and they caught him in the street and took him to a cheka. One of the whorish chekas that were going to make us Soviets very quickly, through blood. You know about the chekas?"

"Yes," Hill said. "Is that the mother?"

"No," said Federico with a bitter grin, and thought for a moment. "Listen. Later when the war was finished and I was in a prison, friends on that side were making a petition for me, though I hadn't asked them to. They went to the mother of this one. And do you know what she said?"

Hill watched him.

"She said, Federico Castaño was like another father to my children. But if they shoot him, well shot he is!"

Bien fusilado está!

The girl, distant through a haze of tobacco smoke and the hum of the café's talk, was herself smoking, and the older woman with her was speaking as though pontifically, one finger upraised. The girl stubbed out her cigarette in an ashtray and turned her head to blow smoke along her arm.

Federico was talking about his own wife, whom he had insisted on marrying un-Catholically, in a civil ceremony, and later those marriages had been annulled, which had suited her well since she did not share his politics, and during his time in jail she had remarried.

He said suddenly, "You don't need to watch that one thus. She's too good for a foreign Protestant. Anyhow, the beast of a mother married her to some kind of marica with money and a title. They don't live together." He stood up and said, "I have to be at the garage at eight."

On the way out they stopped beside the table where the girl sat with the older woman, and Federico was smiling.

"Anda!" the girl said. "It's been months. You're no friend."

"One occupies oneself."

"Doing what? If you would say once, doing what?"

Federico said, "I have a norteamericano whom you know."

She smiled at Hill. "I know him," she said. "It's been time."

"More than a year," Hill said.

"He builds airfields for the Generalísimo," Federico said, never having bothered to ascertain exactly what Hill did, certain that it was politically undesirable.

The older woman, thin and patrician and sour, had been eyeing Federico in his frayed overcoat with distaste, and now she rose.

"You don't go?" she asked the girl.

"No. Not yet."

"Bien," the woman said, and picking up her gloves and handbag left, without saying anything to Hill and Federico. It was good and blunt and Spanish.

Federico gazing after her said, "You did her damage, making her consort with criminals and Yankees."

"She's like Mamá," the girl said soberly. "They go through the world hating." Then she frowned at the old man. "You!" she said, pointing to a chair. "Sit down, you and your American friend. Tell me about yourself."

They sat. "I am an insect of the night," Federico said. "I live in the holes of old blankets."

"The American will tell me," she said, turning to Hill.

Hill said, "He jumps out of sidestreets at me and I walk with him."

"I believe it. He even needs buttons sewn. You wouldn't believe the elegant that he was once, socialist and all. I was in love with him."

"You still are," Federico said smugly.

"But we both married someone else."

"Not I," said the old man. "Your damned church says I didn't."

They bantered along pleasantly, and Hill watched the girl. Her name was Soledad and Federico called her Soles. The expression in her oval face was around the eyes and the dark brows, and there was a calmness in it. Her mouth though full was controlled and straight and he noticed again with something like anger, as he had in Mallorca, that paint overran the line of her upper lip. Her dark-brown heavy hair came back tight to a bun in back, and she wore plain round gold earrings.

She was exactly as he had remembered her so intensely, ever since their brief meeting in Palma at a demoralized expatriates' party.

As time passed it became clear that nothing was going to go as fast as the big Americans had expected. Sour in idleness, they began drifting away back to Morocco, or to Turkey or Greece or the Azores, or home, and it seemed for a time that the girls in the cafés would have to lower their prices within the reach of Spaniards again. Hill went down to pick up twelve hundred dollars helping to dismantle heavy machinery above Casablanca, and took part of the money to Paris to buy a little secondhand Renault with TT plates. When he came back to Madrid the airbase work with Abie was still not ready to begin, and from August to October there were fairs and bullfights in the provincial capitals. He drove to such places sometimes alone and not minding it, or sometimes with Abie or the Argentine singer, or with an English painter named Alistair Turleman to whom he had had a letter of introduction and who lived in a Madrid slum with an undominated Catalan wife.

He had seen a half-naked child weep in the silent night streets of Granada under a cold wind from the mountains. He had sat on the ramparts of a ruined castle in the Gredos with the man who did the fiesta's fireworks and had listened to the gaitillas playing wild all night for the dancing beneath the great black poplars below the wall, and from the darkness beyond that riverside grove had heard the lovecries of the young. And had seen the Quixote country in harvest time, with hard dry faces laughing at him from the threshing floors as they tossed wheat high with wooden-tined pitchforks and the tawny chaff rode away down the wind. And had watched the white egrets among the Andalusian fighting bulls, and had heard the elderly English at Algeciras across the bay from Gibraltar cough hoo, hoo, hoo gently, so as not to hemorrhage.

He had seen and done lots of things, and he sometimes thought he knew little enough about what they had meant to qualify him for writing guidebooks.

One day in Jaca . . . He had gone to Zaragoza for Abie and then fishing in the mountains, and when he came down there was something wrong with the Renault and a wait while they repaired it. It was hot, July. A smell of heated olive oil and garlic lay in the streets, and from windows and doorways as he walked past people stared out at his foreignness. He ate in a hotel and afterward had thick sweet coffee in a café in a cool green-shaded promenade where cold mountain water ran perpetually about the roots of sycamores, or they looked like sycamores, little mason-ried pools into which from his chair he tossed cigarette stubs and watched them be sucked underground. At the end of the promenade was a platform looking north toward the mountains across the valley of the

Aragón which was green and ripe-wheat yellow and coldwater blue and the brown of Spain, with small fields and woods and houses.

He went down a path to a road with an old stone bridge that had somehow escaped destruction in the war, stared at the water for a time, then ascended again steeply to another road lined with poplars and sat down against one of them, the air cold on his damp shirt.

Improbably, two American women came walking down the road. One of them, with blue-washed hair and slanting sunglasses, looked at Hill closely and asked in halting Spanish what hour he had. He thought about answering in Spanish but didn't. They were registered in a summer course in the city. The blue-haired lady talked a great deal with a Long Island accent. She had been in summer courses from San Miguel de Allende, Mexico, to Madrid in an effort to learn Spanish agreeably, and she thought she was going to like the Jaca course.

"They explain in English," she said. "But most of the students are French and they use up time explaining in French, too."

The tall plain pleasant girl with her looked at Hill and they both laughed, but the blue-haired lady did not mind. She was enthusiastic about Spain, and Spaniards. "They're calm," she said. "It's a *settled-down* country. I mean you know where you stand, and that's what we need, more than anything."

Hill agreed that they needed it. They said goodbye finally and separated, and when he turned to look at them again they were a quarter-mile away, walking carefully along the edge of a dry moat and studying the armed modern sentries on the ramparts of an old stone fortress. Beyond them, south of the roofs and trees of Jaca, loomed the slanting lonely mountain called the Peña de Oroel. High up on its side, in a monastery, warrior kings lay buried.

The Catalans bought Abie Elmore out after the Day of Three Kings. They had played their game well and the thing had an inevitability to it and did not cost them much. They bought all the asphalt he had had shipped to the eastern side of the Atlantic, which was a lot, and Hill was never certain how much money Abie had lost. One day after lunch they came to the hotel, and Hill interpreted in the bar at a table by the window. The Catalans explained laughing that their procedure was only to avoid formalities, you understood, and laid big bills of cash money on the table and got Abie's signature, and went away talking Catalan contentedly to one another.

Abie stared at the cash money with black, troubled, amused, part-Cherokee eyes. He said, "Meet my Chinese friend Aw Shit."

Hill grinned crookedly at him in sympathy.

"I never came out on the high side of a deal in my life," Abie said. "I ever tell you about my first wife?"

"No."

Abie said, "She was quite a wife. I was away all the time. It was Venezuela then, dressing tools on an oil rig. One time I came home to Oklahoma for a visit and she said let's quit. It was friendly and nobody mad and I said fine, let old Andy Miller fix it up. He's a lawyer and I'd played football with him in high school, and I said whatever he fixed up would be all right with me."

He paused and lit a cigar, turning its tip in the match flame before putting it in his mouth and pulling on it.

"So I went back to Maracaibo," he said. "Every once in a while one of those crazy-language legal papers would come in the mail and I'd sign it and send it back, and when I got home the next time old Andy had fixed it up fine, by God. She got everything including the chow dog, and a little bit more that it took me seven years to pay off. I went hunting for old Andy and I found him on the sidewalk in front of the Markham Hotel and I knocked him down, and he got up and I knocked him down again, and I told him, Every time I see you from now on, the rest of our God-damn life, I'm going to knock you down. And I will."

Hill had never heard him say that many words in a row. But the asphalt had meant more to him than just money and it had gone to hell. Abie shuffled the bills and pushed some of them across the table.

"There's yours," he said. "I wish it was more. I wish to hell it was what we used to think it was going to be."

Hill counted the money and kept some, and shoved the rest back to his friend. "I didn't do that much," he said. "I was mainly around for company. Keep it for your delinquent alimony."

Abie said swiftly, kicking the bills at him with the hard heel of his hand, "You take a flying jump up my butt, little man. I can earn more than that in three weeks down in Casa, working for the big boys."

"I guess so."

"I know so. You coming down?"

"No."

Abie lay back in his chair and sighed. "It's just that you get so God-damn tired of working for this shithead company and that shithead company. There's always work. They can't make out without little old me when they get to thinking about it. What I was hoping was that I could make out without them."

Ávila, April 1954

IN A TALL chill paneled room with portraits, in the spring of the year, too early in a cold spring, Hill sat watching as Federico moodily ate chickpeas with a spoon and read a book.

Beyond an open door a friend of theirs named Alistair Turleman was shouting into a telephone, "Oiga, oiga! God damn you, oiga!"

Federico glanced up without seeming to see Hill. He had gotten himself complicatedly offended months earlier by something that Hill had done.

Alistair in Spanish yelled at the operator, "Woman, you cut off the marqués in the middle of what he was saying!"

As Hill understood the matter, Shoose was not really a marqués any longer. . . . Federico's offendedness was only for something that Federico assumed Hill had done, after coming across him with Soledad one day in the obscure café where the two of them usually met. Something which Hill, not having done it, might have done if he could have. Nor was it any of Federico's business, what Hill might have but had not done, but with the Spanish all things were personal and their business, and that could get on your nerves sometimes.

He had come up through the mountains the day before, not for the first time. Alistair and Federico had been there in the grim palace for two months now. Alistair, whose feisty Catalan wife had tired of slum poverty and had departed with their child for her parents' home near Barcelona, was there as a sort of superintendent and horse-exerciser and general factotum for the palace's absent owner, his friend and distant relative Don Jesús known as Shoose, and Federico as a down-at-heels socialistic and scholarly intellectual whom Shoose had long admired and liked and had rescued from his job in the garage so that he could work on a book about the unmentionable Republic.

Alistair cursed into the receiver and hung it up so hard that the bell pinged, then came into the dining room without closing the door behind him. He looked as though some poacher had just slaughtered all his pheasants in Devonshire, if he had had any pheasants or any piece of Devonshire, and if a Devonshire landowner would have gone around in such disastrous tweeds as the ones he wore, in sandals and without socks. He had been an aide to Marshal Montgomery during the war, but he damned sure didn't look like it.

He said, "You'd think on a bloody international call with . . . Suppose it had been Franco, negotiating another American bribe? Damn it, I didn't get to say anything about money."

"Did he mention the portrait you're supposed to be painting of him and Lisette and the dachshunds?"

"Doesn't care bugger all about the portrait. Neither do I. Wanted to hear about the new library."

"Ah, the library," said Hill. The contractor and Alistair did not get along, and nothing much had been done there either.

Alistair glanced at the garbanzos on his plate and pushed it away. "Bloody pistol bullets," he said. "Even the dogs eat them."

Federico looked at Alistair over his glasses and said nothing. He did not understand English when it was spoken, although he was something of an Anglophile and could read it not badly and would sometimes quote you lines from Donne or Samuel Johnson or Sidney Webb, miraculously mispronounced. If he was speaking to you . . . His garbanzos were finished, as were Hill's. Out of the chill shadows of the corner, there being no electricity that day, a butler moved in a red-and-black striped silk jacket to take away the plates. Hill poured himself another glass of red wine. It was harsh, but on the other hand none of the three of them was paying for the wine or for the garbanzos or anything else.

Lowering a platter beside Alistair's left shoulder, the butler said, "The Chateaubriands."

Alistair waggled black mustaches at slabs of mutton, sniffing. "Fried in cheap oil, too," he said. "Damn her."

The butler giggled, though he didn't understand English either. "She would do the same to an English ox," he said.

They served themselves in silence. Alistair and Federico had been there eating such food long enough for silence to have become normal, and Hill for one reason or another was mildly at outs with both of them. From the wall portraits watched them. He'd bet none of *them* had subsisted on garbanzos and tough mutton, though since they had been Castilians and Estremadurans it was possible. Shoose, their descendant, did not give a damn about food, or comfort, or beauty except in women and horses.

When alive, he was sure, none of the people in the portraits would have approved of the presence in that room of such types as himself and Alistair and Federico. Several of the paintings were pastoral scenes in the French manner, and the people repeated themselves in different canvases. In one, a round-cheeked young lady was tending sheep and in another she turned up in a marketplace with a basketful of hake balanced on her head, not doing a very convincing job of either task because she was too busy looking at the painter and smiling. She was robust, a good enough approximation of a shepherdess or a fishgirl, which in life would have made her unhappy to hear, since she would have had four or five titles. Shoose in St. Jean de Luz could have had a title or so, they said, if he had wanted them and had behaved better in terms of politics.

The hake were convincing. Dead things in Spanish painting usually were.

Clearly from the kitchen at the end of a corridor a parrot shrieked, "Marica! Maricón!"

Automatically both Hill and Alistair glanced toward the butler, who was watching the chandelier. Hill felt sorry for him, persecuted steadily by the squat harsh woman cook whom Alistair called Old Trumpet-Twat and feared, as did everyone else in that palace.

Cold, and holy dark gray outside, with the spirit of Santa Teresa brooding over everything. On the other side of the mountains, just yesterday, as he had driven up from Madrid in the little Renault that coughed and bucked from a dirty carburetor, it had been clearly April, Spanish April with the cool gusts across the fields of short green wheat, and the tawny Castilian land of always, and the sky El Greco sad and pure with wind-flattened varicolored clouds and here and there a shaft of sunlight shooting down onto the harsh earth. And the rising hills, still April, and the long ascent by the sanitariums from which dying the tubercular could watch with love or despair that Madrid wherein they had sickened, and pines, and then after the top when you were dropping down through thicker pines, the north wind hit you full on from across all of Old Castile and it was winter again, winter still.

Ávila gray, godly mystic gray spraddling out beyond its old wall, without electricity or water either during the day because it had not rained well that year, and last year's storknests on towers, and the three of them hardly speaking now to one another. That was all right. Hill cared little about that. They were three different kinds of hardheaded provincial, each enclosed in a crystal aloneness of his own.

His jaws were tired from working on the rubbery mutton and he was no longer hungry. He finished chewing the piece in his mouth, swallowed it with an effort, and stopped eating. Garbanzos were at any rate filling.

Like two stacked sacks of potatoes the cook wandered down the corridor from the kitchen and stopped just short of the dining room door. She half-shouted toward Alistair, "Oiga, señor!"

The butler turned on her, shocked. He said, "You have no right to be here. No right."

"I'm not inside the comedor."

He repeated weakly, "You have no right."

Past him she said, "Listen, Señor Toormahn, what did Don Jesús tell you for me?"

"For you?" Alistair said with a quaver in his usual fluid Spanish before he picked up confidence. "For you. Nothing at all. I told him we were getting bad food. He said it didn't surprise him. I told him it was making the señor our friend sick. . . ."

It was an effort to awe her with a stranger whom she had not yet managed to scare. It did not work. Old Trumpet-Twat's small eyes above leather cheeks swiveled toward the señor our friend, also known as Hill Cavitt, and dismissed him as the inconsiderable foreign crony of money-less abstract artists and broken-down ex-deputies of the Republic. Aside from the butler, who had problems and was unpolitical, they were all monarchists in that house, like Shoose. On the stable wall behind the palace huge letters in black shouted hopefully:

¡VIVA EL REY DON JUAN III!

She said, "You will have told him also that you do not dominate the workers? That the mantelpiece for the new library remains still in the mud below?"

Alistair said sullenly, "I told him what I wished to tell him. Mud doesn't hurt marble."

Old Trumpet-Twat split her pitted leather face in a cackle, and went waddling back to the kitchen. The butler's hands shook a little as he removed plates. Occupied with a piece of mutton gristle stuck between his back teeth, the señor our friend Hill Cavitt felt comfortably out of the whole mess, which was neither of his contriving nor any concern of his. He had never stayed in Ávila long enough at a time to get tangled up with it. He drank more rough wine, while from the kitchen intermittently the parrot screamed that the butler was a pansy, which was true, and the cook's brass voice encouraged the bird when she was not talking as loudly as possible to one of the eight or nine Estremaduran maids who were all kin to her.

Alistair had said that he was certain she had syphilis. It was his worst insult and seldom had any connection with reality. They were eating the midday meal at twelve o'clock, two hours earlier than any of them wanted it, because it suited her to serve it then.

Flan and iron-tasting coffee behind, they rolled cigarettes with good black Havana tobacco that Hill had obtained in Gibraltar and had brought to Federico, a peace offering that had not yet resulted in peace. The butler cleared the table. Federico, despite his studied detachment, had to glance over at the cigarettes they had made before lighting his own. Alistair's was awry, wrinkled and much fatter toward the fire end that at his mouth. Hill could see that Federico wanted badly to say some-thing about it, but did not because it would have broken the silence.

"Blast!" said Alistair. "The fact is he did tell me something for the old bitch. I'd best go let her know before I forget."

He rose, six-two in unpressed wornout heavy tweeds and sandals, without a necktie or socks, and walked stoopshouldered toward defeat, followed by the butler.

"Federico," Hill said.

Federico looked at him.

"It was all right, that. Nothing happened."

Federico said, using the formal pronoun, "I don't believe you. I don't want to talk about it."

"All right."

"It was clear enough," the old man said. "Why do you come now with lies?"

"I'm tired of having you stare away from me," Hill said. "They're not lies anyhow. I wanted to marry her. I still do."

For a moment Federico's face sagged into doubt. They had not really spoken since three months before, when Federico, after seeing Hill with Soledad in the obscure café, had torn into him at the garage where he worked.

He was slow to change his mind, still not having changed it about beliefs he had held in the years before 1936, beliefs that had cost him no end of trouble and a few years in jail. He repeated, "I don't want to discuss it."

Hill said, "Good."

"She said no?"

Hill nodded.

"Naturally she said no," Federico said with a tinge of satisfaction. "She is a good Catholic and she already has a husband, though God knows not much of one."

"I thought you didn't believe in good Catholics."

"Women, yes," the old man said, forgetting for a professorial mo-ment that he was still angry at Hill. It had been one of the troubles of the Republic, trying to make statesmen out of professors. "Spanish women have to be Catholic," he said. "Otherwise they are whores, without remedy."

Then he remembered he was angry and closed his mouth and did not open it again. Hill was content for the moment to have driven a little wedge into his hostility. Alistair came back from the kitchen with his long blue eyes troubled above the big mustaches. Hill thought ruefully of having thrown a brandy glass at him the night before during a political squabble, though he had missed. He didn't feel honestly sorry for having thrown it, or for having missed, since he had recently given up feeling sorry about things. He just felt a little bad about the vanquished look Old Trumpet-Twat had put into Alistair's eyes.

The woman who ran the cubbyhole tobacco shop looked like a chipmunk. She said in the stately pure Spanish of that region, "I don't see what I can do. You won't name anyone."

Hill said, "I shouldn't have to. Maybe it wasn't you I was looking for."

Her hair was still black. Ageless within fat on her stool behind the counter, she watched him with eyes rolled up small and comfortable in their pouches, and the front teeth peeped out in a chipmunk half-smile that would probably be there even when she was angry. Hill did not know what she was now. Curious, certainly.

She said, "It was I that you asked for, Ana Castro."

And stopped talking as the street door behind him opened to the sound of a little bell, letting in dank air. Hill did not turn around. A short thin old man moved diffidently past his shoulder and to the counter. In the dim kerosene light he counted out three aluminum coins and in return Ana Castro gave him two cigarettes, brown-papered Ideales of firecracker savor, and he hunched his left shoulder up to tuck them away somewhere in his breast. A leather strap passed around the back of his neck, and his gray ill-fitting suit coat was dark with wet, plastered down against scrawny shoulderblades.

"It's bad out," the woman said in a different voice from the one she had used to Hill.

The old man said soberly, "Daughter, it is."

As he turned to leave Hill saw that the strap held up a wooden tray full of little china Virgins. His steps were short and rheumatic and his size was the shrunkenness of extreme old age. The face held stoic defenseless innocence, beneath a tight Castilian beret.

When the old man had gone Hill said angrily, "It's you. Even if she isn't here you're supposed to know."

The fat-rounded shoulders were jiggling; she was laughing. "Hala!" she said. "Fire in the Englishman."

"She's here? In Ávila?"

Ana Castro said, "What are you, a Swede? Your Spanish isn't bad."

"A kind of Mexican," Hill said. "Listen, señora . . ."

"She's here."

"Then, when . . ."

"You're no Mexican," she said. "You don't sing your phrases."

"I used to sing like a nightingale," Hill said.

"Come here when I close, at ten."

"That's eight hours."

"Eight hours," she said, and the chipmunk smile was sad. "And how long do you think she can be sorry later?"

"It's not how you think."

"How I think . . ."

She was older than he had thought, sadder, wiser. She said, "How I think. Go away now."

Before he passed through the door into drizzle, she said, "Mexican?"

"Yes?"

"You love her?"

"Yes."

"Go away," said Ana Castro.

At the top of the hill above the little polluted Adaja, the big stallion grabbed the bit and lit out. Hill had to let him go, gripping hard with unaccustomed thigh muscles, missing the swell of a stock-saddle fork above his knees. The stallion pounded crazy downward weaving among the great gray egg-shapes of rock half-buried in talus and bitter damp tan earth, and Hill bent over and settled into the rhythm of the pounding, letting all the give-a-damn go out of him. His grandfather had said dogmatically never to run a horse down a hill unless it was a forty-dollar pony behind a cow. Never. This one, Grandpapa, you'd play more hell trying to stop him in the rocks than letting him rip. Down, pounding, and near the bottom Hill started pulling him in and to the left, a mouth like iron and even with the jaw forced against the thick stallion neck, you leaning back and both your hands pulling, he kept on for the filthy black river in high long bucks, and you thinking by God I can stay with you forever you big black son of a bitch, go on into the water damn you, go.

And got him turned, and when his last long leap brought him to an abrupt and spraddle-legged stop on the riverbank, Hill's forehead hit the maned twisted neck hard and his butt was a foot out of the small flat saddle. Alistair was waiting on the dappled mare among dead docks and thistles, laughing.

"God damn you, I knew! I knew before you ever got me on him," Hill said, happy too. "I've seen the grooms fight the big bastard before. You thought I couldn't, didn't you?"

Alistair said, "I didn't know. He'd have had you if you'd gone on a bit farther, you know."

Lying, Hill said, "No, he wouldn't."

The stallion shuddered under him, returning from that crazier world, and Hill stroked the hot-sweating neck and was grateful for crazy things.

Alistair said, "At that, you do rather less badly than the grooms. They're afraid of him."

"I'm not afraid of God Almighty," Hill said.

But he was, and in that moment he recognized that he was also afraid of the night. He had never been truly alone with her before.

Empty, and in his life he had not felt so whole. . . . He put his eyes against the smooth round muscle running from her neck to her shoulder and beside his ear she exhaled in a long sigh that caught twice in sounds like tiny sobs.

He said, "We'd go to France. A communist mayor somewhere would marry us and in a house by the sea below Perpignan we could . . ."

"Shut up," Soledad said without opening her eyes. "No. Shut up."

And after a long long time, as though in sleep, he felt her fingers searching on his head. They traced finally the faint elliptical relief of the tantalum plate behind his ear.

"That's it?"

"Yes."

She twisted his head and raising herself against his shoulder, warm and a clinging part of him in the cold stone room, leaned over to kiss the place. Then with her fist she hit him hard on the neck, stunning him.

She said with her forehead against his shoulder, "I don't know why I did that."

"Because you hate me," Hill said.

"I love you."

"Yes," he said.

Later still he said, "And you?"

"And I," she said, and without seeing it he knew the fixity of thought in her eyes. The room was heavy with damp cold and it was right that it should be so. She stirred against him, turning her face upward.

"And I," she said. "I shall spend much time in this house where I was born, and in others like it. I shall speak much with women and old men, about other women's babies and other women's loves."

"You wouldn't have to."

"I have to," she said. "It's all right."

"I suppose you do," Hill said, knowing it really for the first time. "I suppose that yes it is all right."

"Yes," said Soledad.

The unpublished novel, "A Speckled Horse," was written in 1955–56.

Composed in Bulmer types.

BEATRICE WARDE once compared the function of book typography and its accompanying typeface design to that of a crystal goblet. Both should be invisible vehicles to convey their contents. As such, they can be merely utilitarian or, on occasion, they can approach an art form. This book is a "reader" containing stories from a variety of sources over a period of time. To reflect that diversity and to express the nuances in letter design of the Roman alphabet, the designer of this volume has selected a different typeface for each chapter. The name of the typeface used appears following the source notes at the end of each chapter.

Design and typography of this volume was done by George Lenox Design, Austin. The book was composed by G&S Typesetters, Incorporated, Austin; the printing and binding by Edwards Brothers, Incorporated, Ann Arbor.